THE

QUIZ BOOK

1,000 Questions and Answers
About Women and the Things They Love

LESLIE GILBERT ELMAN

CONARI PRESS

First published in 2004 by Conari Press,
an imprint of Red Wheel/Weiser, LLC
York Beach, ME
With offices at:
368 Congress Street
Boston, MA 02210
www.redwheelweiser.com

Typeset in Adobe Garamond by Kathryn Sky-Peck
Cover and interior illustrations by ©2003 Martha Newton Furman.

Printed in the United States of America
Phoenix

11 10 09 08 07 06 05 04

8 7 6 5 4 3 2

The paper used in this publication meets the minimum requirements of the
American National Standard for Information Sciences-Permanence of Paper
for Printed Library Materials Z39.48-1992 (R1997).

Contents

ACKNOWLEDGMENTS

Thanks to Carole and the San Diego beta-testers
for their valuable input.

And huge thanks to Dan for "helping."

INTRODUCTION

*W*hen Alicia Alvrez wrote *The Ladies' Room Reader Revisited*, she made a promise in her author's foreword: "There *will* be a quiz later."

Well ladies, "later" has arrived.

The Ladies' Room Reader Quiz Book picks up where *The Ladies' Room Reader* series left off—with more fascinating facts about females. This time, we ask the questions and you get to show what you know about everyone's favorite gender. (Did you say "the weaker sex"? We didn't think so.)

One hundred 10-question quizzes add up to 1,000 chances to test your knowledge and learn all sorts of stuff about women and the things they love—from food to fashion to their fellow humans (that would be men).

Some of the answers to *The Ladies' Room Reader Quiz Book* quizzes can be found in the first two *Ladies' Room Reader* books. Most of it is fresh information, because we know how much you like new things.

Test your knowledge, quiz your friends, challenge your man. If you think you know all about being a woman, *The Ladies' Room Reader Quiz Book* lets you prove it.

—Leslie Gilbert Elman

1

The Quizzes

1. NOT!

Two are, one isn't. Two did, one didn't.
Pick the one who's **not** . . .

1. Pictured on a U.S. postage stamp
   a. Abigail Adams
   b. Betty Ford
   c. Dolley Madison

2. A Grammy award-winner
   a. Ella Fitzgerald
   b. Billie Holiday
   c. Etta James

3. A wife of Frank Sinatra
   a. Mia Farrow
   b. Ava Gardner
   c. Rita Hayworth

4. Seen topless in a movie
   a. Julie Andrews
   b. Julia Roberts
   c. Sissy Spacek

5. Born a woman
   a. Berthe Morisot
   b. Jan Morris
   c. Toni Morrison

6. An abstract painter
   a. Helen Frankenthaler
   b. Artemisia Gentileschi
   c. Lee Krasner

7. A character in *Alice in Wonderland*

    a. Benjamin Bunny

    b. March Hare

    c. White Rabbit

8. In a James Bond movie

    a. Kim Basinger

    b. Michelle Pfeiffer

    c. Jane Seymour

9. Born in the U.S.A.

    a. Pamela Anderson

    b. Nicole Kidman

    c. Bette Midler

10. An astronaut

    a. Shannon Lucid

    b. Shirley Muldowney

    c. Sally Ride

2. Man or Woman?

*One's a man and one's a woman,
but which is which?*

1. Morgan Fairchild and Morgan Freeman

2. Leslie Nielsen and Leslie Caron

3. Mackenzie Astin and Mackenzie Phillips

4. Isak Dinesen and Izaak Walton

5. Evelyn Waugh and Evelyn Wood

6. George Eliot and George Romney

7. George Sand and George Washington Carver

8. Meredith Willson and Meredith Brooks

9. Gale Storm and Gale Gordon

10. Joyce Kilmer and Joyce Brothers

Did you know . . .

Man Enough to be a Woman is the autobiography of Jayne County (a.k.a. Wayne Rogers), a flamboyant drag queen who was part of Andy Warhol's coterie in the 1970s.

3. What's She Worth?

Who says women aren't good with numbers? Match the dollar value to its significance.

1. $72.39

2. $350

3. $421.27

4. $10,000

5. $32,665

6. $46,782

7. $32.7 million

8. $44.5 million

9. $1 billion

10. $3.46 billion

a. Price paid for first edition of *Pride and Prejudice* at auction in 2001

b. Estimated gross sales of Olsen twins merchandise in 2002

c. Average annual salary of U.S. full-time registered nurses in 2000

d. Total compensation package of highest paid U.S. woman executive in 2000

e. Daily cost for housing a female prisoner on Florida's Death Row

f. Cost of the wedding of Princess Salama to Mohammed, son of Sheik Rashid Bin Saeed El-Maktoum of the United Arab Emirates

g. Average cost of a ticket to Barbra Streisand's 2000 concert tour

h. Stated value of a 27-year-old female slave in 1816

i. Estimated net worth of Queen Beatrix of the Netherlands

j. Weekly salary of actress Mary Pickford in 1916

4. Go-Go Girls

Fill in the blanks with the names of famous women—real and fictional—whose names begin with "Go."

1. Going to eat porridge in the woods_____

2. Going to the chapel with Charlie Chaplin_____

3. Going bareback in Coventry_____

4. Going to create anarchy_____

5. Going under the alias Anna Akhmatova_____

6. Going to take her Nobel Prize home to South Africa_____

7. Going ape with chimps in Africa_____

8. Going to win the first Miss America pageant_____

9. Going to deceive her dad in King Lear_____

10. Going to star in *Harold and Maude*_____

Did you know . . .

The term "go-go girl" originated in the 1960s at the Whisky A Go-Go nightclub in Los Angeles, where the female disk jockey, who was suspended in a cage above the dance floor, danced to the records she played.

5. California Girls

What do you know about women from the Golden State?

1. Who was the first female mayor of San Francisco and the first female senator from California?

    a. Barbara Boxer

    b. Dianne Feinstein

    c. Barbara Mikulski

2. Summer Sanders from Roseville is a world champion in which sport?

    a. Figure skating

    b. Soccer

    c. Swimming

3. Which author from Oakland wrote *The Joy Luck Club?*

    _____

4. Miss Moffit from Long Beach grew up to be which famously feminist tennis star?

    a. Chris Evert

    b. Billie Jean King

    c. Venus Williams

5. Fifth-generation Californian Joan Didion is an award-winning what?

    a. Author

    b. Biologist

    c. Conservationist

6. TV's "French Chef" was born in Pasadena. Who is she?

    _____

7. Edith Head from San Bernardino made her name in which field?

    a. Fashion design

    b. Medicine

    c. Music

8. Alice Stebbins Wells of Los Angeles was the first woman in the United States to become a what?

    a. College professor

    b. Film director

    c. Police officer

9. What California girl was featured in the hit song "Valley Girl"?

    _____

10. *Beauty and the Beat* was a #1 album for which L.A.-based girl band?

    a. The Bangles

    b. The Go-Go's

    c. The Runaways

Did you know . . .

"California Girls" was a #3 hit for the Beach Boys in 1965 and a #3 hit for David Lee Roth in 1985.

6. Patronize Me

In good times and bad, Christians ask for the help and protection of patron saints. Match these female patron saints with their areas of expertise.

1. Agatha   a. Alcoholics

2. Anne   b. Breast disease

3. Catherine of Alexandria   c. Gardeners

4. Catherine of Genoa   d. Grandmothers

5. Cecilia   e. Lawyers

6. Genevieve   f. Lost keys

7. Gertrude of Nivelles   g. Musicians

8. Monica   h. Photographers

9. Veronica   i. Troubled marriages

10. Zita   j. Women in the military

7. With a Name Like That . . .

Choose the true profession for each of these colorfully named women.

1. Maria Tallchief
    a. Ballerina
    b. Politician
    c. Zoologist

2. Cindy Birdsong
    a. Engineer
    b. Nutritionist
    c. Singer

3. I.C. Love
    a. Archaeologist
    b. Fashion designer
    c. Matchmaker

4. Ima Hogg
    a. Agriculturalist
    b. Chef
    c. Philanthropist

5. Wilma Mankiller
    a. Astronaut
    b. Native American leader
    c. Poet

6. Hortense Powdermaker
    a. Anthropologist
    b. 19th-century novelist
    c. Firearms specialist

7. Annie Jump Cannon

    a. Astronomer

    b. Beauty pioneer

    c. Stunt pilot

8. Emma Nutt

    a. Botanist

    b. Psychologist

    c. Telephone operator

9. Theodate Pope Riddle

    a. Architect

    b. Evangelist

    c. Naval officer

10. Frances Gumm

    a. Actress

    b. Chemist

    c. Confectioner

Did you know . . .

Shirley Ellis' sing-along song, "The Name Game," was a top-10 hit in 1965.

8. Female Anatomy Believe it or Not

The female body is an amazing creation. Take a look at these facts and decide if you believe 'em or not.

1. When you're pregnant, your uterus expands to 1,000 times its normal capacity.

    Believe it   Not

2. The ovaries of a newborn girl contain 1.5 million potential eggs.

    Believe it   Not

3. A woman's breasts grow larger after menopause.

    Believe it   Not

4. There is only one type of orgasm.

    Believe it   Not

5. Dry skin causes wrinkles.

    Believe it   Not

6. Blondes have more hair on their heads than brunettes do.

    Believe it   Not

7. Of all your fingernails, the one on your middle finger grows the fastest.

    Believe it   Not

8. The thinner you are, the more likely you are to develop osteoporosis.

    Believe it   Not

9. The only purpose of mother's milk is to provide nutrients to her baby.

    Believe it   Not

10. A woman's labia change color.

    Believe it   Not

9. Mother Lode

Fill in these maternal nicknames.

1. Fairy tale character _____ Goose

2. Comedian Jackie _____ Mabley

3. Singer Gertrude Malissa _____ Rainey

4. Painter Anna Mary Robertson _____ Moses

5. Labor leader Mary Harris _____ Jones

6. Berthold Brecht character _____ Courage

7. Outlaw Kate_____ Barker

8. Blues singer Willie Mae _____ Thornton

9. Political activist Doris _____ Haddock

10. *L'il Abner* character _____ Yokum

Did you know . . .

Most babies in the United States are born on Tuesday.

10. Family Ties

How are these women related?

1. Goldie Hawn and Kate Hudson

   _____

2. Abigail "Dear Abby" Van Buren and Ann Landers

   _____

3. Elizabeth I of England and Mary, Queen of Scots

   _____

4. Florence Griffith Joyner and Jackie Joyner Kersee

   _____

5. Loretta Lynn and Crystal Gayle

   _____

6. Mary Higgins Clark and Carol Higgins Clark

   _____

7. Lynn Redgrave and Natasha Richardson

   _____

8. Ethel Barrymore and Drew Barrymore

   _____

9. Virginia Woolf and Vanessa Bell

   _____

10. Loretta Sanchez and Linda Sanchez

   _____

11. Anything You Can Do

Men and women are different in ways you may not expect. Do you know who . . .

1. Wakes from anesthesia faster?

                    Women   Men

2. Snores more often?

                    Women   Men

3. Lives longer?

                    Women   Men

4. Hears better?

                    Women   Men

5. Sees better at a distance?

                    Women   Men

6. Has a better sense of smell?

                    Women   Men

7. Has more muscle mass?

                    Women   Men

8. Talks more in public?

                    Women   Men

9. Is more susceptible to motion sickness?

                    Women   Men

10. Smiles more often?

                    Women   Men

Did you know . . .

The song "Anything You Can Do," written by Irving Berlin, comes from the Broadway musical *Annie Get Your Gun*.

12. Women 1 to 10

Match the numbers to what they represent.
The answers range from 1 to 10.

1		Bo Derek-Dudley Moore film
2		Children of Rose Fitzgerald Kennedy
3		Elizabeth Taylor's marriages
4		Fingers (including thumb) on Minnie Mouse's hand
5		The Pleiades
6		Spice Girls
7		Witches in *Macbeth*
8		Wives of Henry VIII
9		Women who have served as U.S. attorney general
10		Women who have won the Iditarod sled dog race

13. A Girl's Best Friend

Men can have dogs; we'll take diamonds.
How much do you know about them?

1. Which is the world's largest diamond?

    a. The Cullinan Diamond

    b. The Hope Diamond

    c. Koh-i-noor

2. Which country was the first to mine diamonds?

    a. China

    b. India

    c. South Africa

3. Who wore the first diamond "tennis" bracelet?

    a. Chris Evert

    b. Billie Jean King

    c. Serena Williams

4. What color is the Hope Diamond?

    a. Blue

    b. Pink

    c. White

5. Which company uses the slogan "A diamond is forever"?

    a. Cartier

    b. De Beers

    c. Tiffany & Co.

6. Where is Crater of Diamonds State Park?

    a. Alabama

    b. Arizona

    c. Arkansas

7. How many prongs hold a diamond in a Tiffany setting?

    a. 4

    b. 5

    c. 6

8. When she won the 2001 Oscar for Best Actress, what color diamonds was Halle Berry wearing?

    a. Black and white

    b. Pink and blue

    c. Brown and orange

9. Diamonds are composed of which element?

    a. Calcium

    b. Carbon

    c. Phosphorus

10. Who wore $1-million diamond-and-platinum shoes to the 2002 Academy Awards?

    a. Jennifer Connelly

    b. Laura Harring

    c. Chloe Sevigny

Did you know . . .

Edna MacArthur of Canada had her cremated remains made into a diamond. Intense heat was used to form her ashes into a stone.

14. Eat It or Wear It?

Some you eat and some you wear.
Which is which?

1. Obi	Eat it	Wear it
2. Nori	Eat it	Wear it
3. Sake	Eat it	Wear it
4. Sari	Eat it	Wear it
5. Chanterelle	Eat it	Wear it
6. Chamomile	Eat it	Wear it
7. Chasuble	Eat it	Wear it
8. Cherimoya	Eat it	Wear it
9. Balaclava	Eat it	Wear it
10. Baklava	Eat it	Wear it

15. Stuck in the Middle

Fill in the middle names of these famous women.

1. Joyce _____Oates

2. Julia _____ Howe

3. Charlotte _____ Gilman

4. Zora _____ Hurston

5. Elizabeth _____ Stanton

6. Harriet _____ Stowe

7. Joan _____Cooney

8. Ruth _____ Ginsburg

9. Mary_____ Bethune

10. Helen _____ Brown

Did you know . . .

B@bies Online, a website produced by Southeast Missouri Hospital, ranked the top five middle names for babies born in 2002. For girls: Marie, Elizabeth, Nicole, Ann and Renee. For boys: Michael, James, Joseph, Alan/Allen and Andrew.

16. Playing the Percentages

Match the percentages to what they represent.

1. 2002 *Sports Illustrated* covers featuring women

   a. 0.91%

2. Alcoholics Anonymous members who are women

   b. 5%

3. Commercial airline pilots who are women

   c. 5.7%

4. Expectant mothers who experience morning sickness

   d. 8.7%

5. Televised sports coverage devoted to women's athletics

   e. 12%

6. U.S. wives who earn at least $5,000 per year more than their husbands

   f. 15%

   g. 19%

7. U.S. women 41 to 44 who are childless

   h. 33%

8. U.S. women who are incarcerated

9. U.S. women who say they have used an online dating service

   i. 61%

10. Women who voted in the 2000 U.S. presidential election

    j. 70%

Did you know . . .

Women who work full-time, year-round earn only 76% of what men in the same jobs earn. That's 76 cents for every 1 dollar. Saddest part of all? That's the closest women have yet come to equal pay for equal work.

17. Power of Four

What's the common denominator in each of these groups of four?

1. Sarah, Rebecca, Rachel, Leah

   _____

2. Martha Washington, Pocahontas, Sacagawea, Susan B. Anthony

   _____

3. Carrie, Charlotte, Miranda, Samantha

   _____

4. Susannah Hoffs, Michael Steel, Vicki Peterson, Debbi Peterson

   _____

5. "Believe," "Dark Lady," "Gypsys, Tramps and Thieves," "Half Breed"

   _____

6. Meg, Jo, Amy, Beth

   _____

7. Hollis Stacy, Betsy Rawls, Mickey Wright, Susie Maxwell Berning

   _____

8. *Morning Glory, Guess Who's Coming to Dinner, The Lion in Winter, On Golden Pond*

   _____

9. Angela Bassett, Whitney Houston, Loretta Devine, Lela Rochon

   _____

10. Diane Crump, Patricia Cooksey, Andrea Seefeldt, Julie Krone

    _____

18. Mermaids Multiple Choice

How much do you know about these women with fins?

1. According to legend, mermaids often lack this human faculty.

    a. Sight

    b. Speech

    c. Hearing

2. A mermaid's male counterpart is called a:

    a. Merman

    b. Mermaster

    c. Mermister

3. In ancient Scotland, a mermaid was a symbol for a

    a. Sailor's wife

    b. Sailor's daughter

    c. Prostitute

4. Who wrote the famous tale of "The Little Mermaid"?

    a. Guy de Maupassant

    b. Danny Kaye

    c. Hans Christian Andersen

5. Which actress was the model for Walt Disney's animated Little Mermaid?

    a. Alyssa Milano

    b. Winona Ryder

    c. Pamela Anderson

6. What is a "mermaid's glove"?

    a. Snorkeling gear

    b. A type of marine sponge

    c. Divers' slang for a dangerous reef

7. Which city has a mermaid on its coat of arms?

    a. Helsinki

    b. London

    c. Warsaw

8. Where would you find the Weeki Wachee Mermaids?

    a. California

    b. Florida

    c. Mississippi

9. Darryl Hannah played her in *Splash*.

    a. Madison

    b. Park

    c. Lexington

10. Playing Cher's daughter in *Mermaids* was the first major film role for this actress.

    a. Parker Posey

    b. Maggie Gyllenhaal

    c. Christina Ricci

Did you know . . .

The Golden Mermaid statue, for the year's outstanding bathing beauty, was awarded to Miss America contestants in the 1920s.

19. Measuring Up

Match the measurement to its significance in female anatomy.

1. Average head-to-toe size of a full-term fetus

2. Average height of an adult woman (U.S.)

3. Combined length of the ten longest toenails

4. Fingernail growth per year

5. Hair growth per year

6. Height of the world's tallest woman

7. Length of a human umbilical cord

8. Length of a women's size 8 (U.S.) foot

9. Size of a fetus, head to toe, at 8 weeks

10. World's smallest adult waist measurement

a. 0.56 to 0.8 inch

b. 1.5 inches

c. 6 inches

d. 9.5 inches

e. 13 inches

f. 21.5 inches

g. 26 inches

h. 63.7 inches

i. 7 feet, 3 inches

j. 8 feet, 1.75 inches

20. All Hail the Queen

How much do you know about royal women throughout history?

1. Present-day queen of Denmark

   _____

2. Longest-ruling monarch of England

   _____

3. Julius Caesar's favorite Egyptian queen

   _____

4. Deposed her husband to become Russia's empress

   _____

5. Marie-Antoinette's mother

   _____

6. Became queen of Sweden at age 6

   _____

7. Benefactress of Columbus

   _____

8. The Netherlands' queen since 1980

   _____

9. Last Romanov empress

   _____

10. China's infamous Empress Dowager

    _____

Did you know . . .

All Hail the Queen, rapper Queen Latifah's 1989 debut album, sold more than 1 million copies. The Queen's real name is Dana Owens.

21. Who Thought of That?

We give you the invention; you tell us whether a man or a woman was responsible for it.

1. Tampon   Man   Woman

2. Brassiere   Man   Woman

3. Guillotine   Man   Woman

4. Pantyhose   Man   Woman

5. Disposable diapers Man   Woman

6. Dishwasher   Man   Woman

7. Barbie doll   Man   Woman

8. Pap test   Man   Woman

9. Birth-control pill Man   Woman

10. Windshield wiper   Man   Woman

22. Is She for Real?

Which of these famous foodies are real women?

1. Aunt Jemima   For real   Not for real

2. Betty Crocker   For real   Not for real

3. Marie Callender   For real   Not for real

4. Baby Ruth   For real   Not for real

5. Granny Smith   For real   Not for real

6. Sara Lee   For real   Not for real

7. Little Debbie   For real   Not for real

8. Wendy of Wendy's   For real   Not for real

9. Mrs. Fields   For real   Not for real

10. Mrs. Smith   For real   Not for real

Did you know . . .

Candy maker Leo Hirschfield named
Tootsie Rolls in honor of his daughter
Clara, whose nickname was Tootsie.

23. Girl Groups

Shang-a-lang and da -doo-ron-ron, fill in the blanks on these girl group hits.

1. "I Met Him on a _____": the Shirelles' first record.

2. "He's a _____": A #1 hit for the Crystals.

3. "_____ of Love": Where the Dixie Cups were going in 1964.

4. "Please Mr. _____": Entreaty from the Marvelettes.

5. "_____ Too Late": The Poni-Tails' lament.

6. "Mr. _____": The Bobbettes' ode to their high school teacher.

7. "My Boyfriend's _____": Warning from the Angels.

8. "Leader of the _____": Chart-topper from the Shangri-Las.

9. "He's So _____": Sang the Chiffons in 1963.

10. "_____ in the Rain": Favorite activity of the Ronettes in 1964.

24. Ode to Florence

Her name means "prosperous and blooming," and who could argue? Show what you know about famous Florences.

1. *Brady Bunch* mom _____

2. Pseudonym of English writer
   Florence Smith _____

3. Where would you find a Florence flask?

   a. In a man's breast pocket

   b. In a chemistry lab

   c. In the barrel of a gun

4. Actress who portrayed Flo in the film *Alice Doesn't Live Here Anymore* _____

5. Actress who portrayed Flo on the TV
   sitcom *Alice* _____

6. Full name of the character Flo on the TV
   sitcom *Alice* _____

7. Which U.S. city of Florence has the largest population?

   a. Florence, Alabama

   b. Florence, Kentucky

   c. Florence, South Carolina

8. Crimean War nurse _____

9. Who was Florence Mills?

   a. Stage performer of the Harlem Renaissance

   b. Pulitzer Prize-winning journalist

   c. First president of Smith College

10. Who was Florence Sabin?

    a. First female governor of New Jersey

    b. Medical researcher

    c. German abstract painter

25. Marriage-Minded

Here's a quiz for anyone who's ever considered a walk down the aisle.

1. True or false: The older you are when you get married, the more likely you are to stay married.

2. Who is generally credited with making the white wedding gown fashionable?

    a. Queen Elizabeth II

    b. Jacqueline Kennedy

    c. Queen Victoria

3. What does a couple do with a *chupa* at a Jewish wedding?

    a. Stand under it

    b. Step on it

    c. Wear it

4. True or false: Couples who are unmarried and living together break up more often than married couples.

5. In some African-American wedding ceremonies, what does the couple jump over?

    a. Broom

    b. Bucket

    c. Rope

6. What color does the bride wear in a traditional Chinese wedding ceremony?

    a. Black

    b. Red

    c. Yellow

7. True or false: Between 1950 and 1980, the likelihood of a divorced woman's remarrying increased.

8. At U.S. military weddings, the couple may walk through an arch formed by
   a. Rifles
   b. Sabers
   c. Tanks

9. What's the symbol for the first wedding anniversary?
   a. Paper
   b. Tin
   c. Wood

10. True or false: Seventy-five percent of women in the U.S. have been married at least once by age 30.

Did you know . . .

Mae West once said, "Marriage is a great institution, but I'm not ready for an institution."

26. Cälorie Count

*Match these everyday activities to the number of
calories they burn for a 145-pound woman
in a half hour.*

1. Brushing teeth   a. 22

2. Computer work   b. 26

3. Cooking   c. 48

4. Gardening   d. 74

5. Grocery shopping   e. 82

6. Rearranging furniture   f. 83

7. Sleeping   g. 87

8. Vacuuming   h. 117

9. Washing dishes   i. 157

10. Watching TV   j. 218

27. Smells Like . . .

Forget celebrity look-alikes. You can be a celebrity smell-alike if you match these famous women to their "celebrity fragrances."

1. Cindy Adams	a. Girlfriend
2. Cher	b. Still
3. Patti LaBelle	c. Gossip
4. Jennifer Lopez	d. Manifesto
5. Miss Piggy	e. Moi
6. Stephanie Powers	f. Now & Forever
7. Joan Rivers	g. Rare Orchid
8. Isabella Rossellini	h. Shocking
9. Elizabeth Taylor	i. Uninhibited
10. Mae West	j. White Diamonds

Did you know . . .

Two episodes of *The Simpsons* mention a fictional celebrity fragrance called Meryl Streep's Versatility. It comes in an Oscar-shaped bottle.

28. Title Characters

Two big-name actresses, one title role.
Do you remember who was who?

1. In *Desperately Seeking Susan*, who played Susan?

   a. Rosanna Arquette   b. Madonna

2. In *Whatever Happened to Baby Jane*, who played Jane?

   a. Joan Crawford   b. Bette Davis

3. In *All About Eve*, who played Eve?

   a. Anne Baxter   b. Bette Davis

4. In *Julia*, who played Julia?

   a. Jane Fonda   b. Vanessa Redgrave

5. In *Hush Hush Sweet Charlotte*, who played Charlotte?

   a. Bette Davis   b. Olivia de Havilland

6. In the movie musical *My Sister Eileen*, who played Eileen?

   a. Betty Garrett   b. Janet Leigh

7. In the movie musical *Gypsy*, who played Gypsy Rose Lee?

   a. Rosalind Russell   b. Natalie Wood

8. In the original movie version of *Thoroughly Modern Millie*, who played Millie?

   a. Julie Andrews   b. Mary Tyler Moore

9. In the 1970s cult film *What's the Matter with Helen?*, who played Helen?

   a. Debbie Reynolds   b. Shelley Winters

10. In the movie version of *Agnes of God*, who played Agnes?

    a. Anne Bancroft   b. Meg Tilly

29. Birds Do It

Think your sex life is weird? See how much you know about mating in the animal kingdom.

1. At what age does a female hamster reach sexual maturity?

    a. 2 days

    b. 2 months

    c. 2 years

2. How many penises does a male iguana have?

    a. 1

    b. 2

    c. 4

3. How does a male whooping crane get a female ready for sex?

    a. By dancing for her

    b. By biting her

    c. By singing to her

4. What does a male octopus use to impregnate a female?

    a. His tentacle

    b. His penis

    c. His mouth

5. What's unusual about most species of whiptail lizards?

    a. They're all male

    b. They're all female

    c. They have sex for pleasure

6. Which is true of most kinds of sea bass?

    a. They're all male

    b. They're all female

    c. They can change gender

7. Where do seahorse eggs grow to maturity?

    a. In the female's stomach

    b. In the male's pouch

    c. Under a rock

8. How long is a typical elephant pregnancy?

    a. 9 months

    b. 12 months

    c. 22 months

9. What does a male proboscis monkey use to attract a female?

    a. Food

    b. Foreplay

    c. Facial features

10. How long does the sex act between a bull and a cow last?

    a. 5 seconds

    b. 5 minutes

    c. 35 minutes

Did you know . . .

The female black widow spider doesn't necessarily eat her mate after sex, but the female praying mantis usually does.

30. She Said What?

Match these words of wisdom with the women who said them.

1. "I base my fashion taste on what doesn't itch."

2. "An archaeologist is the best husband a woman can have; the older she gets, the more interested he is in her."

3. "The test for whether or not you can hold a job should not be the arrangement of your chromosomes."

4. "The trouble with some women is that they get all excited about nothing—and then marry him."

5. "If the world were a logical place, men would ride side saddle."

6. "Why are women . . . so much more interesting to men than men are to women?"

7. "Nobody can make you feel inferior without your consent."

8. "I've given my memoirs far more thought than any of my marriages. You can't divorce a book."

9. "My passport photo is one of the most remarkable photographs I have ever seen—no retouching, no shadows, no flattery—just stark me."

10. "I've never had a humble opinion in my life. If you're going to have one, why bother to be humble about it?"

who said it?

a. Bella Abzug   number_____

b. Joan Baez   number_____

c. Rita Mae Brown   number_____

d. Cher   number_____

e. Agatha Christie   number_____

f. Anne Morrow Lindbergh   number_____

g. Gilda Radner   number_____

h. Eleanor Roosevelt   number_____

i. Gloria Swanson   number_____

j. Virginia Woolf   number_____

31. Kiss Me, Kate

They called her the first lady of cinema. How much do you know about Katharine Hepburn and her films?

1. Kate runs a research library. Spencer Tracy plans to install a computer to replace her. Name the film.
    a. *Adam's Rib*
    b. *Desk Set*
    c. It doesn't exist

2. Which was the last film Kate made with Spencer Tracy?
    a. *Woman of the Year*
    b. *Guess Who's Coming to Dinner*
    c. *Summertime*

3. True or false: Katharine Hepburn starred in a film with John Wayne.

4. Kate went "royal" in a handful of films. Which queen did she portray in *The Lion in Winter*?
    a. Eleanor of Aquitaine
    b. Elizabeth I of England
    c. Marie Antoinette

5. What fashion choice made Kate infamous in the 1930s?
    a. Baring her midriff
    b. Piercing her ears
    c. Wearing slacks

6. True or false: Katharine Hepburn and Audrey Hepburn were half-sisters.

7. Kate is a Chinese peasant. Walter Huston is her father-in-law. Name the film.

    a. *A Bill of Divorcement*

    b. *Dragon Seed*

    c. It doesn't exist

8. Kate is a missionary. Humphrey Bogart is a sailor. Name the film.

    a. *The African Queen*

    b. *Christopher Strong*

    c. *Holiday*

9. True or false: Katharine Hepburn once played Elizabeth Taylor's aunt.

10. Kate starred in both the Broadway and movie versions of

    a. *Driving Miss Daisy*

    b. *The Philadelphia Story*

    c. *Woman of the Year*

Did you know . . .

Katharine Hepburn and Spencer Tracy, one of the all-time great screen couples, appeared in nine films together.

32. Color Full

*Match each color to the description
that suits it best.*

1. Red

2. Orange

3. Yellow

4. Green

5. Blue

6. Violet

7. Black

8. White

9. Gray

10. Pink

a. Character in early *Peanuts* comics

b. Color of jealousy

c. Laa-Laa of the Teletubbies is this color

d. Mrs. _____, The suspicious maid in the Clue board game

e. One-time color of brothel lights

f. "Panthers" founded by Maggie Kuhn

g. Rapper/singer Alecia Moore

h. Frederick's of Hollywood's revolutionary lingerie color

i. Traditional color of Buddhist monks' robes

j. Viagra color

33. More Likely

Who is more likely to . . .

1. Remarry after divorce

   Men   Women

2. Contract a sexually transmitted disease

   Men   Women

3. Be on a diet

   Men   Women

4. Be color blind

   Men   Women

5. Speed while driving

   Men   Women

6. Be diagnosed with prostate cancer

   Men   Women

7. Complete 4 years of college

   Men   Women

8. Recycle

   Men   Women

9. Smoke

   Men   Women

10. Commit suicide

    Men   Women

Did you know . . .

Women are three times more likely than men to contract autoimmune diseases such as lupus, multiple sclerosis, diabetes and rheumatoid arthritis. This could have something to do with the way a woman's body processes proteins.

34. Nobel Women

How much do you know about female Nobel Prize laureates?

1. Who was the first woman to win a Nobel Prize?

    a. Marie Curie

    b. Rita Levi-Montalcini

    c. Gerty Cori

2. Which is the only category in which a woman has not won a Nobel Prize?

    a. Chemistry

    b. Economics

    c. Physics

3. What American author of *Tar Baby* and *Beloved* won the Nobel Prize in literature?

    a. Zora Neale Hurston

    b. Toni Morrison

    c. Alice Walker

4. Aung San Suu Kyi won the 1991 Nobel Peace Prize for her work in which country?

    a. Burma

    b. China

    c. Laos

5. In 1997, American Jody Williams won the Nobel Peace Prize for her campaign against what?

    a. Female circumcision

    b. Landmines

    c. Slavery

6. Best known for her book *The Good Earth*, who was the first American woman to win the Nobel Prize in literature?

    a. Pearl S. Buck

    b. Willa Cather

    c. Clare Booth Luce

7. Barbara McClintock won the Nobel Prize in physiology or medicine for her research in what field?

    a. Genetics

    b. Gerontology

    c. Immunology

8. In which country did Nobel laureate Mother Teresa do most of her work?

    a. Bhutan

    b. India

    c. Pakistan

9. Who was the only woman to win two Nobel Prizes?

    a. Mother Teresa

    b. Dorothy Crowfoot Hodgkin

    c. Marie Curie

10. Nobel laureate Gertrude Belle Elion developed drugs to treat which ailment?

    a. Epilepsy

    b. Leukemia

    c. Stroke

Did you know . . .

Irene Joliot-Curie, the daughter of Nobel laureates Marie and Pierre Curie, is also a Nobel laureate. She shared the Nobel Prize in chemistry with her husband Frederic Joliot-Curie, in 1935.

35. Women's Timeline

What happened when in women's cultural history?
Match the events to the dates—it's tougher
than you think!

1. 1892

2. 1893

3. 1914

4. 1917

5. 1920

6. 1931

7. 1941

8. 1958

9. 1971

10. 1973

a. Barbie doll introduced

b. First female member joins U.S. Congress

c. First issue of *Vogue* magazine published

d. *The Joy of Cooking* first published

e. Mother's Day becomes an official holiday in the U.S.

f. Ms. is accepted as a prefix by the U.S. Government Printing Office

g. Women in New Zealand granted full voting rights

h. Women in U.S. granted full voting rights

i. Women in Switzerland granted full voting rights

j. *Wonder Woman* comic debuts

36. Mostly Martha

How many Marthas can you name?

1. Modern dance pioneer

   _____

2. Domestic "diva"

   _____

3. First first lady of the United States

   _____

4. Third first lady of the United States

   _____

5. *Rambling Rose* director

   _____

6. Leader of the Vandellas

   _____

7. "Big Mouth" comedienne

   _____

8. Original MTV veejay

   _____

9. Beatles' song that fits the category

   _____

10. Massachusetts island

    _____

Did you know . . .

St. Martha, who provided hospitality to Jesus in her home, is the patron saint of cooks, dieticians and homemakers.

37. First Women

Match these ground-breaking women with their accomplishments.

1. Bridgett Bishop

2. Elizabeth Blackwell

3. Louise Brown

4. Nadia Comaneci

5. Gertrude Ederle

6. Janet Guthrie

7. Mary Kies

8. Arabella Mansfield

9. Valentina Tereshkova

10. Victoria Woodhull

a. First woman to drive in the Indianapolis 500

b. First woman to pass the bar in the United States

c. First woman to graduate from a U.S. medical school

d. First "test-tube baby"

e. First woman to swim the English Channel

f. First woman to run for U.S. president

g. First woman in space

h. First U.S. woman to be granted a patent

i. First woman to be executed as a witch in Salem, Massachusetts

j. First woman to score a perfect "10" in Olympic gymnastics competition

38. Chick Flicks

*Romantic or empowering, sappy or snappy,
love 'em or hate 'em—you know you've
seen at least one.*

1. *You've Got Mail* was a remake of what 1940 chick flick?

   _____

2. Who played the young CC Bloom in *Beaches*?

   _____

3. Which of these Doris Day flicks did not pair Doris with Rock Hudson?

   a. *Lover Come Back*

   b. *Pillow Talk*

   c. *That Touch of Mink*

4. In *Thelma & Louise*, who played Thelma?

   _____

5. In the same film, who played Louise?

   _____

6. When (or more precisely where) did Harry meet Sally?

   _____

7. Where do the lovers plan to rendezvous in *An Affair to Remember*?

   a. Eiffel Tower

   b. Empire State Building

   c. Trafalgar Square

8. True or false: Julia Roberts and Richard Gere were married to each other in real life.

9. Which was the first chick flick to pair Sandra Bullock and Hugh Grant?

    a. *Miss Congeniality*

    b. *Notting Hill*

    c. *Two Weeks Notice*

10. Shirley Maclaine plays Debra Winger's mother. Name the chick flick.

_____

Did you know . . .

My Big Fat Greek Wedding, the surprise hit of 2002, grossed more than $200 million and passed *Pretty Woman* as the highest grossing romantic comedy of all time.

39. I Love to Tell the Story

Match these famous women with their autobiographies.

1. Rosalynn Carter

2. Patty Duke

3. Geri Halliwell

4. Lillian Hellman

5. Brenda Lee

6. Loretta Lynn

7. Susan McDougal

8. Queen Noor of Jordan

9. Suzanne Somers

10. Esther Williams

a. *If Only*

b. *Little Miss Dynamite*

c. *The Woman Who Wouldn't Talk*

d. *First Lady from Plains*

e. *Keeping Secrets*

f. *The Million-Dollar Mermaid*

g. *Still Woman Enough*

h. *An Unfinished Woman*

i. *Leap of Faith: Memoirs of an Unexpected Life*

j. *Call Me Anna*

40. The Cinderella Syndrome

How much do you know about that old fairy tale belle of the ball?

1. Who wrote the tale of Cinderella we know best?

    a. Carlo Collodi

    b. The Brothers Grimm

    c. Charles Perrault

2. Where did the oldest known version come from?

    a. China

    b. Egypt

    c. Greece

3. In what year did Disney's animated Cinderella debut?

    a. 1940

    b. 1950

    c. 1960

4. Which comedian starred in the film Cinderfella?

    a. Milton Berle

    b. Jerry Lewis

    c. Henny Youngman

5. Which *Brady Bunch* kid had a Cinderella complex?

    a. Bobby

    b. Cindy

    c. Jan

6. What time is Cinderella's "deadline" for leaving the ball?

    a. Dawn

    b. Midnight

    c. Sunset

7. Which rap group had a DJ called Spinderella?

    a. Run DMC

    b. Salt-N-Pepa

    c. TLC

8. Who played Cinderella in the original 1957 version of Rodgers & Hammerstein's Cinderella?

    a. Julie Andrews

    b. Mary Martin

    c. Lesley Ann Warren

9. Which one-named singer starred in the 1997 version of Rodgers & Hammerstein's Cinderella?

    a. Aaliyah

    b. Ashanti

    c. Brandy

10. Which is the Fairy Godmother's song in Disney's animated *Cinderella*?

    a. "Bibbidi-Bobbidi-Boo"

    b. "Impossible"

    c. "A Dream Is a Wish Your Heart Makes"

Did you know . . .

Helene Stanley, a film ingénue in the 1940s and 1950s, was Disney's live-action model for Cinderella, Sleeping Beauty, and the wife in *One Hundred and One Dalmatians*.

41. Person or Place

You never know how fashion inspiration will strike. Some of these fashions were inspired by people; some by places. Which is which?

1. Angora   Person   Place

2. Ascot   Person   Place

3. Bikini   Person   Place

4. Damask   Person   Place

5. Denim   Person   Place

6. Fedora   Person   Place

7. Leotard   Person   Place

8. Nehru jacket   Person   Place

9. Raglan sleeves   Person   Place

10. Tuxedo   Person   Place

42. Chocolate Covered

It's sweet and smooth and you might even crave it . . . um . . . periodically. But how much do you know about chocolate?

1. What is it called when brown chocolate develops a whitish coating?

    a. Bleed

    b. Blight

    c. Bloom

2. True or false: Dark chocolate and milk chocolate contain the same amount of caffeine.

3. Peter Paul brought the world Mounds and Almond Joy chocolate bars. For whom was the company named?

    a. The founder

    b. The founder's sons

    c. Saint Peter and Saint Paul

4. True or false: The United States is the world's largest per capita consumer of chocolate.

5. Which country is considered the "birthplace" of chocolate?

    a. China

    b. Mexico

    c. Switzerland

6. True or false: Women crave chocolate more often than men do.

7. What kind of frosting is used on a German chocolate cake?

    a. Coconut and pecan

    b. Marshmallow

    c. Whipped cream

8. Which came first?

    a. Angel food cake

    b. Devil's food cake

9. True or false: Cocoa butter is low in cholesterol.

10. Which is *not* a filling in a Sky Bar?

    a. Fudge

    b. Vanilla

    c. Raspberry

Did you know . . .

The melting point of cocoa butter is just below 98.6°F, which is why chocolate literally melts in your mouth.

43. Me Me Me

It all begins with "me"—like the names of these famous women, real and fictional.

1. American anthropologist

   _ _ _ _ _ _ _ ME_ _

2. "There's No Business Like Show Business" singer

   _ _ _ _ _ ME_ _ _ _

3. Wife of Emperor Claudius I

   _ _ _ _ _ _ _ ME_ _ _ _ _ _

4. Lorraine Bracco's role on *The Sopranos*

   _ _ . ME_ _ _

5. Gorgon of ancient Greece

   ME_ _ _ _

6. Florentine, and French queen

   _ _ _ _ _ _ _ _ _ _ _ ME_ _ _ _

7. "Peachy" Australian soprano

   _ _ _ _ _ _ ME_ _ _

8. Euripides' Greek tragic heroine

   ME_ _ _

9. Vivian Vance's alter-ego

   _ _ _ _ _ ME _ _ _

10. Israel's first female Prime Minister

    _ _ _ _ _ ME _ _

44. Shop 'til You Drop

It takes a great mind to be a great shopper, and this quiz proves it.

1. Where is the world's largest shopping mall?

    a. Bloomington, Minnesota

    b. Alberta, Canada

    c. Jakarta, Indonesia

2. Where is the world's largest department store?

    a. London

    b. New York

    c. Paris

3. What category of product had the most coupons distributed in 2000?

    a. Breakfast cereal

    b. Frozen food

    c. Household cleaners

4. Which U.S. retailer was known for its Blue Light Specials?

    a. Kmart

    b. Target

    c. Wal-Mart

5. How much did Americans spend on dog and cat food in 2002?

    a. $100 million

    b. $1 billion

    c. $10 billion

6. Which retailer had Andy Warhol drawing illustrations of shoes for its catalog?

    a. Bloomingdale's

    b. I. Miller

    c. Nordstrom

7. What is a BOGO sale?

    a. Boys Out, Girls Only

    b. Before Our Grand Opening

    c. Buy One, Get One

8. Which department store was the first to issue charge cards?

    a. Dayton-Hudson

    b. Filene's

    c. Marshall Field

9. What was the first type of clothing sold by Lane Bryant?

    a. Lingerie

    b. Maternity wear

    c. Swimwear

10. How many trips to the grocery store were made per household in the United States in 2002?

    a. 52

    b. 73

    c. 104

Did you know . . .

Retailers call the Friday after Thanksgiving "Black Friday" because the rush of shoppers on that day takes them out of the "red" (financial loss) and into the "black" (profit) for the year.

45. Butterfly Kisses

Ancient people throughout the world equated the butterfly with the soul. Let your soul take flight with this quiz.

1. Monarch butterflies are known for doing what?

    a. Dancing

    b. Migrating

    c. Singing

2. When butterflies are puddling, what are they doing?

    a. Absorbing nutrients

    b. Bathing

    c. Mating

3. Which pasta is named for butterflies?

    a. Cavatelli

    b. Farfalle

    c. Linguini

4. About how long does it take for Monarch butterflies to copulate?

    a. 16 seconds

    b. 16 minutes

    c. 16 hours

5. How many wings do butterflies have?

    a. 2

    b. 4

    c. 6

6. What's special about Queen Alexandra's Birdwing?

    a. It's the world's largest butterfly

    b. It's the world's smallest butterfly

    c. It's the only butterfly found in Antarctica

7. How fast do the fastest butterflies fly?

    a. 100 miles per hour

    b. 30 miles per hour

    c. 5 miles per hour

8. How much does an adult butterfly grow?

    a. 1/2 inch to 1 inch in its lifetime

    b. 1 to 2 inches in its lifetime

    c. Adult butterflies don't grow

9. What do a butterfly's scales do?

    a. Give its wings color

    b. Make noise

    c. Protect its eyes

10. What makes the Mourning Cloak stand out among butterflies?

    a. It's the only pure black butterfly

    b. It can swim

    c. It has the longest lifespan of all butterflies

46. Miss Thing

Match these celebrities to the pageant titles they once held.

1. Halle Berry
2. Delta Burke
3. Zsa Zsa Gabor
4. Kim Novak
5. Diane Sawyer
6. Sharon Stone
7. Tiffani-Amber Thiessen
8. Vanessa Williams
9. Oprah Winfrey
10. Michelle Yeoh

a. Miss New York
b. Miss Junior America
c. Miss Fire Prevention
d. Miss Crawford County
e. Miss Teen All American
f. Miss Malaysia
g. Miss Hungary
h. America's Junior Miss
i. Miss Deepfreeze
j. Miss Orlando Action Princess

Did you know . . .

Erika Harold, Miss America 2003, received a $50,000 scholarship as part of her prize winnings.

47. Old Testament Women

Fill in the names of these Biblical women.

1. Samson's downfall

   _____

2. Sister of Moses

   _____

3. King David's great-grandmother

   _____

4. Jacob's wives

   _____

5. Kenite murderess

   _____

6. Mother of the prophet Samuel

   _____

7. First lady

   _____

8. Helped Joshua at Jericho

   _____

9. Principal figure in the feast of Purim

   _____

10. Prophetess and judge

    _____

48. O' Baby

Match each of these women—real and fictional—to the description that suits her best.

1. Helen O'Connell

2. Flannery O'Connor

3. Sinead O'Connor

4. Rosie O'Donnell

5. Madalyn Murray O'Hair

6. Scarlett O'Hara

7. Georgia O'Keeffe

8. Kate O'Leary

9. Tatum O'Neal

10. Dolores O'Riordan

a. 1973 Oscar winner

b. American painter

c. American short-story writer

d. Big-band singer

e. Chicago cow owner

f. The Cranberries lead singer

g. *Gone With the Wind* heroine

h. Noted atheist

i. "Nothing Compares 2 U" singer

j. Talk-show host and comedienne

49. The Beauty Treatment

Since the earliest days of womanhood, we've been painting, plucking and primping ourselves. Why? We can't answer that. But can you answer these beauty questions?

1. What color did high-ranking ancient Egyptian women paint their nails?

    a. Red

    b. Black

    c. Gold

2. Which cosmetics pioneer created the first make-up especially for motion pictures?

    a. Elizabeth Arden

    b. Max Factor

    c. Estee Lauder

3. Which product made Maybelline a household name?

    a. Lipstick

    b. Mascara

    c. Perfume

4. To cover up red spots, make-up artists use cosmetics in which color?

    a. Blue

    b. Green

    c. Pink

5. Which famous writer inspired Avon's name?

    a. Virginia Woolf

    b. Lucy Maud Montgomery

    c. William Shakespeare

6. Whose slogan was "Does she or doesn't she?"

   a. Clairol

   b. L'Oréal

   c. Revlon

7. What was Noxzema originally marketed to do?

   a. Remove makeup

   b. Reduce wrinkles

   c. Soothe sunburn

8. Eye shadow doesn't last forever. When should you throw out your old ones?

   a. 12 months

   b. 18 months

   c. 2 years

9. Mary Kay Cosmetics' top salespeople sometimes drive around in this car

   a. Gold Mercedes

   b. Pink Cadillac

   c. Silver Rolls Royce

10. Who brought waterproof mascara to the world?

    a. Helena Rubinstein

    b. Elizabeth Arden

    c. Revlon

Did you know . . .

After serving as the "face" of Revlon for 11 years, model Cindy Crawford was replaced in 2000. She was 34 at the time.

50. She's a Buckeye

They call Ohio the "Buckeye State." These famous women have called it home.

1. "This is what 50 looks like," she said
   _____

2. *Carmen Jones* actress_____

3. Pretenders singer_____

4. First woman to fly solo around the world
   _____

5. Sharp-shooting cowgirl_____

6. "Domestic" humorist and newspaper columnist
   _____

7. Cartoonist for the single woman
   _____

8. 1930s architecture photographer
   _____

9. Comedienne wife of "Fang"
   _____

10. Silent-screen vamp_____

Did you know . . .

A buckeye is a kind of chestnut that looks like the eye of a buck deer.

51. Signature Songs

They've sung a lot of songs, but each of these women is known for one special tune. Match these vocalists to their "signature" songs.

1. Shirley Bassey   a. "Fever"

2. Doris Day   b. "God Bless America"

3. Gloria Gaynor   c. "Goldfinger"

4. Lena Horne   d. "Harper Valley P.T.A."

5. Peggy Lee   e. "I Am Woman"

6. Edith Piaf   f. "I Will Survive"

7. Helen Reddy   g. "La Vie en Rose"

8. Jeannie C. Riley   h. "Que Sera Sera"

9. Kate Smith   i. "Stand By Your Man"

10. Tammy Wynette   j. "Stormy Weather"

52. Queen of the Nile

How much do you know about the legendary Egyptian queen Cleopatra?

1. How old was Cleopatra when she became queen of Egypt?

    a. 12

    b. 18

    c. 25

2. What was unusual about her husband?

    a. He was her brother

    b. He was her father

    c. He was her son

3. Where would Cleopatra have worn her kohl?

    a. Around her eyes

    b. Around her head

    c. Around her waist

4. What was her primary language?

    a. Egyptian

    b. Greek

    c. Latin

5. Historians say she wasn't beautiful. Where did they see her portrait?

    a. On temple walls

    b. Inside the pyramids

    c. On coins

6. Even so, she managed to charm which Roman emperor?

    a. Julius Caesar

    b. Augustus Caesar

    c. Nero

7. When she met him, how was she disguised?

    a. As a maid

    b. As a man

    c. As a carpet

8. Who was the father of Cleopatra's twins?

    a. Mark Antony

    b. Lepidus

    c. Tiberius

9. How did she die?

    a. She was murdered

    b. She died in battle

    c. She committed suicide

10. How was she buried?

    a. Alone

    b. With her first husband

    c. With her lover

Did you know . . .

Cleopatra was not born in Egypt. She was born in Macedonia, which was part of Greece.

53. In Your Dreams

Are these sleep facts true in the light of day, or only in your dreams?

1. In a 1998 National Sleep Foundation poll, women surveyed slept an average of 8 hours a night.

   In the light of day   In your dreams

2. Pregnant women sleep best during the second trimester of pregnancy.

   In the light of day   In your dreams

3. More women than men suffer from restless legs syndrome.

   In the light of day   In your dreams

4. Sleep-eating is a sleep disorder similar to sleep-walking and sleep-talking.

   In the light of day   In your dreams

5. More men than women say that they suffer from insomnia.

   In the light of day   In your dreams

6. Exercising right before bedtime helps you sleep better.

   In the light of day   In your dreams

7. Babies need less sleep than adults do.

   In the light of day   In your dreams

8. Pregnant women don't snore.

   In the light of day   In your dreams

9. Women have more trouble sleeping during menstruation.

   In the light of day   In your dreams

10. The warmer the room, the easier it is to fall asleep.

    In the light of day   In your dreams

54. A Price Above Rubies

*Test your "brilliance" with these questions
about gemstones.*

1. Ancient Greeks believed amethyst protected against what?

    a. Drunkenness

    b. Infidelity

    c. Miscarriage

2. What color is tanzanite?

    a. Olive green

    b. Golden yellow

    c. Bright blue

3. What was the principal stone in Princess Diana's engagement ring?

    a. Emerald

    b. Ruby

    c. Sapphire

4. Where do most of the world's emeralds come from?

    a. Chile

    b. Colombia

    c. Senegal

5. In ancient Greece, what were emeralds said to prevent?

    a. Toothache

    b. Eyestrain

    c. Hemorrhoids

6. Which stone was used in "mourning jewelry"?

    a. Jet

    b. Opal

    c. Topaz

7. Which of these stones was considered to be unlucky?

    a. Garnet

    b. Opal

    c. Turquoise

8. Which gem was ground up to make paint for medieval monks?

    a. Aquamarine

    b. Diamond

    c. Lapis lazuli

9. Which of these isn't really a stone?

    a. Agate

    b. Amber

    c. Jasper

10. Traditionally, which term describes the color of high-quality rubies?

    a. Pigeon's blood

    b. Quail's eye

    c. Swallow's foot

Did you know . . .

"Who can find a virtuous woman? For her price is far above rubies. The heart of her husband doth safely trust in her" comes from the Old Testament, Proverbs 31:10-11.

55. This Is a Bust

Big or small, we're all blessed with breasts. How much do you know about yours?

1. Breasts are composed mainly of
    a. Fat
    b. Muscle
    c. Ligaments

2. Where would you find your Montgomery's glands?
    a. In your armpit
    b. Around your nipple
    c. In your upper chest

3. When was the first specialized mammography machine developed?
    a. 1944
    b. 1955
    c. 1966

4. True or false: A woman's nipples change color during pregnancy.

5. Which is the most common bra size in the United States?
    a. 34 B
    b. 36 B
    c. 36 C

6. How much does the average D cup breast weigh?
    a. 2 pounds
    b. 4 pounds
    c. 8 pounds

7. Where was the Wonderbra invented?

    a. Canada

    b. England

    c. United States

8. True or false: Large-breasted women produce more milk than small-breasted women.

9. Who designed the cone-shaped bras Madonna wore on her 1990 Blonde Ambition tour?

    a. Dolce & Gabbana

    b. Jean-Paul Gaultier

    c. Christian Lacroix

10. Where should you measure yourself to determine your bra size?

    a. Around your upper rib cage

    b. Across your nipples

    c. Both

Did you know . . .

Shot in a 2002 gun battle between police and drug pushers in Rio de Janeiro, a woman was saved by her silicone breast implants. They slowed the bullet enough to prevent it from damaging her vital organs.

56. Gentlemen Prefer Blondes

For this quiz, so do we. What do you know about your fair-haired sisters?

1. *Legally Blonde* star

   _____

2. Blondie lead singer

   _____

3. The movies' "Blonde Venus"

   _____

4. Dagwood's comic-strip wife

   _____

5. Nameless "Blonde in T-bird" of *American Graffiti*

   _____

6. Blonde at the helm of Hewlett-Packard

   _____

7. Nickname of roller derby's Joan Weston

   _____

8. Gossip columnist and author of *Natural Blonde*

   _____

9. Author of *Gentlemen Prefer Blondes*

   _____

10. Dorothy Parker's blonde tale

   _____

57. Fashionable Women

Show what you know about these female fashion trendsetters.

1. Which British designer is credited with introducing the miniskirt?

    a. Georgina Godley

    b. Mary Quant

    c. Vivienne Westwood

2. By what name is model Lesley Hornby better known?

    a. Dovima

    b. Twiggy

    c. Veruschka

3. Vera Wang is best known for designing what?

    a. Menswear

    b. Shoes

    c. Wedding gowns

4. Who was the first black model to be featured on the cover of American *Vogue*?

    a. Naomi Campbell

    b. Iman

    c. Beverly Johnson

5. Which material did Norma Kamali turn into a high-fashion staple in the 1980s?

    a. Fleece

    b. Leather

    c. Washable silk

6. Which 1980s pop group immortalized Katharine Hamnett's "Choose Life" T-shirts?

    a. Abba

    b. Duran Duran

    c. Wham!

7. When you think of Laura Ashley, which fabric comes to mind?

    a. Calico

    b. Lycra

    c. Stretch denim

8. With which fashion designer did Donna Karan begin her career?

    a. Anne Klein

    b. Calvin Klein

    c. Ralph Lauren

9. What fashion item made Diane von Fürstenberg famous?

    a. Hand-knit sweater

    b. Jeweled pocketbook

    c. Wrap dress

10. Which symbol is Gloria Vanderbilt's trademark?

    a. Rose

    b. Swan

    c. Tiger

Did you know . . .

American model Lauren Hutton holds the record for the most appearances on the cover of *Vogue* with 25.

58. Double Your Pleasure

Two is better than one when it comes to the initials of these famous females.

1. Second first lady

    A_____ A_____

2. U.S. speed-skating gold medalist

    B_____ B_____

3. French fashion legend

    C_____ C_____

4. American pioneer in the care of the mentally ill

    D_____ D_____

5. Groundbreaking cookbook author

    F_____ F_____

6. *The Female Eunuch* author

    G_____ G_____

7. Gossip columnist called "the Hat"

    H_____ H_____

8. "I Love Rock 'n' Roll" singer

    J_____ J_____

9. World's most tattooed woman

    K_____ K_____

10. Celebrated beauty and maybe the mistress of England's Edward VII

    L_____ L_____

59. Rose Fever

"Rose is a rose," said Gertrude Stein. We're not sure what she meant, but she'd probably ace this quiz about America's favorite flower. What's your rose IQ?

1. Which new variety was introduced in 2002?

    a. Cappuccino

    b. Green Tea

    c. Hot Cocoa

2. Which holiday ranks #1 for rose purchases?

    a. Christmas

    b. Mother's Day

    c. Valentine's Day

3. How long is a "long-stemmed" rose?

    a. 12 inches

    b. 15 inches

    c. 18 inches

4. What part of the rose holds the scent?

    a. Petals

    b. Leaves

    c. Both

5. What color is a Dolly Parton rose?

    a. Yellow

    b. Orange-red

    c. Salmon

6. How did tea roses get their name?

    a. They smell like tea

    b. They're used to make tea

    c. They were traditional decorations at tea parties

7. What are thrips?

    a. Garden pests

    b. Roses that bloom three times a season

    c. Leaves with three leaflets

8. Which is true about cutting rose stems?

    a. You should cut them on an angle

    b. You should cut them underwater

    c. Both

9. Rose hips are nutritionally loaded with which vitamin?

    a. A

    b. B

    c. C

10. How did cabbage roses get their name?

    a. They look like cabbage

    b. They smell like cabbage

    c. They taste like cabbage

Did you know . . .

Roses for perfume are picked at night when their scent is the strongest.

60. M . . . M . . . Good

Name these women with m . . m . . matching initials.

1. She played Marcia Brady.

   M_____M_____

2. Founder of the alternative childhood education schools that bear her name.

   M_____M_____

3. "The Morning After" singer.

   M_____M_____

4. Female disciple of Jesus

   M_____M_____

5. Pulitzer-Prize-winning poet and baseball fan.

   M_____M_____

6. Astronomer known for her discovery of a comet in 1847.

   M_____M_____

7. Late actress and Greek minister of culture.

   M_____M_____

8. First black woman to win a Best Supporting Actress Tony.

   M_____M_____

9. Folk heroine who sold "cockles and mussels, alive, alive oh!"

   M_____M_____

10. "Midnight at the Oasis" singer.

    M_____M_____

Did you know . . .

M&M candies were named for Mars and Murrie, the founders of the company.

61. Did She Really?

Women have done some amazing things. Which of these statements are true about women's accomplishments?

1. A woman gave birth to sixty-nine children.

   Really   Not really

2. The oldest woman to climb Mt. Everest was 60.

   Really   Not really

3. No woman ever rowed a boat across the Atlantic Ocean.

   Really   Not really

4. A woman gave birth to twins who had different fathers.

   Really   Not really

5. No woman has been the head of state in a predominantly Muslim country.

   Really   Not really

6. A woman was the first person to go over Niagara Falls in a barrel.

   Really   Not really

7. A woman voluntarily sat in a bath of maggots for 90 minutes.

   Really   Not really

8. A woman holds the record for the fastest run up the Empire State Building.

   Really   Not really

9. A woman wrote the world's best-selling diary.

   Really   Not really

10. A woman survived a fall of more than 33,000 feet without a parachute.

    Really   Not really

62. Initially

These fundamentally female concepts stand for something—can you tell what it is from their initials?

1. DAR

_____

2. YWCA

_____

3. GSA

_____

4. NOW

_____

5. ERA

_____

6. HRT

_____

7. WAC

_____

8. MADD

_____

9. LWV

_____

10. WCTU

_____

63. Bay State Babes

Massachusetts has produced women of great accomplishment. What do you know about women from the Bay State?

1. Which poet was known as the "Belle of Amherst"?

    a. Emily Dickinson

    b. Sylvia Plath

    c. Anne Sexton

2. What do Sophia Smith and Mary Lyon have in common?

    a. They were the first women to graduate from Harvard

    b. They founded women's colleges in Massachusetts

    c. They opened Boston's first library

3. Which Olympic figure skater hails from Woburn?

    a. Tenley Albright

    b. Tonya Harding

    c. Nancy Kerrigan

4. Which disco queen was born Adrian Donna Gaines in Boston?

    a. Gloria Gaynor

    b. Thelma Houston

    c. Donna Summer

5. She's the "I Don't Want to Wait" singer from Rockport

    a. Paula Cole

    b. Juliana Hatfield

    c. Aimee Mann

6. What did Eleanor Raymond from Cambridge do in 1948?

    a. Became mayor of Boston

    b. Opened a college for the blind

    c. Designed a solar-powered house

7. In 2001, which woman from Adams became the youngest female governor in U.S. history?

    a. Jane Alexander

    b. Jane Byrne

    c. Jane M. Swift

8. Which TV interviewer from Boston was the first female co-host of *The Today Show*?

    a. Katie Couric

    b. Jane Pauley

    c. Barbara Walters

9. Anne Whitney of Watertown was highly regarded in which field of art?

    a. Etching

    b. Sculpture

    c. Watercolor painting

10. What was the connection between Deborah Sampson of Middleboro and Robert Shurtliff?

    a. "He" was her alias

    b. He was her doctor

    b. He was her husband

Did you know . . .

"Boston Marriage" was a 19th-century term used to describe a relationship between two single women who were long-time friends and roommates.

64. Power of Three

What do these groups of three have in common?

1. Monica, Phoebe, Rachel

   _____

2. Natalie Maines, Martie Maguire, Emily Robison

   _____

3. Lee Meriwether, Eartha Kitt, Julie Newmar

   _____

4. Anne, Charlotte, Emily

   _____

5. Zsuzsa, Zsofia, and Judit Polgar

   _____

6. Patty, Maxene, LaVerne

   _____

7. Clotho, Lachesis, Atropos

   _____

8. Olga, Masha, and Irina Prozorov

   _____

9. Maureen Connolly, Margaret Court, Steffi Graf

   _____

10. Cynthia Cooper, Coleen Rowley, Sherron Watkins

   _____

65. The Sopranos

We mean the operatic kind! Match these leading roles to their character descriptions—then please explain why so many of them die at the end of the show.

1. Norma _____

2. Tosca _____

3. Lucia di Lammermoor _____

4. Violetta in *La Traviata* _____

5. Aïda _____

6. Carmen _____

7. *Girl of the Golden West* leading lady _____

8. La Gioconda _____

9. Salome _____

10. Madam Butterfly _____

a. The soprano is an Ethiopian slave in love with an Egyptian soldier. When he's convicted of treason and sentenced to be buried alive, she sneaks into his tomb so they can die together.

b. The soprano is Minnie, a California saloonkeeper. She falls in love with Dick, a bank robber, protects him from the posse trying to capture him, and rides off into the sunset with him in the end.

c. The soprano is a singer in love with a painter. He is arrested and tortured in jail. She tries to save him from execution, but she's unsuccessful. So she commits suicide out of grief.

d. The soprano is a Druid high priestess. When her unfaithful Roman lover is sentenced to death, she throws herself onto his funeral pyre.

e. The soprano is the sister of a Scottish nobleman who marries her off to a man she doesn't love. She murders her new husband on their wedding night, goes mad and dies moments later.

f. The soprano is a ballad singer in Venice. To save the man she loves—so that he can marry someone else—she offers herself to the opera's villain. Ultimately, she can't face fulfilling that promise, and stabs herself to death instead.

g. The soprano has tuberculosis. She loves Alfredo, but his father asks her to break off the relationship. When she and Alfredo finally reconcile, she's desperately ill and dies soon after.

h. The soprano is hopelessly in love with John the Baptist, who has been imprisoned by her stepfather Herod. After John spurns her, she persuades Herod to execute him. But her triumph is short-lived, as Herod's soldiers crush her to death in the end.

i. The soprano is a 15-year-old Japanese girl who marries an American soldier. When he leaves her, she's sure he's coming back. But when he finally returns with his new American wife, she kills herself.

j. The soprano is a gypsy who works in a Spanish cigarette factory. Madly in love, a young soldier gives up his career for her. When she jilts him and takes up with a bullfighter, he murders her.

Did you know . . .

Maria Callas, one of the great sopranos of all time, performed in her first starring role as Tosca in Athens in 194 2. Her last role also was Tosca, performed in London in 1965.

66. I Do, I Do

Being in a bridal party isn't only about wearing a goofy dress. Everyone has a job to do, but—according to Emily Post—who does what?

1. Makes the first toast at the reception

   _____

2. Holds the bride's bouquet at the ceremony

   _____

3. Escorts the groom's mother to her seat

   _____

4. Pays for the bride's wedding ring_____

5. Pays for the bride's gown_____

6. Organizes a bridal shower_____

7. Pays for the honeymoon_____

8. Holds the bride's ring during the ceremony

   _____

9. Escorts the bride up the aisle_____

10. Stands first in the receiving line_____

Did you know...

Newspaper columnist Emily Post wrote the first edition of *Etiquette* in 1922. After her death in 1960, her granddaughter-in-law and great-granddaughter-in-law continued the family etiquette "franchise" with updated guides to social protocol.

67. Swingin' Girls of Song

Name the swingin' chicks mentioned in these songs of the 1960s and 1970s.

1. "Because Love Grows (Where My _____ Goes)/And nobody knows like me."

2. "And then Along Comes _____/And does she want to give me kicks, and be my steady chick . . ."

3. "Just Walk Away _____/You won't see me follow you back home."

4. "_____ the Prima Donna/Broke my heart."

5. "Help Me _____, Help, help me _____."

6. "Keep away from-a Runaround _____."

7. "_____ in Disguise . . . with glasses."

8. "So Take a Letter _____, address it to my wife . . ."

9. "Sweet _____/Good times never seemed so good."

10. "_____ Juniper, hair of golden flax."

68. Olympians

Hundreds of women from around the world compete at the summer and winter Olympic Games. Can you match these global Olympic stars to their events?

1. Princess Anne of England   a. Speed skating

2. Birgit Fisher   b. Equestrian events

3. Dawn Fraser   c. Alpine skiing

4. Daina Gudzineviciute   d. Track and field

5. Sonja Henie   e. Gymnastics

6. Janica Kostelic   f. Marathon

7. Catriona LeMay Doan   g. Trap shooting

8. Merlene Ottey   h. Canoeing

9. Naoko Takahashi   i. Figure skating

10. Ludmilla Turischeva   j. Swimming

Did you know . . .

The first modern Olympics took place in 1896. Women were not allowed to compete until the second modern Olympics—in 1900.

69. She's Got Spirit

Which of these famous women were high school cheerleaders?

1. Sandra Bullock   Rah, rah, rah   Ha, ha, ha

2. Laura Welch Bush   Rah, rah, rah   Ha, ha, ha

3. Mariah Carey   Rah, rah, rah   Ha, ha, ha

4. Hillary Rodham Clinton   Rah, rah, rah   Ha, ha, ha

5. Calista Flockhart   Rah, rah, rah   Ha, ha, ha

6. Jennifer Lopez   Rah, rah, rah   Ha, ha, ha

7. Madonna   Rah, rah, rah   Ha, ha, ha

8. Julia Roberts   Rah, rah, rah   Ha, ha, ha

9. Meryl Streep   Rah, rah, rah   Ha, ha, ha

10. Renee Zellweger   Rah, rah, rah   Ha, ha, ha

70. It's Me, Margaret

Their close friends might call them Maggie, Meg or even Peg, but we think of them as the world's best-known Margarets.

1. *Gone With the Wind* author_____

2. U.S. birth-control pioneer_____

3. First female prime minister of Great Britain

   _____

4. *M*A*S*H* character called "Hot Lips"

   _____

5. Actress best known as "The Wicked Witch of the West"

   _____

6. "Notorious" Korean-American comedienne

   _____

7. Presidential daughter and mystery writer

   _____

8. First woman elected to U.S. Congress and Senate

   _____

9. First official female photojournalist of World War II

   _____

10. 1940s child star and Oscar winner_____

Did you know . . .

With more than 6 million copies in print, Judy Blume's 1970 book, *Are You There God? It's Me, Margaret*, is one of the top-selling young adult novels of all time.

71. Holy Women

Each of these women became famous for her religious calling. What do you know about these spiritual sisters?

1. Which American-based religion was founded by Mary Baker Eddy?

    a. First Church of Christ, Scientist

    b. Mormonism

    c. United Church of Christ

2. Elizabeth Bayley Seton was the first American-born what?

    a. Methodist minister

    b. Rabbi

    c. Saint

3. In 1974, Episcopal Church pioneer Betty Bone Schiess led a successful campaign to do what?

    a. Abolish school prayer

    b. Allow women to be ordained as priests

    c. Publish Bibles in Communist China

4. What was Khadijah's relationship to the prophet Muhammad?

    a. Daughter

    b. Mother

    c. Wife

5. Which best describes Sister Aimee Semple McPherson?

    a. Activist

    b. Evangelist

    c. Nun

6. Mother Ann Lee led members of this religious group from England to the United States.

a. Jehovah's Witnesses

b. Seventh-Day Adventists

c. Shakers

7. In what year was Sally Priesand, the first female rabbi in the U.S., ordained?

a. 1910

b. 1972

c. 1993

8. What's special about Samding Dorji Phagmo in the Tibetan Buddhist tradition?

a. She is the head of a Buddhist monastery

b. She's the Dalai Lama's wife

c. She's the Dalai Lama's mother

9. In what country was St. Frances Xavier Cabrini born?

a. Argentina

b. Italy

c. United States

10. Rabi'a is considered a female saint among followers of which religion?

a. Sufism

b. Taoism

c. Zoroastrianism

72. Just Marilyn

Marilyn Monroe will forever be remembered as the world's greatest sex symbol. What do you know about Hollywood's best-loved blonde?

1. True or false: Marilyn was a natural blonde.

2. In which film did Marilyn play Sugar Cane, a ukulele-strumming singer?

    a. *Bus Stop*

    b. *Niagara*

    c. *Some Like It Hot*

3. True or false: The mole on Marilyn's chin was real.

4. Which film featured the famous scene of Marilyn's dress blowing up above her knees?

    a. *Monkey Business*

    b. *River of No Return*

    c. *The Seven-Year Itch*

5. True or false: Marilyn appeared in *Playboy*.

6. Which baseball player became Marilyn's second husband?

    a. Joe DiMaggio

    b. Mickey Mantle

    c. Ted Williams

7. True or false: Marilyn's figure was surgically enhanced.

8. Which playwright was Marilyn's third husband?

    a. Arthur Miller

    b. Clifford Odets

    c. Harold Pinter

9. True or false: Marilyn was never nominated for an Academy Award.

10. Which was Marilyn's last film?

     a. *Don't Bother to Knock*

     b. *The Misfits*

     c. *The Prince and the Showgirl*

Did you know . . .

In *How to Marry a Millionaire*, Marilyn played a near-sighted woman who refused to wear her glasses in public. In real life, Marilyn wore glasses—but not in public.

73. Lone Star Women

What do you know about women from Texas? Maybe more than you think.

1. Which is a classic album from Janis Joplin of Port Arthur?

    a. *Diamond*

    b. *Emerald*

    c. *Pearl*

2. Babe Didrikson was another Texan from Port Arthur. What was her field of endeavor?

    a. Athletics

    b. Journalism

    c. Medicine

3. Irene Ryan from El Paso became a TV icon on which show?

    a. *The Beverly Hillbillies*

    b. *Bewitched*

    c. *Gilligan's Island*

4. This lady from Lakeview was the governor of Texas from 1991 to 1995.

    a. Laura Bush

    b. Barbara Jordan

    c. Ann Richards

5. Molly Ivins is one outspoken Lone Star woman. What does she do for a living?

    a. Lawyer

    b. Newspaper columnist

    c. Politician

6. Selena, from Lake Jackson, was famous for singing what type of music?

    a. Calypso

    b. Salsa

    c. Tejano

7. Which of the original Charlie's Angels was *not* a Lone Star woman?

    a. Farrah Fawcett

    b. Kate Jackson

    c. Jaclyn Smith

8. El Paso-born Sandra Day O'Connor has held some important jobs, but *not* this one.

    a. Arizona state senator

    b. U.S. Secretary of State

    c. U.S. Supreme Court justice

9. This *Ship of Fools* author was born in Indian Creek.

    a. Willa Cather

    b. Kate Chopin

    c. Katherine Anne Porter

10. Just call her "Mommie Dearest" from San Antonio.

    a. Joan Crawford

    b. Bette Davis

    c. Ava Gardner

Did you know . . .

In 1924, Miriam Amanda "Ma" Ferguson became the first female governor of Texas. A staunch opponent of the Ku Klux Klan, she passed a law that would have forced klansmen to be unmasked. The local courts did not uphold it.

74. Mind Your Manners

Are you more familiar with fine dining or fast food? This test will tell, as you decide whether these rules of the table are in "perfect taste" or a "recipe for disaster."

1. The dessert fork should be placed above the dinner plate.

   Perfect taste   Recipe for disaster

2. It is acceptable to eat asparagus using your fingers.

   Perfect taste   Recipe for disaster

3. Cut your entire steak into small pieces before your first bite.

   Perfect taste   Recipe for disaster

4. Wait staff should always serve diners from the right.

   Perfect taste   Recipe for disaster

5. If you burp at the table, don't draw attention to yourself by saying "excuse me."

   Perfect taste   Recipe for disaster

6. At a formal dinner party, a woman should not be seated next to her husband or companion.

   Perfect taste   Recipe for disaster

7. Salad may be properly served after the main course.

   Perfect taste   Recipe for disaster

8. It is acceptable to blow on your soup to cool it.

   Perfect taste   Recipe for disaster

9. If you bite into a piece of bone or gristle, just chew and swallow like nothing is wrong.

   Perfect taste   Recipe for disaster

10. Your red wine glass has a relatively short stem and a rounded bowl.

    Perfect taste   Recipe for disaster

75. Notorious

There are good girls and there are bad girls. These girls were very, very bad.

1. Who was Bonnie Parker's partner in crime?

    a. Clyde Barrow

    b. Butch Cassidy

    c. Parker Stevenson

2. Who were Lizzie Borden's alleged murder victims?

    a. Her children

    b. Her husband and his lover

    c. Her parents

3. Which art-world big did Valerie Solanas shoot in 1968?

    a. Pablo Picasso

    b. Jackson Pollock

    c. Andy Warhol

4. For what crime was actress Winona Ryder arrested?

    a. Arson

    b. Shoplifting

    c. Vehicular homicide

5. How did Charlotte Corday murder Jean-Paul Marat?

    a. Stabbing

    b. Poisoning

    c. Explosives

6. What was Typhoid Mary's profession?

    a. Cook

    b. Housekeeper

    c. Nurse

7. What made Christine Keeler notorious?

    a. Bank fraud

    b. Drug trafficking

    c. Sex scandals

8. Mata Hari was a World War I spy, but for whom?

    a. France

    b. Germany

    c. United States

9. Why are Patricia Krenwinkel, Susan Atkins and Leslie Van Houten in prison?

    a. Kidnapping

    b. Murder

    c. Treason

10. What line of crime did Mary Read and Anne Bonney pursue?

    a. Embezzlement

    b. Piracy

    c. Train robbery

Did you know . . .

During the French Revolution Marie Gresholtz Tussaud was hired to make wax "death masks" of people who were executed on the guillotine. In 1802, after the Revolution, she opened Madame Tussaud's wax museum in London. In addition to the death masks, it featured a Chamber of Horrors exhibit of torture equipment.

76. Heart Throbs

As long as there have been teenagers, there have been teen idols. Match these baby-faced boy singers to their hit songs.

1. Frankie Avalon

2. David Cassidy

3. Tony DeFranco

4. Leif Garrett

5. Andy Gibb

6. Rick Nelson

7. New Kids on the Block

8. Donny Osmond

9. Bobby Sherman

10. Rick Springfield

a. "Heartbeat is a Love Beat"

b. "Hello Mary Lou"

c. "I Just Want to be Your Everything"

d. "I Think I Love You"

e. "I Was Made for Dancing"

f. "I'll be Loving You (Forever)"

g. "Jessie's Girl"

h. "Julie, Do Ya Love Me?"

i. "Puppy Love"

j. "Venus"

Did you know . . .

David Cassidy, Donny Osmond and Andy Gibb all starred in stage productions of *Joseph and the Amazing Technicolor Dreamcoat*.

77. You Jane

Well, maybe not you, *but these women—real and fictional—are Jane. Can you name them?*

1. *Emma* author_____

2. *Father Knows Best* mother portrayer

   _____

3. Hull-House founder_____

4. Space-age cartoon wife_____

5. Actress and former head of the National Endowment for the Arts _____

6. Queen of England for 9 days

   _____

7. Nominated for a Best Director Oscar

   _____

8. Tragic fictional governess

   _____

9. Tarzan's love interest_____

10. Author and *New York Times* personal health columnist_____

Did you know . . .

Editor Jane Pratt started *Jane* magazine in 1997.

78. Easy as Pie

Oh go ahead! Cut yourself a slice and answer these questions about one of America's favorite desserts.

1. Which pie doesn't get baked?

    a. Grasshopper pie

    b. Lemon Meringue pie

    c. Pecan pie

2. Where was Key lime pie invented?

    a. California

    b. Florida

    c. New York

3. True or false: Shoofly pie is filled with molasses and brown sugar.

4. Which is not a sweet pie?

    a. Chess pie

    b. Mincemeat pie

    c. Shepherd's pie

5. What's the common filling for Funeral pie?

    a. Apricots

    b. Prunes

    c. Raisins

6. True or false: Boston cream pie is traditionally made with a graham cracker crust.

7. What's the main ingredient of meringue?

    a. Cream

    b. Egg whites

    c. Flour

8. Which variety of apple would you *not* use in an apple pie?

   a. Granny Smith

   b. Jonathan

   c. Red Delicious

9. True or false: Pies are an American invention.

10. What's the best way to describe Mississippi mud pie?

    a. Chocolaty

    b. Coffee-flavored

    c. Crunchy

Did you know . . .

January 23 is designated as National Pie Day in the United States.

79. We Love Lucy

She'll always be the queen of TV comedy. How much do you know about America's favorite redhead?

1. What was Lucy Ricardo's maiden name?

   _____

2. What was her hometown? _____

3. True or false: Lucy's real-life children, Lucie Arnaz and Desi Arnaz, Jr., appeared on *I Love Lucy*.

4. What was the name of Ricky Ricardo's nightclub?

   _____

5. Who was Little Ricky's babysitter? _____

6. True or false: The *I Love Lucy* theme song has words.

7. Where was Lucy for the famous grape-stomping episode?

   _____

8. What part of her body did Lucy set on fire during the William Holden episode? _____

9. True or false: Bob Hope, John Wayne and Rock Hudson were guest stars on *I Love Lucy*.

10. What product is Lucy selling in the episode called "Lucy Does a TV Commercial"? _____

Did you know . . .

I Love Lucy debuted in October 1951 and has never been off the air since. Somewhere in the world right now, someone is loving Lucy.

80. Comic Relief

Even in the comics, a girl's gotta earn a living.
Match these characters from the comics
to their daily occupations.

1. Broom-Hilda

2. Barbara Gordon a.k.a.
   Batgirl

3. Jean Grey a.k.a.
   Marvel Girl

4. Mari McCabe a.k.a.
   Vixen

5. Miss Peach

6. Diana Prince a.k.a.
   Wonder Woman

7. Sue Richards a.k.a.
   Invisible Girl

8. Brenda Starr

9. Tommie Thompson
   from Apartment 3G

10. Winnie Winkle

a. Reporter

b. Teacher

c. Witch

d. Nurse

e. Fashion model

f. Wife and mother

g. Librarian

h. Stenographer

i. Student and actress

j. U.S. Army major

Did you know . . .

One of the few female cartoonists to make it big was
Marjorie Henderson Buell, who first drew Little Lulu for the
Saturday Evening Post in 1935. She patterned the little girl with
the long black curls after herself as a child.

81. She Is Love

How much do you know about these women—real and fictional—whose names are filled with "Love"?

1. TV's *Party of Five* star _____

2. Lead singer of Hole _____

3. Darlene Love made her name in which field?

    a. Education

    b. Music

    c. Zoology

4. The 1960s TV "superspy" portrayed by Teresa Graves

    _____

5. Wife of TV's Thurston Howell III

    _____

6. Sarah Breedlove, America's first black female millionaire, is better known by what name?

    a. Sarah Chalke

    b. Sarah Vaughan

    c. Madam C.J. Walker

7. Star of *Deep Throat* _____

8. Country chart-topper who sang "You Can Feel Bad (If It Makes You Feel Better)"_____

9. Rapper and former MTV Lip Service presenter

    _____

10. Nancy Harkness Love helped the U.S. effort during World War II as what?

    a. Codebreaker

    b. Pilot

    c. Spy

82. More or Less

*If you've been reading the labels on what you eat,
you'll know which of these foods has . . .*

1. More calories?

    a. 8 ounces of whole milk   b. A 12-ounce beer

2. More carbohydrate grams?

    a. 1 medium banana   b. 1 medium plantain

3. More sodium?

    a. 1 tablespoon of black caviar

    b. An Entenmann's cheese Danish

4. More cholesterol?

    a. 4 ounces of shrimp   b. 4 ounces of swordfish

5. More fat?

    a. ½ cup Breyer's chocolate ice cream

    b. 2 slices of Oscar Meyer bacon

6. More vitamin C?

    a. 1 cup cantaloupe   b. 1 orange

7. More potassium?

    a. 1 cup baked beans   b. 1 cup broccoli

8. More iron?

    a. 1 cup cooked chickpeas   b. 1 cup cooked spinach

9. More dietary fiber?

    a. 1 cup frozen raspberries   b. 1 cup frozen okra

10. More calcium?

    a. 1 cup low-fat cottage cheese

    b. 1 cup plain low-fat yogurt

83. Shakespeare's Women

Match these Shakespearian roles to their character descriptions.

1. Beatrice

2. Cordelia

3. Cressida

4. Desdemona

5. Juliet

6. Katharina

7. Lady Macbeth

8. Ophelia

9. Titania

10. Viola

a. Wife of a nobleman. After convincing her husband to commit murder, she can't live with the guilt and kills herself.

b. Benedick's love in *Much Ado About Nothing*.

c. Hamlet's would-be bride. When he won't marry her, she goes mad herself.

d. King Lear's youngest daughter, and the only one who truly loves him. Too bad he doesn't understand that until she's dead.

e. Queen of the fairies.

f. Daughter of a Trojan priest. She spends the first half of the play seducing a man and the second half cheating on him.

g. Spends most of the time dressed as a boy in *Twelfth Night*, a comedy of mistaken identity.

h. Wife of Othello. When he thinks she's been unfaithful to him, he kills her.

i. Foul-tempered "shrew" whose father marries her off to a foul-tempered man.

j. Tragic 14-year-old. When her lover thinks she's dead, he kills himself. When she finds out, she kills herself.

Did you know . . .

When Shakespeare's plays were originally produced, women did not perform on stage. All the female roles were played by boys.

84. The Healers

They say nurturing is in a woman's nature. That's certainly true of these famous women in the world of medicine.

1. Virginia Apgar created the Apgar Score to diagnose what?

    a. Health problems in newborns

    b. Heart disease

    c. Osteoporosis

2. What health organization credits Clara Barton as its founder?

    a. American Red Cross

    b. Juvenile Diabetes Foundation

    c. World Health Organization

3. Toxicologist Alice Hamilton is known for the study of what?

    a. Miscarriage

    b. Poisons

    c. Tuberculosis

4. Dr. Frances Kelsey of the U.S. Food and Drug Administration caused a furor in the 1960s when she fought the use of which drug?

    a. Acetaminophen

    b. Erythromycin

    c. Thalidomide

5. In 1990, Antonia Novello became the first woman to hold which job?

    a. Chief of Surgery at Bethesda Naval Hospital

    b March of Dimes president

    c. U.S. Surgeon General

6. To serve rural Kentucky, Mary Breckinridge created a traveling network of what?

    a. Nurse-midwives

    b. Surgeons

    c. Veterinarians

7. Psychiatrist Elizabeth Kübler-Ross is known for her work in which field?

    a. Child abuse

    b. Death and dying

    c. Domestic violence

8. Bacteriologist Alice Evans identified the organism that causes brucellosis, which can be transmitted to humans through what?

    a. Blood transfusions

    b. Milk

    c. Raw vegetables

9. Nurse Florence Wald is credited with introducing what European medical practice to the United States?

    a. Hospice care

    b. Lamaze childbirth

    c. Thalassotherapy

10. Blalock-Taussig surgery, developed in part by Dr. Helen Taussig, is performed on which organ?

    a. Brain

    b. Heart

    c. Uterus

Did you know . . .

The American Nurses Association's Mary Mahoney Award honors work to improve race relations. In 1879, Mary Mahoney became the first black woman to graduate from a U.S. nursing school.

85. Flower Power

How does your garden grow? With silver bells and cockleshells . . . and maybe some of these flowers.

1. Which flower was named for a character in Greek mythology?

    a. Aster

    b. Carnation

    c. Narcissus

2. Singer Billie Holiday was known to wear this flower in her hair. _____

3. True or false: Poinsettias are poisonous.

4. Botanists call this flower gypsophila, but you probably know it by this name.

    a. Baby's breath

    b. Lily of the valley

    c. Queen Anne's lace

5. Miss Miller, the Henry James title character who fits this theme.

    _____

6. True or false: The chrysanthemum is a royal symbol in Japan.

7. Zinnias were named for

    a. Dr. Johann Gottfried Zinn

    b. The metallic element zinc

    c. Zinfandel wine

8. The botanical name for this flower is Helianthus, in honor of the Greek god Helios. _____

9. Roses are the #1 selling flower in the United States in terms of dollar value. What's #2?

    a. Carnations

    b. Lilies

    c. Tulips

10. Which flower comes in bearded and beardless varieties?

    _____

86. Jersey Girls

*Match these women from the Garden State
with their accomplishments.*

1. Carol Blazejowski

2. Debby Boone

3. Millicent Fenwick

4. Lauryn Hill

5. Whitney Houston

6. Clara Louise Maass

7. Keshia Knight Pulliam

8. Eva Marie Saint

9. Elizabeth Coleman White

10. Christine Todd Whitman

a. Developer of the first cultivated blueberry

b. First female governor of New Jersey

c. Fugees' lead singer

d. Gray-haired, pipe-smoking congresswoman

e. *North by Northwest* leading lady

f. Rudy Huxtable on *The Cosby Show*

g. "Saving All My Love for You" singer

h. Women's basketball trailblazer

i. Yellow fever nursing pioneer

j. "You Light Up My Life" singer

Did you know . . .

Singer Tom Waits, who was born in California, wrote and recorded the song "Jersey Girl." It was later covered by Jersey boy Bruce Springsteen.

87. You Should Be Dancing

Okay twinkle-toes, here's your chance to show your stuff. 5 . . . 6 . . . 7 . . . 8 . . . Dance!

1. How many people dance a *pas de deux*?

    a. 1

    b. 2

    c. 3

2. Where did the mambo originate?

    a. Cuba

    b. Florida

    c. Mexico

3. You just performed an "arm breaker" and a "comb." What kind of dance are you doing?

    a. Contra

    b. Jive

    c. Paso doble

4. What made Twyla Tharp famous?

    a. Ballet dancing

    b. Choreography

    c. Folk dancing

5. When did people start doing the Lindy Hop?

    a. 1890s

    b. 1920s

    c. 1950s

6. If a ballerina is on *pointe*, where is she?

    a. Above her partner's head

    b. Backstage waiting for her cue

    c. On her toes

7. Where do you place your hands in country line dancing?

    a. On your partner's shoulders

    b. At your waist

    c. In the air

8. Which dance was banned because it was considered scandalous?

    a. Polka

    b. Quadrille

    c. Waltz

9. How is a hora performed?

    a. In a circle

    b. Alone

    c. With a partner

10. What style of dancing requires a "caller"?

    a. Foxtrot

    b. Salsa

    c. Square dancing

88. On the Scene

You know the whos and whats of women's history, but how about the wheres? Match these milestone events to the places where *they happened.*

1. 7-year-old Megan Kanka is murdered

2. First college sorority founded

3. First female mayor in the United States elected

4. First Tupperware party is held

5. First U.S. woman receives a driver's license

6. Katharine Gibbs opens her first secretarial school

7. *Roe v. Wade* originated

8. Rosa Parks keeps her seat on a city bus

9. Site of the first Million Mom March

10. Site of the first Women's Rights Convention

a. Argonia, Kansas

b. Chicago

c. Dallas County, Texas

d. Detroit

e. Hamilton Township, New Jersey

f. Macon, Georgia

g. Montgomery, Alabama

h. Providence, Rhode Island

i. Seneca Falls, New York

j. Washington, D.C.

89. Stamping Ground

*Name these famous women, gummed and perforated
on U.S. postage stamps.*

1. U.S. first lady and delegate to the United Nations

   _____

2. *The Age of Innocence* author_____

3. Revolutionary flagmaker_____

4. *Atlas Shrugged* author _____

5. America's best-known female Impressionist painter

   _____

6. "What a Difference a Day Makes" singer, known as Queen
   of the Blues_____

7. Royal patron of Christopher Columbus, and financier of
   his voyages_____

8. Kewpie creator_____

9. First black woman to hold a U.S. cabinet post

   _____

10. Creator of the VFW's annual poppy drive

    _____

Did you know . . .

The first woman to design a U.S. postage stamp was
Esther Althea Richards, a Philadelphia art professor who
created the 10-cent Great Smoky Mountains stamp for a
National Parks series in 1934.

90. Read the Label

There are a lot of strange ingredients in the stuff you have around the house. Do you know what they do? Here's your chance to prove it!

1. What's the best thing to do with ascorbic acid?

    a. Swallow it

    b. Use it to strengthen your nails

    c. Wash your hair in it

2. In what type of products are you most likely to find calcium thioglycolate?

    a. Floor cleaners

    b. Hair removers

    c. Processed cheese

3. What does FD&C mean when it's written before a color additive?

    a. Food, Drug & Cosmetic

    b. Federal Dye & Color

    c. Food Dye & Color

4. Why is there guar gum in your salad dressing?

    a. To add color

    b. To add saltiness

    c. To thicken it

5. What is sodium lauryl sulfate (SLS)?

    a. Antibiotic

    b. Coloring additive

    c. Detergent

6. Which of these are you likely to find in ice cream?

    a. Fumaric acid

    b. Seaweed

    c. Turmeric

7. What did the original formula of Coca-Cola contain?

    a. Cocaine

    b. Cocoa

    c. Coconut

8. You'll find propylene glycol in marshmallows. Where else will you find it?

    a. Antifreeze

    b. Apple juice

    c. Toothpaste

9. Which is the most common artificial food coloring?

    a. Blue

    b. Red

    c. Yellow

10. What is monosodium glutamate (MSG)?

    a. Artificial sweetener

    b. Flavor enhancer

    c. Preservative

91. Valentine's Day

Show us your romantic side! How much do you know about Valentine's Day?

1. Valentine's Day is always celebrated on this date

   _____

2. True or false: More candy is sold in the United States on the week leading up to Valentine's Day than during any other week in the year.

3. If you engage in osculation on Valentine's Day, what are you doing?

   a. Eating breakfast in bed

   b. Getting married

   c. Kissing

4. According to Hallmark, who receives more valentine cards?

   Men   Women

5. What simple symbol can be used to designate a "kiss" on a valentine card? _____

6. When were candy "Conversation Hearts" introduced?

   a. 1860s

   b. 1920s

   c. 1940s

7. Who expects to spend more on Valentine's Day gifts for their significant others?

   Men   Women

8. For Valentine's Day, the majority of men buy flowers for their wives or significant others. For whom do the majority of women buy Valentine's Day flowers?

   a. Their husbands or significant others

   b. Their moms

   c. Themselves

9. It's not true that 50 million roses were sold for Valentine's Day 2002. Is the real number higher or lower?

   Higher   Lower

10. What is Esther Howland's connection to Valentine's Day?

   a. She invented the heart-shaped box for chocolates

   b. She made the first valentines in the United States

   c. She invented edible panties

Did you know . . .

You could spend Valentine's Day in Valentine, Texas, or Valentine, Nevada. According to the U.S. Census Bureau, they're the only towns called Valentine in the United States.

92. Which Happened First?

Two events in women's history, similar but different.
Which happened first?

1. a. A woman climbs Mt. Everest

    b. A woman serves on a U.S. Navy submarine

2. a. A woman invents the chocolate-chip cookie

    b. Women study at the Cordon Bleu

3. a. A female professor teaches at Harvard Medical School

    b. A woman graduates from Harvard Medical School

4. a. Women officially compete in the Boston Marathon

    b. A woman earns a Ph.D. from Boston University

5. a. Girls are permitted to play in Little League Baseball

    b. A woman is hired as a Major League Baseball scout

6. a. A woman walks at the South Pole

    b. A woman walks in space

7. a. Women join the FBI as agents

    b. Women join the Kiwanis Club

8. a. Pregnancy Discrimination Act passed in the U.S.

    b. La Leche League founded

9. a. A woman serves as Poet Laureate in the United States

    b. A woman serves as Poet Laureate in England

10. a. Mensa accepts women

    b. The U.S. Military Academy at West Point accepts
    women

93. Lä Lä Lädies

Identify these ladies with a little "la" in their names.

1. Canadian singer who likes her "la" in lower case
   _. _. la _ _

2. "Bring me your tired, your poor . . ." poet
   _ _ _ _ LA _ _ _ _ _

3. Clark Kent's female colleague _ _ _ _ LA _ _

4. Xena: Warrior Princess _ _ _ _ LA _ _ _ _ _

5. First woman to win the Nobel Prize for literature
   _ _ L _ A LA _ _ _ _ _ _

6. Film noir blonde famous for her seductive hairstyle
   _ _ _ _ _ _ _ _ LA _ _

7. Lord Byron's "Lady" lover _ _ _ _ _ _ _ _ LA _ _

8. Polish harpsichord virtuoso _ _ _ _ _ LA _ _ _ _ _ _ _

9. Actress who rose to fame in King Kong's paw circa 1976
   _ _ _ _ _ _ _ LA _ _ _

10. TV's Jessica Fletcher _ _ _ _ LA LA _ _ _ _ _ _

Did you know . . .

The La's, a band from Liverpool, England, had a hit with "There She Goes" in 1990.

94. When She Was Born . . .

. . . she didn't have the name she has now. Match these famous women with their original names.

1. Taylor Dayne

2. Carmen Electra

3. Cass Elliot

4. Emme

5. Whoopi Goldberg

6. Jamaica Kincaid

7. Pat Nixon

8. Anne Rice

9. Dusty Springfield

10. Sojourner Truth

a. Isabella Baumfree

b. Ellen Naomi Cohen

c. Caryn Johnson

d. Melissa Miller

e. Howard Allen O'Brien

f. Mary Isabel Catherine Bernadette O'Brien

g. Tara Leigh Patrick

h. Elaine Potter Richardson

i. Thelma Catherine Ryan

j. Leslie Wunderman

95. Lady Be Good

Ladies turn up in all sorts of places.
Like these, for example.

1. Lady who launched King Arthur into legend
   LADY ___ ___ _____

2. Lady in a Beatles' song
   LADY ____ _____

3. Wife of Lyndon Baines Johnson
   LADY _____ _____

4. Eliza Doolittle's transformation____ ____ ___ LADY

5. Drink made with gin, grenadine, light cream and egg
   white _____ LADY

6. Bob Dylan's instruction to a lady ____ LADY ____

7. Ladylike name for Cypripedium orchids
   LADY_____

8. John Dillinger's downfall LADY _____ _____

9. Spongecake biscuit LADY_____

10. D.H. Lawrence's title character Oliver Mellors
    LADY _____ _____

Did you know . . .

The Russian word for ladybug is *bózhe koróva*. Literally translated it means "God's little cow."

96. Pair Shaped

Professionally—and sometimes romantically—they're linked forever in our minds. Can you match these male-female working pairs?

1. Tai Babilonia

2. Justine Carrelli

3. Betty Comden

4. Lynn Fontanne

5. Eydie Gorme

6. Virginia Johnson

7. Carole King

8. Ginger Rogers

9. Valerie Simpson

10. Jayne Torvill

a. Nickolas Ashford

b. Fred Astaire

c. Bob Clayton

d. Christopher Dean

e. Randy Gardner

f. Gerry Goffin

g. Adolph Green

h. Steve Lawrence

i. Alfred Lunt

j. William Masters

97. Oh, You Beautiful Doll!

As long as there have been girls, there have been dolls for them to play with. Open up the toy chest and see what you remember about these childhood favorites.

1. What was special about Ideal's Beautiful Crissy?

    a. She talked

    b. Her hair grew

    c. She drove a car

2. Playskool's Dressy Bessy had a male counterpart. What was his name?

    a. Dapper Dan

    b. Dressy Wesley

    c. Bo Buttons

3. Who was Barbie's little sister?

    a. Midge

    b. Scooter

    c. Skipper

4. What did Remco's Heidi doll do when you pushed her belly button?

    a. Giggle

    b. Sing

    c. Wave

5. Which doll changed expressions when you moved her arm?

    a. Cheerful Tearful

    b. Betsy Wetsy

    c. Liddle Kiddle

6. "She's flat and that's that"—what kind of doll are we talking about?

    a. Flathead

    b. Flatsy

    c. Flattop

7. What made Mattel's Dancerina dance?

    a. Tugging her tutu

    b. Tying her shoes

    c. Touching her tiara

8. Where did the characters of Holly Hobbie and Rainbow Brite make their first appearance?

    a. Greeting cards

    b. Storybooks

    c. TV cartoons

9. Which company manufactured Ginny dolls?

    a. Hasbro

    b. Tonka

    c. Vogue Dolls

10. 1990s fashion doll Gene has a last name. What is it?

    a. Marshall

    b. Maxwell

    c. Tierney

Did you know . . .

In 1971, just as the women's liberation movement was hitting its stride, Ideal introduced Bizzie Lizzie, a battery-operated doll that could dust, iron and vacuum. She only lasted a year.

98. Goddess Bless

Match these mythological female figures to what they represented and protected.

1. Artemis	a. Agriculture
2. Athena	b. Children
3. Demeter	c. Fire
4. Fortuna	d. Hearth
5. Freya	e. Hunt
6. Kishimo-jin	f. Love and sex
7. Kwan-yin	g. Luck
8. Nut	h. Mercy
9. Pele	i. Sky
10. Vesta	j. Wisdom

Did you know . . .

Green Goddess salad dressing, made from anchovies, mayonnaise and tarragon vinegar, was invented at the Palace Hotel in San Francisco and named in honor of a 1920s play called *The Green Goddess*.

99. Queen of Scots

She was beautiful, romantic and tragic. How much do you know about Mary, Queen of Scots?

1. Where was she born?
    a. England
    b. France
    c. Scotland

2. How old was she when she became queen of Scotland?
    a. 1 week
    b. 1 month
    c. 1 year

3. How old was she when she was engaged to the man who would become her first husband?
    a. 1 year
    b. 2 years
    c. 5 years

4. Who was her first husband?
    a. Edward IV of England
    b. Francois II of France
    c. Philip II of Spain

5. How many husbands did she have?
    a. 2
    b. 3
    c. 4

6. How many children did she have?
    a. 0
    b. 1
    c. 2

7. What would have made Mary stand out among other women of her day?

    a. Her eye color

    b. Her weight

    c. Her height

8. The "casket letters" were a big problem for Mary because they implicated her in a crime. What was it?

    a. Embezzlement of treasury funds

    b. Her husband's murder

    c. Queen Elizabeth I's assassination

9. Mary was known to be extremely fond of which sport?

    a. Curling

    b. Golf

    c. Ice skating

10. How did she die?

    a. She was beheaded

    b. She was hanged

    c. She was shot

100. Handy with a Needle

Needle arts and fiber work have always been a woman's province. How much do you know about them?

1. If you're tatting, what are you doing?
    - a. Mending a garment
    - b. Making lace
    - c. Sharpening scissors

2. Where would you put an antimacassar?
    - a. On your dresser
    - b. On the back of a chair
    - c. In front of the window

3. Which woman from Greek mythology was known for her weaving skills?
    - a. Arachne
    - b. Electra
    - c. Penelope

4. Besides being a style of needlepoint, bargello is what?
    - a. A type of boat
    - b. A type of flower
    - c. A museum in Italy

5. The NAMES Project quilt honors victims of what?
    - a. AIDS
    - b. Child abuse
    - c. Nuclear disasters

6. Where would you use a granny square?
    - a. In an afghan
    - b. In a quilt
    - c. In a tapestry

7. What were often depicted in mourning embroideries?

    a. Daisies

    b. Rosebushes

    c. Willow trees

8. Which U.S. first ladies had quilt blocks named for them?

    a. Martha Washington and Bess Truman

    b. Lucy Webb Hayes and Rachel Jackson

    c. Dolley Madison and Frances Folsom Cleveland

9. Blackwork is a style of what?

    a. Embroidery

    b. Knitting

    c. Rug-making

10. What does the word "crochet" mean in French?

    a. Cradle

    b. Hook

    c. Lace

Did you know . . .

The word "spinster," used to describe an unmarried woman, may have come from the fact that, centuries ago, a single woman usually lived with her family and did work for them. One of her primary jobs would have been spinning wool and flax into yarn.

2

The Answers

1. NOT!

1. (b) The U.S. Postal Service does not picture living people on its postage stamps. A person will not be considered for a postage stamp sooner than 10 years after his or her death. (The exception is a former U.S. president, who may receive a memorial stamp on his first birthday following death.) So, while former First Ladies Dolley Madison and Abigail Adams have been pictured on stamps, Betty Ford has not.

2. (b) Billie Holiday, the legendary vocalist, never won a Grammy award because she died about a year after the Grammys were introduced. Ella Fitzgerald won the first of her thirteen Grammys at the first Grammy presentation in 1958. Etta James won a Grammy in 1994 for Best Jazz Vocal on an album called "Mystery Lady." It was a collection of songs originally performed by Billie Holiday.

3. (c) Actress Rita Hayworth was married five times, including once to Orson Welles, but she was never married to Frank Sinatra. Ava Gardner was the second of Sinatra's four wives. Mia Farrow was the third.

4. (b) The body bared in *Pretty Woman* did not belong to actress Julia Roberts. She had a body double handle all the revealing scenes. On the other hand, the demure Julie Andrews appeared topless in *S.O.B.*, directed by her husband, Blake Edwards. Sissy Spacek has appeared topless in a few films, most notably as a topless housecleaner in *Welcome to L.A.*

5. (b) English writer Jan Morris was born James Morris. Her experience with sex-change surgery was documented in her book, *Conundrum*. Berthe Morisot was a French Impressionist painter. Toni Morrison is a Nobel Prize-winning author.

6. (b) Artemisia Gentileschi was a 17th-century Italian Baroque painter whose work could be tender or quite terrifying, as in her graphic portrayal of Judith beheading Holofernes. Helen Frankenthaler and Lee Krasner are modern artists.

7. (a) Benjamin Bunny was the featured character in a tale by Beatrix Potter. The English writer and illustrator wrote her first book as a gift for a sick child in the 1890s. Since then, generations of children have come to love her sweet tales and gentle watercolor illustrations. The March Hare and the White Rabbit were characters from Lewis Carroll's *Alice in Wonderland*.

8. (b) Michelle Pfeiffer has never been a Bond girl. Kim Basinger played Domino in the 1983 Bond film *Never Say Never Again*, and Jane Seymour played Solitaire, a psychic tarot card reader in 1973's *Live and Let Die*.

9. (a) Pamela Anderson of *Baywatch* fame was born in British Columbia, Canada. Both Nicole Kidman and Bette Midler were born in Hawaii.

10. (b) Shirley Muldowney was the first woman to win a U.S. national drag-racing title. Shannon Lucid and Sally Ride both were space shuttle astronauts. Ride flew two *Challenger* missions. Lucid flew once on *Discovery* and twice on *Atlantis*.

8-10 correct: Not bad
4-7 correct: Not for nothing
1-3 correct: Not good

2. Man or Woman?

1. Morgan Fairchild (woman), born Patsy McClenny, rose to fame playing conniving vixens on late-night soaps such as *Falcon Crest*, and gained infamy playing a "lipstick lesbian" on the TV series *Roseanne*. Morgan Freeman (man) is an award-winning actor who received Oscar nominations for his roles in *Driving Miss Daisy* and *The Shawshank Redemption*.

2. Leslie Nielsen (man) is an actor and star of the *Naked Gun* movies. Leslie Caron (woman) is the sylphlike French actress who danced with Gene Kelly in *An American in Paris* and starred in the movie musical *Gigi*.

3. Mackenzie Astin (man), son of Patty Duke and John Astin, is an actor who had an ongoing role as Andy Moffett in the TV series *The Facts of Life*. Mackenzie Phillips (woman), born Laura Mackenzie Phillips, is the daughter of singer John Phillips. She starred as Julie Cooper in the TV series *One Day at a Time*.

4. Isak Dinesen (woman) is the pen name of Baroness Karen Blixen, the Danish author of *Out of Africa*. Izaak Walton (man) was a 17th-century English conservationist, and author of *The Compleat Angler*.

5. Evelyn Waugh (man)—full name Evelyn Arthur St. John Waugh—was an early 20th-century English novelist whose works include *A Handful of Dust* and *Brideshead Revisited*. Evelyn Wood (woman), a former schoolteacher, created Reading Dynamics, a pioneering speed-reading program.

6. George Eliot (woman) is the pen name of Mary Ann Evans, 19th-century English author of *Middlemarch* and *Silas Marner*. George Romney (man) was the chairman of American Motors Corporation and governor of Michigan.

7. George Sand (woman) is the pen name of 19th-century French novelist Amandine-Aurore-Lucile Dudevant, known for her feminist views and her love affair with Frederic Chopin. George Washington Carver (man) was an American botanist known for developing more than 300 products made from peanuts.

8. Meredith Willson (man) is the writer and composer of *The Music Man*. Meredith Brooks (woman) is a rock singer who scored a hit with "Bitch" in 1997.

9. Gale Storm (woman), star of the popular 1950s TV series *My Little Margie*, was born Josephine Owaissa Cottle in Texas in 1922. Gale Gordon (man), born Charles T. Aldrich, Jr., was a comic actor and colleague of Lucille Ball. He was best known as Theodore J. Mooney, Lucy's boss on *The Lucy Show*.

10. Joyce Kilmer (man), full name Alfred Joyce Kilmer, was an

American poet whose most famous work was "Trees" ("I think that I shall never see, a poem lovely as a tree . . ."). Joyce Brothers (woman) is a TV psychologist, talk-show guest and game-show fixture.

8-10 correct: Gender specific
4-7 correct: Gender issues
1-3 correct: Gender bender

3. What's She Worth?

1. (e) Aileen Wuornos, a convicted serial killer, spent almost 11 years on Florida's Death Row before her execution in October 2002. Daily cost for her upkeep was about $72.39. Total cost for her Death Row incarceration was an estimated $282,455.

2. (h) In an estate appraisal from Loudon County, Virginia, dated December 30, 1816, a 27-year-old female slave named Milly was valued at $350. A 50-year-old female slave named Katy, presumably past her child-bearing years, was valued at $100. Moses, a 22-year-old male slave, was valued at $600.

3. (g) Barbra Streisand's 2000 concert tour, which included just four performances, grossed over $27 million. The average ticket price was $421.27.

4. (j) Mary Pickford, the actress known as "America's Sweetheart," signed a contract with Famous Players Company for a weekly salary of $10,000. It was 1916 and she was 20 years old.

5. (a) At a Christie's London auction, three first-edition Jane Austen novels sold for a combined total of £59,572 (about $82,805). *Pride and Prejudice* was the most expensive of the three, selling for about $32,665. When she wrote the book in 1813, Austen was paid £110 (about $412.50 in 1813 dollars).

6. (c) The U.S. Department of Health & Human Services calculated that the national average annual earnings for full-time registered nurses was $46,782 in 2000.

7. (d) In 2000, Heather Killen, a senior vice president at Yahoo!, earned $32.7 million. She was the highest-paid executive woman in the United States. Staggering as her compensation package was, it was just 11% of the package earned by the highest-paid male executive in the U.S. John Reed of Citigroup took in $293 million that year.

8. (f) The *2003 Guinness Book of World Records* lists the $44.5-million wedding of Princess Salama to Mohammed as the world's most expensive wedding. The couple from the United Arab Emirates was married in Dubai in May 1981. The party lasted 7 days and was held in a specially built stadium that seated 20,000 guests.

9. (b) Mary-Kate and Ashley, the Olsen twins, are among the wealthiest teens in Hollywood. In 2002, when they turned 16, the actresses were expecting to realize $1 billion in gross sales of branded merchandise, including videos, books, dolls, accessories and a line of clothing made for Wal-Mart stores.

10. (i) With a net worth of $3.46 billion, Queen Beatrix of the Netherlands is the wealthiest modern queen on Earth, according to the *2003 Guinness Book of World Records*. By comparison, Britain's Queen Elizabeth II is worth a mere $330 million.

> *8-10 correct: Worth a fortune*
> *4-7 correct: Worth a second look*
> *1-3 correct: Mrs. Butterworth*

4. Go-Go Girls

1. Goldilocks. The original go-go girl was immortalized by the Brothers Grimm. One little girl, three bears and some porridge make the story "just right."

2. Paulette Goddard. Born Pauline Marion Goddard Levy in 1914, she joined the Ziegfeld Follies when she was just 13 years old and married for the first time at age 15. She worked with Charlie Chaplin in *Modern Times* and *The Great Dictator* and married him in 1940. Actor Burgess Meredith was her third husband. Author Erich Maria Remarque was her fourth.

3. Lady Godiva. Godiva was the wife of the 12th-century English noble Leofric, Earl of Mercia. Her famous ride, naked through the streets of Coventry, was a social protest to demand that her husband lower taxes. She is also credited with building monasteries in England.

4. Emma Goldman. Lithuanian-born Goldman arrived in the United States in 1885 at age 16. She soon joined a group of Socialist sympathizers, draft protestors and anarchists who wreaked havoc during the 1900s. Though she was deported to the Soviet Union in 1919, her legacy of protest lives on.

5. Anna Andreyevna Gorenko. Generally considered Russia's greatest female poet, she wrote under the name Anna Akhmatova. Her work was banned by the Soviet government from 1921 to 1940, and again throughout the 1950s. She died in 1966.

6. Nadine Gordimer. South African writer Gordimer won the Nobel Prize for literature in 1991. Her major works include *The Conservationist* and *Burger's Daughter*.

7. Jane Goodall. Born in England in 1934, Goodall worked during graduate school as a waitress to save money for her first trip to Africa. She is world-renowned for her pioneering work studying chimpanzees in Tanzania.

8. Margaret Gorman. Gorman became the first Miss America pageant winner in 1921 representing Washington, D.C. as a 16-year-old high-school student. She was known as Miss Washington throughout her reign, until the 1922 pageant when a new Miss Washington joined the competition. It was then that Gorman, who was defending her title, became known as Miss America.

9. Goneril. The eldest of King Lear's three daughters, Goneril was one of Shakespeare's less sympathetic female roles.

10. Ruth Gordon. Though she began her acting career when she was a teenager, Gordon is best known for the roles she played as a septuagenarian. She won an Academy Award for her work in 1968's *Rosemary's Baby* and became a cult-film heroine playing the 70-something love interest of a teenage boy in 1971's *Harold and Maude*.

8-10 correct: You go, girl!
4-7 correct: Get up and go
1-3 correct: Go try another quiz

5. California Girls

1. (b) In 1978, Dianne Feinstein became the first female mayor of San Francisco—her hometown. In 1992, she achieved another milestone by becoming the first female U.S. senator from California. Her senate colleague Barbara Boxer followed two years later.

2. (c) Summer Sanders swam her first full lap in the pool at age 3 and was in an organized swim program by the time she was 4. At age 20, the Stanford University student won the first of her four Olympic medals at the 1992 Barcelona Olympics.

3. Amy Tan. Born in Oakland in 1952 to Chinese immigrant parents, Tan has chronicled the unique perspectives of first-generation Chinese-Americans and their parents in such books as *The Joy Luck Club* and *The Kitchen God's Wife*.

4. (b) Billie Jean King (maiden name: Moffit) started playing tennis at 11. By 29, she had been named *Sports Illustrated's* "Sportsperson of the Year"—the first woman to receive that honor. She was ranked #1 in women's tennis seven times between 1966 and 1974, and was the first female athlete to earn more than $100,000 in one year.

5. (a) When author Joan Didion was born in Sacramento in 1934, she was part of the fifth generation of her family to be born in the Golden State. Her works include *Salvador*, *Miami* and the essay collections *Slouching Toward Bethlehem* and *The White Album*.

6. Julia Child. Often imitated, but never equaled, Child started her public television show, *The French Chef*, in 1963. Since then, the effervescent chef has hosted numerous television cooking shows, written countless books and articles, and paved the way for all celebrity chefs.

7. (a) Edith Head was a renowned costume designer for films, starting with *She Done Him Wrong* (1933) and ending with *Dead Men Don't Wear Plaid* (1982). She received thirty-five Academy Award nominations and won eight, including Oscars for *All About Eve*, *Roman Holiday*, *Sabrina* and *The Sting*.

8. (c) In 1910, Alice Stebbins Wells was sworn in as a police woman in the Los Angeles Police Department, making her the first female police officer in the United States. The LAPD provided her with a book of rules and a first-aid manual, but she had to design and sew her own uniform.

9. Moon Unit Zappa. Frank Zappa's 1982 song "Valley Girl" was a dig at the bratty girls of California's San Fernando Valley. It featured his 14-year-old daughter, Moon Unit, teaching the world important expressions like "Gag me with a spoon" and "Grody to the max." Bitchin'.

10. (b) The Go-Go's hit #1 in 1981 with their debut album, *Beauty and the Beat*. It featured the hit singles "Our Lips are Sealed" and "We Got the Beat." The five-woman group

featured singer Belinda Carlisle, guitarists Charlotte Caffey and Jane Weidlin, bassist Kathy Valentine and drummer Gina Schock.

8-10 correct: L.A. Woman
4-7 correct: Valley Girl
1-3 correct: California Dreamin'

6. Patronize Me

1. (b) To crush St. Agatha's faith, a 3rd-century Roman lawman ordered her to work in a brothel. When she refused to entertain customers there, she was beaten and her breasts were cut off. In some accounts of St. Agatha's life, her wounds are healed by St. Peter. Thus women suffering from breast diseases ask for her intercession.

2. (d) Mother of the Virgin Mary and grandmother of Jesus, St. Anne quite naturally is the patron saint of grandmothers.

3. (e) In defense of her faith, St. Catherine of Alexandria debated fifty pagan philosophers in the 4th century. Her arguments in favor of Christianity were so convincing she became a most persuasive advocate for the Church, and the patron saint of lawyers.

4. (i) Women in troubled marriages turn to St. Catherine of Genoa for comfort. At age 16, she married a sorry excuse for a husband. He spent all their money, treated her horribly and cheated on her repeatedly. Her faith eased her distress. Impressed by her commitment, her wayward husband eventually converted. They lived together celibately for the rest of their lives.

5. (g) When the music was played at St. Cecilia's wedding, she sang a silent hymn to Jesus, vowing always to be faithful to him. That's why she's associated with musicians, singers, composers and musical instrument makers.

6. (j) In the 5th century, St. Genevieve led an expedition to bring food and supplies to Paris when it was under siege. Thus she became a patron saint for women in the military. She's also a patron saint of Paris, where people sometimes pray to her in times of crisis.

7. (c) St. Gertrude of Nivelles became a patron saint of gardeners because good weather on her feast day, March 17, meant it was time to begin the spring planting. She is also said to guard against infestations of mice and rats. So, fittingly, she's also the patron saint of cats.

8. (a) The 4th-century North African St. Monica had a miserable life. Married to a foul-tempered, verbally abusive adulterer, and forced to live with her unsympathetic mother-in-law to boot, St. Monica drank heavily. Faith helped her overcome her addiction.

9. (h) St. Veronica was the woman who wiped the face of Jesus as he carried the cross to Calvary. The image of his face became imprinted on her cloth. Similarly, when photographs are developed, the photo image "miraculously" appears on blank photographic paper. Thus St. Veronica became associated with photographs.

10. (f) St. Zita, from 13th-century Italy, lived a pious life as a domestic servant. As part of her work, she kept the keys to her master's household. Who better to protect against losing the keys to yours?

8-10 correct: Heavenly
4-7 correct: Slice of heaven
1-3 correct: Heaven forbid!

7. With a Name Like That . . .

1. (a) Maria Tallchief was known as America's prima ballerina in the 1940s and 1950s. Born in Oklahoma to a Native American father and Scots-Irish mother, she trained in Europe, where she met and married renowned choreographer George Balanchine. When he founded the New York City Ballet, she became its principal ballerina. After she retired from dancing, she founded the Chicago City Ballet.

2. (c) The aptly named Cindy Birdsong was a member of the Supremes, Motown's premier female group. She joined the trio when original member Florence Ballard left in 1967.

3. (a) Archaeologist Iris Cornelia (I. C.) Love is best known for her 1969 discovery at Knidos in Turkey. She unearthed an ancient temple devoted to Aphrodite, the Greek goddess of love. How appropriate!

4. (c) Judging by what he named his daughter, you might think Ima Hogg's father, a former Texas governor, had a cruel sense of humor. Fact is, she was named for the heroine in a poem written by one of her ancestors. "Miss Ima" donated a great deal of money to found mental health centers in Texas, presented her family estate to Texas to be used as a historical park, and funded Houston's museums and cultural arts.

5. (b) In 1987, Wilma Mankiller became the principal chief of the Cherokee Nation, the second largest Native American tribe in the United States. She's the first woman in modern history to lead a Native American people.

6. (a) In 1933, American anthropologist Hortense Powdermaker published her first book. *Life in Lesu* was a study of a village on the South Pacific island of New Ireland, but she was more interested in studying life closer

to home. Her work in the community of Indianola, Mississippi, was one of the first scholarly examinations of racial issues in the American South. That led to her joining the faculty at Queens College in New York, where she started the Department of Anthropology and Sociology.

7. (a) There are billions and billions of stars in the universe. Annie Jump Cannon wanted to classify them all. While working at the Harvard College Observatory in the 1910s and 1920s, she devised a system to categorize stars by their temperature and color. The system is a fundamental part of astronomy today, and every astronomer owes Annie gratitude for bringing some order into the universe.

8. (c) Emma Nutt wasn't any old telephone operator. She was the first female telephone operator in the United States. When telephones were invented, the same young boys who used to deliver telegrams manned switchboards, but they were too rambunctious to sit still and patch calls through. So phone companies hired women to do the job. Emma Nutt was the first. She started work on September 1, 187 8.   Today, September 1 is officially recognized as Emma Nutt Day (no kidding!).

9. (a) Theodate Pope Riddle wasn't permitted to attend college-level architecture classes in the late 1800s, so she hired tutors to teach her at home. She became the first woman to become a licensed architect in New York and Connecticut. Hill-Stead, the family home she built for her parents in Connecticut, is now a museum.

10. (a) You know the actress Frances Gumm better by her stage name, Judy Garland. She was born in Minnesota in 1922 and made her first film at age 14. She was 17 when she starred as Dorothy in *The Wizard of Oz*.

8-10 correct: Name brand
4-7 correct: Name dropper
1-3 correct: Name your poison

8. Female Anatomy
Believe it or Not

1. Believe it. Before you become pregnant, your uterus is about the size of a pear. It expands to 1,000 times its original capacity to hold a growing fetus.

2. Believe it. The body of a newborn girl contains 1.5 million oocytes, the cells that can develop into eggs. Typically, only 500 of them make it all the way to ovulation. That means during a woman's lifetime her ovaries release about 500 eggs for fertilization.

3. Not. As your body's estrogen levels  decrease after menopause, breasts lose some of their fatty deposits and their gland structure begins to break down. So, breasts shrink slightly after menopause.

4. Not. Depending on whom you ask, women can experience two, or possibly three, kinds of orgasms. A vulvar orgasm occurs when the clitoris is stimulated. A uterine orgasm is produced by vaginal stimulation. Then there's the mysterious "G" spot (named for a scientist called Grafenberg). Located on the front wall of the vagina about 1 inch into the vaginal canal, this spot, if stimulated, can produce orgasms in some women.

5. Not. The primary cause of wrinkles is sun exposure. Smoking can weaken the collagen bonds that keep your skin firm. And simply using your face—to smile, laugh, frown or squint—can cause creases over time.

6. Believe it. Typically, blondes have about 120,000 hair follicles on their heads, brunettes have about 100,000, and redheads have about 80,000. To compensate for the disparity, blondes tend to have finer hair, while brunettes and redheads have thicker, coarser hair.

7. Believe it. We're not sure why someone measured this, but it's true. The middle fingernail tends to grow faster than the other nails. Pinky nails grow most slowly.

8. Believe it. Women are about four times more likely than men to suffer from osteoporosis. Smaller, more slender women suffer from it more often than large, heavy-boned women.

9. Not. It's true that mother's milk provides a baby with nutrients, but that's not the only thing it does. A woman's milk also contains disease-fighting white blood cells and antibodies that help pass the mother's immunities to her baby and protect it from disease.

10. Believe it. Strange as it sounds, the inner lips of the vulva—known as the *labia minora*—change color at different times and for different reasons. First, they generally darken as you age. Second, the color becomes darker or more intense after you have children. Third, they darken when you become sexually aroused and return to their natural color when the arousal ends.

> *8-10 correct: I know my body*
> *4-7 correct: I know somebody*
> *1-3 correct: I ain't got nobody*

9. Mother Lode

1. "Mother" Goose. Some say Mother Goose was Elizabeth Goose of Charlestown, Massachusetts, and that her son-in-law, a printer named Thomas Fleet, published a book of children's stories called *Mother Goose's Melodies* in 1719. These people really existed, but the book probably didn't, which is why most historians maintain that Mother Goose was really the creation of French fairy-tale writer Charles Perrault.

2. "Moms" Mabley. Onstage, dressed in a housecoat and Hawaiian shirt, Jackie "Moms" Mabley looked like a harmless frump, but her comedy was filled with stinging social commentary. She was a regular at Harlem's Apollo Theater, where she performed for 35 years.

3. "Ma" Rainey. They say Ma Rainey taught legendary blues diva Bessie Smith to sing. It's certainly true that "Ma" earned her nickname when she married dancer-comedian William "Pa" Rainey. She was a beloved jazz-blues singer of the 1920s.

4. "Grandma" Moses. Self-taught artist Anna Mary Robertson Moses started painting in her 70s. When a New York City art collector spotted her naïve depictions of rural life, he promised to make her famous—and he did. She had her first one-woman show at the age of 80, and created more than 1,500 paintings before her death at age 101.

5. "Mother" Jones. This little old lady in a black bonnet was a powerful weapon for the 19th-century labor movement, organizing demonstrations wherever workers were treated unfairly. She even led marches of United Mine Workers' wives armed with mops and brooms. She died at 100 and is buried in the United Mine Workers' cemetery in Illinois.

6. Mother Courage. *Mother Courage and Her Children*, written in 1939 at the beginning of World War II, was Berthold Brecht's commentary on the disintegration of human values during wartime. Mother Courage sacrifices her family for the sake of her business. Brecht intended her to be a completely unsympathetic character, then cast his wife in the role for the original production.

7. "Ma" Barker. Former FBI director J. Edgar Hoover claimed Ma Barker was a vicious criminal, but he might have been lying. Ma's sons were in the murderous Barker-Karpis gang of the 1930s, but no crime was pinned on Ma. Nevertheless, the FBI gunned her down and Hoover tried to defend its actions. Real criminals never bought Hoover's story. As one said, "The old woman couldn't organize breakfast."

8. "Big Mama" Thornton. In 1953, before Elvis had a hit with "Hound Dog," Big Mama Thornton was belting it out to blues audiences in the American South. In 1984, she was inducted into the Blues Foundation's Hall of Fame.

9. "Granny D." In 1999, at the age of 89, Doris "Granny D" Haddock walked across America to draw attention to the need for political campaign finance reform. From Pasadena, California, to Washington, D.C., she walked 10 miles a day for 14 months. When snow threatened her progress she strapped on cross-country skis and kept going.

10. "Mammy" Yokum. Tough and tiny Mammy Yokum was a guardian of decency in the *Li'l Abner* comic strip, even though she smoked a corncob pipe and boasted a lethal punch. Her famous line is: "Good is better than evil because it's nicer."

8-10 correct: Maternal instinct

4-7 correct: Mother's little helper

1-3 correct: Mama mia!

10. Family Ties

1. Mother and daughter. Actress Kate Hudson's father is musician Bill Hudson, whom Goldie Hawn married in 1976 and divorced in 1980. Kate was born in 1979.

2. Sisters. The two newspaper advice columnists were identical twins. Born Esther Pauline Friedman (Landers) and Pauline Esther Friedman (Van Buren) on July 4, 1918 in Sioux City, Iowa, they were friendly (and, for a time, not-so-friendly) rivals. Landers died in 2002.

3. Cousins. England's Queen Elizabeth I and Mary, Queen of Scots, were first cousins once removed, to be precise. The rival queens were locked in a power struggle for years, until Elizabeth had Mary imprisoned for nineteen years and executed in 1587. Ironically, they never met face-to-face.

4. Sisters-in-law. The late Florence Griffith Joyner, Olympic sprinter and world-record holder in the 100- and 200-meter dash, was married to Al Joyner, brother of Olympic heptathlon champion Jackie Joyner Kersee.

5. Sisters. Country singers Loretta Lynn and Crystal Gayle (real name: Brenda Gail) are two of Ted and Clara Webb's eight children. Loretta was already an established Nashville star when she wrote Crystal's first single, "I've Cried (the Blue Right Out of My Eyes)," which went to #23 on the *Billboard* charts.

6. Mother and daughter. Best-selling suspense novelists Mary Higgins Clark and Carol Higgins Clark are mother and daughter.

7. Aunt and niece. Sisters Lynn and Vanessa Redgrave are highly acclaimed actresses. Natasha Richardson is the daughter of Vanessa Redgrave and director Tony Richardson, which makes her Lynn Redgrave's niece.

8. Great-aunt and grand-niece. Ethel Barrymore was the most famous and highly paid actress of the 1920s. Her brother, actor John Barrymore, was the grandfather of actress Drew Barrymore, which makes Ethel Drew's great-aunt.

9. Sisters. Virginia Woolf and her sister, Vanessa Bell, both were members of the Bloomsbury group of authors and artists in London during the early 20th century. Woolf earned a worldwide reputation for her writing, which included *To the Lighthouse* and *A Room of One's Own*. Bell was a painter of modest achievements. She's best known for the vivid letters she wrote to her sister, which have become a kind of historical chronicle of the Bloomsbury group's activities.

10. Sisters. In 2002, the Sanchez sisters became the first sisters ever elected to the U.S. Congress. Both are Democrats who represent districts in California's Orange County.

8-10 correct: Mastered the theory of relativity

4-7 correct: Everything's relative

1-3 correct: Poor relation

11. Anything You Can Do

1. Women. On average, women wake from anesthesia in about 7 minutes. It takes men closer to 11 minutes.

2. Men. If you've ever shared a bed with a man, you know the answer to this one. Studies show that about 44% of men are habitual snorers, as opposed to about 28% of women. One reason for this is obstructive sleep apnea, a condition that causes the throat muscles to block air passages during sleep. It affects more men than women.

3. Women. A 2000 report from the Centers for Disease Control stated that the average life expectancy for women in the U.S. is 79.5 years. For men it's 74.1 years.

4. Women. Most women would say that they listen better than the men they know. Fact is, women hear better too. From early childhood, females are more sensitive to sound and better able to detect sound. Everyone's hearing deteriorates over time, but men's hearing tends to go slightly earlier than women's.

5. Men. Women's hearing may last longer than men's, but women's sight usually deteriorates faster. In general, men are more sensitive to visual stimuli and their distance vision remains stronger, longer.

6. Women. A woman's nose is keener than a man's, especially when she's pregnant. This goes for a woman's sense of taste as well (since taste and smell are physiologically related). Some biologists believe that this heightened sensitivity to taste and smell is what causes some women to suffer nausea when they're pregnant.

7. Men. Generally speaking, men have about 8% more muscle mass and 11% less body fat than women. Thus, with few exceptions, men are stronger than women. But women do have some muscular advantages. They generally have better fine-motor skills to do precision tasks, and some studies have shown that women have better muscular endurance than men.

8. Men. At meetings and large social gatherings, men yak more often and for longer periods than women do. But when it comes to talking on the phone with friends, women take the prize. Sociologists think the difference comes down to the way each gender is conditioned by society. Men are comfortable drawing attention to themselves in a crowd. Women use conversation to make more personal, intimate connections.

9. Women. A Penn State University study placed men and women in a chamber that simulated the visual effects of motion. All of the subjects had some unpleasant reaction to the test, but women reported more upsetting and longer lasting effects.

10. Women. In everyday encounters, or even just walking down the street, women smile more often than men do. Maybe it's because women instinctively understand that, like Mama said, "You catch more flies with honey than with vinegar." Maybe it's because people smile at women more often, so women smile back more often.

8-10 correct: Can do

4-7 correct: Can try

1-3 correct: Can it

12. Women 1 to 10

1. Women who have served as attorney general of the United States. Janet Reno, who was attorney general during the Clinton administration, is the only woman to serve as U.S. attorney general to date.

2. Women who have won the Iditarod. Two women have won the annual Iditarod sled-dog race between Anchorage and Nome, Alaska. Libby Riddles did it first in 1985 and Susan Butcher did four times, in 1986, 1987, 1988 and 1990.

3. Witches in *Macbeth*. In the opening scene of Shakespeare's famous "Scottish play," Macbeth's fate is foretold by the three "weird sisters."

4. Fingers, including thumb, on Minnie Mouse's hand. Virtually all cartoon characters are drawn with four fingers (including a thumb). The style makes the cartoons faster and easier to draw, and cartoonists feel the hands are just as expressive minus one digit.

5. Spice Girls. That would be Baby, Ginger, Posh, Scary and Sporty Spice, if you're counting.

6. Wives of Henry VIII. England's famous Tudor king was known for marrying often and for disposing of his wives in unpleasant ways. Here's the countdown: Catherine of Aragon (divorced), Anne Boleyn (beheaded), Jane Seymour (died after childbirth), Anne of Cleves (divorced), Catherine Howard (beheaded), Catherine Parr (outlived him).

7. The Pleiades. The Pleiades of Greek mythology, daughters of Atlas and Pleione, are sometimes called the Seven Sisters. It was said that Zeus, king of the gods, turned the sisters into stars and put them in the sky to protect them from Orion, a hunter who was pursuing them. The constellation known as the Pleiades is one of the most important to astronomers. It's near the constellation of Orion.

8. Elizabeth Taylor's marriages. Elizabeth Taylor has been married eight times to seven different men (she married and divorced actor Richard Burton twice). Her other hus-bands include: hotel heir Nicky Hilton, actor Michael Wilding, producer Mike Todd, actor Eddie Fisher, U.S. Senator John Warner, and construction worker Larry Fortensky.

9. Children of Rose Fitzgerald Kennedy. The mother of President John F. Kennedy and U.S. Senators Robert F.

Kennedy and Edward M. Kennedy gave birth to nine children in all. They include Joseph P. Kennedy, Jr., Kathleen, Eunice, Patricia, Jean and Rosemary. Mrs. Kennedy died in 1995 at the age of 105.

10. Bo Derek-Dudley Moore film. As the object of Dudley Moore's desire in *10*, Bo Derek briefly made a headful of braids a fashion choice for some women.

8-10 correct: Count on me

4-7 correct: Don't count me out

1-3 correct: Down for the count

13. A Girl's Best Friend

1. (a) At 530.20 carats, the Cullinan Diamond, named for the South African mine where it was found, is the world's largest diamond. Today it's housed in the Tower of London with the British Crown Jewels. It's set in the scepter of King Edward VII.

2. (b) The first recorded history of diamond mining comes from India, more than 3,000 years ago.

3. (a) Tennis star Chris Evert wore her favorite diamond "line" bracelet while playing in the 1987 U.S. Open. When it flew off her wrist during the match, the official stopped play while Chris gathered up the stones. Reporters referred to it as the "tennis bracelet" and the name stuck. In 2002, jeweler Harry Winston created a $29,000, 12-carat tennis bracelet especially for Serena Williams. Hers had an extra-secure clasp!

4. (a) The Hope Diamond is the world's largest deep-blue diamond. Its history dates to the 1600s, but it was named for Englishman Henry Philip Hope, who owned it in the 1830s. Sold to pay off Mr. Hope's debts, the diamond made its way from England to Paris to the United States.

In 1949, jeweler Harry Winston bought the gem and eventually donated it to the Smithsonian Institution in Washington, D.C., where you can see it today.

5. (b) Since 1947, "A diamond is forever" has been the slogan of De Beers, the world's largest diamond mining, production and marketing corporation.

6. (c) Crater of Diamonds State Park, near Murfreesboro, Arkansas, covers the site where more than 100,000 diamonds were found in the early 20th century. For generations, it was the only working diamond mine in the United States. Now tourists go there to hunt for diamonds, and the largest U.S. commercial diamond mine is located on the Colorado-Wyoming border.

7. (c) The six-prong Tiffany setting is named for the New York jeweler Tiffany & Co., which introduced it in the late 1890s. Unlike earlier settings that held the diamond flush and surrounded by precious metal, the Tiffany setting holds the diamond in an open "basket" so that the entire stone can be seen and savored.

8. (c) To accept her Oscar for *Monster's Ball*, Halle Berry wore a form-fitting brown dress accessorized by a brown-and-white diamond bracelet, matching ear clips and the vivid orange $3-million Pumpkin diamond ring, courtesy of the jeweler Harry Winston.

9. (b) Diamonds are made from concentrated carbon. The molecules are squeezed together by intense pressure some 100 miles below Earth's surface.

10. (b) Laura Elena Harring, star of the 2001 film *Mullholland Drive*, wore platinum shoes studded with 464 diamonds to the Academy Awards in 2002.

> *8-10 correct: Flawless gem*
> *4-7 correct: Carbon copy*
> *1-3 correct: Cubic zirconia*

14. Eat It or Wear It?

1. Wear it. An obi is the sash used to bind a Japanese kimono.

2. Eat it. Nori is the edible, dried seaweed used to wrap sushi. It's rich in protein, vitamins, iron and calcium.

3. Eat it. Actually, you would drink it. Sake is Japanese wine made from fermented rice. It's usually served warm in tiny porcelain cups.

4. Wear it. A sari is a traditional garment worn by Hindu women.

5. Eat it. Chanterelles are bright yellow or orange wild mushrooms that grow in the Pacific Northwest and the northeastern United States.

6. Eat it. Chamomile flowers look like daisies. They're dried and used to brew a fragrant yellow tea that is believed to have soothing properties.

7. Wear it. At least you would if you were a Roman Catholic priest. A chasuble is the sleeveless tunic worn over the priest's robes during Mass.

8. Eat it. Cherimoyas are also known as custard apples. They grow in the tropics and taste like a combination of mango, pineapple and strawberry.

9. Wear it. A balaclava is a close-fitting knitted hood that covers the head, ears and neck, leaving only the face exposed. It was named for the town of Balaklava on the Crimean peninsula of what is now the Ukraine. Balaklava was the site of the famous Charge of the Light Brigade during the Crimean War.

10. Eat it. Baklava is a sweet pastry from Greece and Turkey, made with layers of phyllo dough and drenched in honey.

8-10 correct: Dressed for success
4-7 correct: Well dressed
1-3 correct: Is that what you're wearing?

15. Stuck in the Middle

1. Joyce Carol Oates won the 1970 National Book Award for her novel *Them*, and is among the more prolific modern writers. In addition to literary novels, countless short stories and essays about boxing, she has written psychological thrillers under the pen name Rosamond Smith.

2. Julia Ward Howe, a vocal campaigner for women's suffrage and the abolition of slavery, wrote "Battle Hymn of the Republic" in 1862.

3. Charlotte Perkins Gilman, a 19th-century feminist writer, examined the social oppression of women from a variety of perspectives. Her psychological short story "The Yellow Wallpaper" is a reading-list staple for women's-studies majors. Her *Women and Economics*, written in 1898, was one of the first books to discuss the way women's financial dependence on men can limit their progress toward social equality.

4. Zora Neale Hurston was a key figure of the Harlem Renaissance of the 1930s. She's best known for the novel, *Their Eyes Were Watching God*.

5. Elizabeth Cady Stanton, along with Lucretia Mott, organized the first Women's Rights Convention in 1848. Three years later, she met Susan B. Anthony and together they advanced the causes of women's suffrage and women's rights.

6. Harriet Beecher Stowe is best known for her 1852 anti-slavery novel, *Uncle Tom's Cabin*. Her works included other fictionalized accounts of slavery, as well as a non-fiction book called *A Key to Uncle Tom's Cabin*, which gave factual information to support her position against slavery. She was the daughter of a Connecticut minister and the sister of Henry Ward Beecher, a preacher and a vocal abolitionist.

7. Joan Ganz Cooney, a TV producer at public pelevision station WNET in New York, co-founded Children's Television Workshop in 1968. The company's first

production was *Sesame Street,* an educational series for children. It debuted in 1969 and hasn't been off the air since.

8. Ruth Bader Ginsburg, the second woman to become a U.S. Supreme Court justice, founded the American Civil Liberties Union: Women's Rights Project and served as a U.S. Court of Appeals judge in Washington, D.C., before her 1993 Supreme Court nomination. Her daughter, Jane Ginsburg, is a professor at Columbia University Law School.

9. Mary McLeod Bethune started her first school for black women in 1904 with $1.50 and five students in a rented house in Daytona Beach, Florida. Through incredible perseverance, she was able to secure corporate sponsorship to help the school flourish and grow. Eventually her all-female Bethune College merged with all-male Cookman Institute to form Bethune-Cookman College. In 1935, she formed the National Council of Negro Women.

10. Helen Gurley Brown, a former advertising copywriter and author of the racy 1962 book *Sex and the Single Girl,* became the editor-in-chief of *Cosmopolitan* magazine in 1965 and held that position until 1996. Under her leadership, the magazine became a virtual bible for women who were ready for candid talk about life and sex (not necessarily in that order).

8-10 correct: Middle class
4-7 correct: Middle of the road
1-3 correct: Middle of nowhere

16. Playing the Percentages

1. (c) Of the fifty-three issues of *Sports Illustrated* published in 2002, only three issues featured women on the cover, and one of those was the annual swimsuit issue. The other two pictured female college athletes and Olympic gold-medalist

skater Sarah Hughes. That's 5.7% of the total, which is higher than the year before, but lower than 2000, when seven covers featured women.

2. (h) Most people believed that women couldn't become alcoholics when Alcoholics Anonymous was founded in 1935. They figured drinking was a man's curse, but they were wrong. Ever since the first woman got sober through AA in 1939, female participation in the organization has grown, and it has spawned a number of women-only groups. As of 2001, 33% of Alcoholics Anonymous members were women.

3. (b) The International Society of Women Airline Pilots estimates that 4,000 of the 80,000 commercial airline pilots flying today are women. That's 5% of the total, and most of those women fly for U.S.-based air carriers. However, Aer Lingus, the national carrier of Ireland, has the highest percentage of women pilots for a single airline.

4. (j) The bad news is that 70% of expectant mothers experience some symptoms of morning sickness during pregnancy. The good news is that 30% don't. Also, remember that morning sickness generally does not last throughout an entire pregnancy and that each pregnancy is different. Even if you experienced morning sickness with your first child, that doesn't necessarily mean you'll have it with your second.

5. (d) A 1999 study of gender in televised sports conducted by the Amateur Athletic Foundation of Los Angeles found that just 8.7% of televised sports coverage was devoted to women's athletics. That was up from 5% in 1989.

6. (f) In most married households, the man earns more than the woman, but not always. The 2000 U.S. Census reported that in 15% of married couples, the wife out-earns her husband by at least $5,000 per year. In unmarried couples, that rises to 22%.

7. (g) The rate of childless women in their 40s has been rising steadily. In 2000, it was 19%, compared with 10% in 1980.

8. (a) The 2000 U.S. Census reported that 0.91% of women between the ages of 18 and 64 were in jail. At the same time, 11.7% of men in that age group were incarcerated.

9. (e) A 2003 *People* magazine poll found that 12% of women had used an online dating service to find a man. Of the men surveyed, 16% said they'd logged on to find love.

10. (i) Since 1984, women have consistently had a stronger showing than men at the presidential polls. In 2000, 61% of registered female voters—citizens over the age of 18—cast their votes for president. In the same year, 58% of registered male voters did.

8-10 correct: Percentage wise

4-7 correct: Statistical average

1-3 correct: Fuzzy numbers

17. Power of Four

1. Old Testament matriarchs. These women were the wives of the Old Testament patriarchs. Sarah was married to Abraham. Rebecca was married to Isaac. Rachel and Leah, who were sisters, both married Jacob.

2. The only four real women to be pictured on U.S. currency. In 1862, Pocahontas became the first real woman depicted on U.S. currency. (Lady Liberty had been there before.) Her image was part of a tableau called "Introduction of the Old World to the New World" on a $10 note. Martha Washington had her portrait on $1 silver certificates from the 1880s. Susan B. Anthony dollar coins were issued in 1979, and the Sacagawea golden dollar coin was introduced in 2000.

3. *Sex and the City* girls. The main characters of the HBO series—Carrie, Charlotte, Miranda and Samantha—were played by Sarah Jessica Parker, Kristin Davis, Cynthia Nixon and Kim Cattrall, respectively.

4. The Bangles. Members of the 1980s girl group, whose hits included *Manic Monday* and *Walk Like an Egyptian*.

5. Cher's four U.S. #1 solo hits. Sonny and Cher hit #1 on the *Billboard* charts in 1965 with "I Got You Babe." As a solo performer, Cher scored four U.S. #1s. Her first was 1971's "Gypsys, Tramps and Thieves," followed by "Half Breed" (1973), "Dark Lady" (1974), and "Believe" (1999). She also scored a U. K. #1 in 1990 with "The Shoop Shoop Song (It's in His Kiss)."

6. The March sisters. You may know them better as the title characters of Louisa May Alcott's *Little Women*.

7. The only four women to win the Ladies Professional Golf Association U.S. Open three or more times. Betsy Rawls did it in 1951, 1953, 1957 and 1960; Mickey Wright in 1958, 1959, 1961 and 1964; Susie Maxwell Berning in 1968, 1972 and 1973; Hollis Stacy in 1977, 1978 and 1984.

8. The four films for which Katharine Hepburn won Best Actress Oscars. *Morning Glory* (1933) was Hepburn's third film and it brought her first Best Actress Oscar. It took another 34 years for her to win the second, for *Guess Who's Coming to Dinner* (1967), followed by *The Lion in Winter* (1968) and *On Golden Pond* (1981). She was nominated for Oscars twelve times.

9. Stars of *Waiting to Exhale*. These four actresses brought Terry MacMillan's best-seller to the big screen in 1995.

10. The only four women to ride in the Kentucky Derby. Diane Crump broke the Kentucky Derby jockey gender barrier when she rode Fathom in 1970. Patricia Cooksey rode So Vague in the 1984 Derby, and Andrea Seefeldt rode Forty Something in 1991. Julie Krone was the first woman to ride in two Kentucky Derby races, 1992 and 1995. She also became the first woman to win a Triple Crown horse-racing event, when she won the Belmont Stakes in 1993.

8-10 correct: Four-midable

4-7 correct: Four-tunate

1-3 correct: Four-get about it

18. Mermaids Multiple Choice

1. (b) In many legends, mermaids are unable to speak. Irish legends about mermaids who marry mortal men often say that their children are doomed to be silent as well.

2. (a) Merman legends aren't as scarce as you may think. In fact, there's one contained in the tales of *1,001 Arabian Nights*. Just as mermaids must give up their underwater lives to marry mortal men, mortal women who marry mermen are prevented from returning to land.

3. (c) In ancient Scotland and England, mermaids were equated with prostitutes or courtesans. Shakespeare used "mermaid" as a euphemism for a woman of easy virtue.

4. (c) The original tale of "The Little Mermaid" was written by Danish author Hans Christian Andersen in the 1800s.

5. (a) Alyssa Milano was a teenage star of TV's *Who's the Boss?* when her face and body were used as the model for "Ariel," the title character of Disney's *The Little Mermaid*. The animated film was released in 1989.

6. (b) If you're ever diving in Morecambe Bay on England's west coast, you may encounter a variety of spiky-fingered sea sponge that the locals call "mermaid's glove."

7. (c) The mermaid known as Syrena is the symbol of Warsaw, Poland. Legend says that the Polish hero Prince Kazimierz became hopelessly lost during a hunting trip in the area that is now Warsaw. Syrena rose from the Vistula River, which now runs through the city's center, and guided him to safety.

8. (b) For more than 50 years, the Weeki Wachee Waterpark on Florida's Gulf Coast (near Tampa) has been known for

its live-action "mermaid" show. The mermaids, who perform underwater, breathe through air hoses that are strategically placed around their lagoon.

9. (a) In the 1984 film *Splash*, starring Darryl Hannah and Tom Hanks, Hannah plays a mermaid named Madison. She was named for Madison Avenue in New York City. According to the U.S. Social Security Administration, Madison was the second-most popular name for girls born in 2001.

10. (c) In 1990, Christina Ricci was just 9 years old when she made her movie debut in *Mermaids*. She played Kate Flax, a water-loving little girl, and spent much of her on-screen time wearing a 1960s-style bathing cap.

8-10 correct: Water baby

4-7 correct: Treading water

1-3 correct: Chicken of the Sea

19. Measuring Up

1. (f) A baby carried to full term generally measures about 21.5 inches.

2. (h) Women in the United States average almost 5 feet 4 inches tall, according to Centers for Disease Control statistics.

3. (i) We're not making this up. The *2003 Guinness Book of World Records* reports that Louise Hollis of the United States grew her toenails to a combined length of 7 feet 3 inches. We're trying to resist making barefoot and pregnant jokes, but Hollis rarely wears shoes and is the mother of 12.

4. (b) Fingernails grow about 1.5 inches per year. That rate slows as you age.

5. (c) Your hair grows about .5 inch per month, or 6 inches per year.

6. (j) At 8 feet 1.75 inches, China's Zeng Jinlian was the world's tallest woman when she died in 1982. She was over 5 feet tall by the time she was 4, and her rapid growth caused her to suffer from scoliosis, or curvature of the spine.

7. (g) A human umbilical cord, the tube through which nutrients flow from a mother's body to a growing fetus, measures about 26 inches.

8. (d) To fit a size-8 shoe, the most common size in the United States, a woman's foot generally measures about 9.5 inches.

9. (a) At 8 weeks, a growing fetus measures about the size of a bean, or 0.56 to 0.8 inch.

10. (e) The world's smallest adult waist measurement, 13 inches, belonged to 1930s Englishwoman Ethel Granger, who got a little help from her corset.

8-10 correct: Measure of success
4-7 correct: Made to measure
1-3 correct: Desperate measures

 20. All Hail the Queen

1. Margrethe II. Although she is Denmark's second Queen Margrethe, she is the first queen to rule Denmark in her own right. (Medieval Queen Margrethe I ruled jointly with her adolescent son.) A true Renaissance woman, Denmark's modern-day queen is a highly regarded artist and designer.

2. Victoria. She became queen in 1837 at age 18 and ruled until 1901, a few months shy of her 82nd birthday— almost 64 years. In addition to being the queen of the United Kingdom of England and Ireland and empress of India, she was the mother of nine children.

3. Cleopatra. We tend to think of her as the one and only, but the woman we call Cleopatra was actually the seventh Egyptian queen to bear that name. Both Julius Caesar and Marc Antony were her lovers.

4. Catherine the Great. This German princess married Peter III of Russia, and a rotten guy he was, too. Sick of Peter's philandering (and possibly the tiniest bit hypocritical), Catherine asked her own lover to help her seize the throne. In 1762, shortly after Peter became emperor, Catherine had him deposed and proclaimed herself empress of Russia. She reigned for 34 years.

5. Maria Theresa. The first Hapsburg woman to inherit her father's kingdom, Maria Theresa was empress of the Austro-Hungarian Empire for much of the 18th century. Though she ruled jointly with her husband, Francis, she was the more powerful and savvy monarch. During their marriage, she gave birth to sixteen children—eleven daughters and five sons—the youngest of whom became the French queen Marie-Antoinette.

6. Christina. Here is a woman to be reckoned with. Christina ascended to Sweden's throne in 1632 when she was just 6 years old. Described as "highly intelligent" and (ahem) "mannish," she refused to marry and frequently dressed in men's clothing. In her 20s, she converted to Catholicism—forbidden in Sweden—so she abdicated the throne to her cousin and lived the rest of her life in Italy.

7. Isabella. Queen of Castile, a province in Spain, she married Ferdinand of Aragon, another Spanish province, in 1469. They merged their kingdoms and ruled together. Isabella may have been Christopher Columbus' biggest fan. She certainly was the one most active in paying for his voyage to the New World.

8. Beatrix. Born in 1938, Beatrix became queen of the Netherlands in 1980 when her mother, Queen Juliana, abdicated after ruling for 31 years. She is one of the world's wealthiest women.

9. Alexandra. The granddaughter of England's Queen Victoria married Russia's Czar Nicholas II in 1894. Bolshevik revolutionaries assassinated them, along with their five children, in 1917.

10. Cixi or Tz'u-hsi. Known as the Empress Dowager, or, less flatteringly but more appropriately, "Dragon Lady," Cixi held sway in China from 1861 until her death in 190 8. As the emperor's concubine, she gave birth to his only son and began her rise to power. She ruled jointly with her son and later her nephew, and outlived them both.

8-10 correct: Kneel before me, peasant
4-7 correct: Blue blood
1-3 correct: Throne it all away

21. Who Thought of That?

1. Man. Denver physician Earle Cleveland Haas invented the modern tampon in 1929. (He also had been the president of a company that developed the flexible ring for the contraceptive diaphragm.) The idea of "internal protection" from menstrual flow was not new. Ancient Egyptians made "tampons" from papyrus. Romans used wool. And in Indonesia, women used vegetable fibers.

2. Woman. Mary Phelps Jacobs holds the U.S. patent for the "backless brassiere." Jacobs was not an inventor by trade. She was a woman who, back in 1914, wanted an undergarment to wear with a sheer evening gown. The corsets available at the time did not fit her needs, so she developed her own makeshift bra from silk handkerchiefs.

3. Man. Marie-Antoinette lost her head on this French execution machine that was named for the man who invented it in 1789—Joseph-Ignace Guillotin.

4. Man. You knew it had to be, right? No woman would come up with a garment *that* uncomfortable. The truth is

a woman may have had something to do with the origin of pantyhose. Allen Gant of the Glen Raven hosiery company in North Carolina is generally credited as the inventor of pantyhose, although it is sometimes said that his wife, Ethel, conceived of the product in the 1950s, when she was pregnant and couldn't wear a girdle and stockings.

5. Woman. Marion Donovan Butler, a Connecticut mother and former *Harper's Bazaar* editor, developed a waterproof covering for diapers that kept them from leaking, but didn't pinch or bind the way rubber panties did. Her design, known as the "Boater," was patented in the 1940s and was the forerunner of today's flexible disposable diapers.

6. Woman. Josephine Cochrane of Shelbyville, Illinois, received a patent for a mechanical dishwasher in 1886. The wife of a local politician, Cochrane often hosted dinner parties in her home. Her household staff  was overwhelmed by the number of dishes to wash, and Cochrane was exasperated by the amount of china the staff broke in the process. Her mechanical dishwasher won praise for its ingenuity, but it was not an immediate success, reportedly because women of the day claimed to find dishwashing a "relaxing" activity.

7. Woman. Ruth Handler is credited as the "mother" of the Barbie doll. She certainly was the mother of Barbara Handler, for whom the doll was named. (Her son, Ken, was later immortalized as Barbie's male counterpart.) With her husband, Elliot, Ruth Handler was one of the founders of the Mattel toy company.

8. Man. The "Pap test," used for early detection of cervical cancer, was named for its inventor, George Papanicolaou, a Greek-born American scientist. Also known as the "Pap smear," the test was introduced in 1928.

9. Man. Actually, it was two men. Gregory Pincus and John Rock are credited with developing the birth-control pill,

which prevents pregnancy by preventing ovulation. The pill was introduced in 1960.

10. Woman. Mary Anderson of Alabama was the first person in the United States to patent a design for a windshield wiper that could be controlled from inside a car. She developed her wipers for public streetcars and patented the idea in 1905. By 1915, windshield wipers were standard equipment on all U.S. automobiles.

> *8-10 correct: Always thinking*
> *4-7 correct: Quick thinking*
> *1-3 correct: What are you thinking?*

22. Is She for Real?

1. Not for real. The name Aunt Jemima comes from a 19th-century New Orleans-style jazz tune. Chris Rutt, an entrepreneur who packaged pre-mixed pancake flour for sale in grocery stores, thought the name and the idea of Southern hospitality (embodied in a smiling "mammy" figure) created the perfect image for his product. For the 1893 Chicago World's Fair, a real-life "Aunt Jemima" was hired to serve pancakes at a promotional event. Her name was Nancy Green, and she went on to act as the "face" of Aunt Jemima products until her death in 1923.

2. Not for real. "Betty Crocker" was invented by the Washburn Crosby Company, makers of baking products. The name Crocker honored an outgoing company president. Betty was chosen because it sounded friendly. Originally, Betty Crocker was a faceless entity who answered consumers' mail to the company. Later, a portrait was commissioned, and Betty's face has graced product packaging ever since.

3. For real. Marie Callender started baking and selling pies in southern California in the 1940s. Her son, Don, opened the first Marie Callender's restaurant in 1964. Today, the company operates 160 restaurants.

4. For real. The Baby Ruth candy bar, introduced in the 1920s, was named for Ruth Cleveland, the daughter of then-U.S. President Grover Cleveland.

5. For real. Legend has it that the Granny Smith apple was named for Australia's Mary Anne Smith in the 19th century.

6. For real. Charles Lubin renamed his chain of Chicago-area bakeries the Kitchens of Sara Lee, in honor of his 8-year-old daughter. Their first signature product was a cream cheesecake, introduced in 1949.

7. For real. McKee Foods founder O.D. McKee wanted an appealing name for his company's line of family-pack snack cakes, so he named them after his granddaughter, Debbie. That's her face, circa 1960, on the box.

8. For real. In 1969, when Dave Thomas opened his first fast-food restaurant, he named it for his 8-year-old daughter. Her name was Melinda Lou, but everyone in the family called her Wendy.

9. For real. Debbi Fields, a young mother, opened her first cookie store in Palo Alto, California in 1977. Today there are more than 700 Mrs. Fields franchised cookie stores in twelve countries.

10. For real. Her name is on pie boxes in virtually every supermarket freezer case in the United States, but the real Amanda Smith started her baking career selling slices of pie at the Pottstown, Pennsylvania, YMCA in the 1920s.

8-10 correct: The real deal
4-7 correct: Known to fake it
1-3 correct: Phony baloney

23. Girl Groups

1. "I Met Him on a Sunday" was the first record made by the Shirelles, a group of girlfriends from Passaic High School in New Jersey. They wrote some of their own songs, including "I Met Him on a Sunday," which they first performed at a high school talent show.

2. "He's a Rebel" was a #1 hit for the Crystals in 1962, but it's not clear who actually sang on the record. Music producer Phil Spector brought in a number of singers and musicians to work on the song, and their work is almost certainly on the final recording.

3. "Chapel of Love" was a hit for the Dixie Cups, a trio from New Orleans.

4. "Please Mr. Postman" made the Marvelettes one of Motown's hottest commodities. They hit #1 on the charts in 1961, well before their Motown rivals, the Supremes. Alas, the Marvelettes passed on recording "Baby Love," the hit that made the Supremes stars.

5. "Born Too Late" was the Poni-Tails' lament about falling for an older guy. The Ohio trio had already explored that theme in a previous recording—"It's Just My Luck to Be 15"—which went nowhere in the charts. "Born Too Late" hit #7.

6. "Mr. Lee" was written about a teacher some of the Bobbettes knew in Harlem. Though the 1957 song wound up praising Mr. Lee, the singers really hated the man. If you have any doubts, investigate the sequel—"I Shot Mr. Lee."

7. "My Boyfriend's Back," one of the all-time girl-group classics, was recorded by the New Jersey-based Angels in 196 3. Legend has it that the songwriters were inspired by a fight they'd heard between a young girl and the boy who was harassing her. "My boyfriend's back and there's gonna be trouble . . ." The rest is history.

8. "Leader of the Pack" by the Shangri-Las hit #1 on the charts in 1964. The production engineer reportedly brought his motorcycle into the studio to record the engine revving.

9. "He's So Fine" by the Chiffons was #1 on the pop and R&B charts in March 1963. It was best known for its catchy "doo-lang" chorus until the 1970s, when George Harrison was accused of plagiarizing "He's So Fine" for his hit "My Sweet Lord."

10. "Walking in the Rain" wasn't as well-known as the Ronettes' "Be My Baby" and "Baby I Love You," but it did earn a Grammy for best sound effects.

8-10 correct: Child of the 1950s
4-7 correct: Shopping for saddle shoes
1-3 correct: Ike who?

24. Ode to Florence

1. Florence Henderson. You probably know her best as Carol Brady, but Henderson had a successful career as a singer before she joined the sitcom cast.

2. Stevie Smith. English writer Florence Margaret Smith, better known as Stevie, published her first book of poems when she was in her 30s, illustrated with her own eccentric doodles. Sometimes wry and cynical, sometimes downright morose, Smith was inspired by everything from Grimm's *Fairy Tales* to the teachings of the Church of England. Though she published from the 1930s onward, her work didn't really catch on with a broad audience until the 1960s.

3. (b) A Florence flask is a glass laboratory flask with a long neck and a round bottom. Some chemists say it earned its name because it's built like a woman (these guys don't date much). The fact is it was named after the bottles used for wine in Florence, Italy.

4. Diane Ladd received an Oscar nomination for her role as the feisty waitress Flo in 1974's *Alice Doesn't Live Here Anymore*. In an ironic turn, she joined the cast of the TV sitcom *Alice* for one season. Her character, Belle Dupree, replaced the sitcom character Flo.

5. Polly Holliday took over the role of Flo in the TV sitcom *Alice*, based on *Alice Doesn't Live Here Anymore*. She won two Golden Globe awards for her acting on the show, and starred in a spin-off called *Flo*, which ended almost as soon as it hit the air.

6. When the film was adapted for the TV show, Flo got a full name. It's Florence Jean Castleberry. And if you don't like it, you can "Kiss mah grits!" (Sorry, we couldn't resist.)

7. (a) With a population of just over 36,000, Florence, Alabama, named for the Italian city of Florence, is the largest of the three mentioned here. There also are cities called Florence in Arizona, California, Colorado, Kansas, Mississippi, New Jersey, Oregon and Wisconsin (not to mention Florence Lakes, Florida).

8. Florence Nightingale. They called England's Florence Nightingale "The Lady with the Lamp" because she walked through battlefield hospitals at night talking to the wounded soldiers. Her focus on hygiene and sanitation was new to battlefield medicine, and helped reduce the spread of disease and infection. In the 1860s, she founded the world's first training school for nurses.

9. (a) Poet Langston Hughes said that *Shuffle Along*, a 1921 revue in which Florence Mills appeared, marked the beginning of the Harlem Renaissance. Mills, the daughter of former slaves, rose to become such a major musical theater star that impresario Florenz Ziegfeld invited her to become a featured player in his Ziegfeld Follies. She passed on his offer, deciding instead to help create an all-black revue to rival Ziegfeld's all-white one.

10. (b) In the National Statuary Hall at the U.S. House of Representatives in Washington, D.C., the state of

Colorado is represented by a statue of Florence Sabin. She was a pioneering medical researcher who contributed to the understanding of how tuberculosis develops and spreads. She was also the first woman to become a full professor at Johns Hopkins Medical School and the first to be inducted into the National Academy of Sciences.

8-10 correct: Go with the Flo

4-7 correct: Low Flo

1-3 correct: No Flo

25. Marriage-Minded

1. True. The National Center for Health Statistics reports that 59% of brides who married at age 18 or younger were divorced within 15 years. Of those who married at age 20 or over, 36% were divorced after 15 years.

2. (c) When Queen Victoria married Prince Albert in 1840, she wore white from head to toe. Before her, most royal brides wore heavily brocaded gowns in a variety of colors (except green, which implied loose morals). An ordinary bride simply wore her best dress for her wedding. But Victoria started a trend that has survived to this day.

3. (a) The *chupa* is the traditional wedding canopy used at Jewish weddings to symbolize the tents of the ancient people of Israel. It's usually made from a pretty cloth and held up by poles in each of the corners. The bride and groom stand beneath the *chupa* while the wedding ceremony is performed.

4. True. The chance of a first marriage breaking up within 5 years is about 20%. The chance of an unmarried-and-living-together couple breaking up within 5 years is 49%.

5. (a) Jumping the broom is done at some African-American weddings. The tradition probably came from Africa and symbolized the sweeping away of the couple's old life and the clean start of a new one. Slaves in the American South, who were not legally permitted to marry, jumped the broom to symbolize a marital union.

6. (b) Both the bride and groom wear red, the color of good fortune, in a traditional Chinese wedding ceremony. The bride's face is typically hidden beneath a red veil trimmed with tassels.

7. False. In the 1950s, about 65% of divorced women remarried. By 1980, the figure had dropped to 50%. This could be due to the fact that divorce had lost much of its negative stereotype by the 1980s, and to the fact that a woman's earning power—and thus her ability to support herself—has increased over the years.

8. (b) At weddings of commissioned officers in the U.S. military, the wedding couple sometimes exits the chapel under an arch of sabers or swords held by ushers and guests in military uniform.

9. (a) Traditional anniversary symbols grow more durable and valuable with each year of marriage. So, the first year is symbolized by paper. The tenth year is tin. Twenty-five years is silver, fifty years is gold, and seventy-five is diamond. Real traditionalists buy married couples gifts made from these materials on the corresponding anniversaries.

10. True. About three-quarters (75%) of women in the United States have been married at least once by age 30, and about half have cohabited with a romantic partner without being married.

8-10 correct: White wedding
4-7 correct: Civil ceremony
1-3 correct: Left at the altar

26. Calorie Count

1. (f) If you brushed your teeth for half an hour, you'd use 83 calories. Of course, you'd never brush for a full 30 minutes. Dentists recommend brushing for 2 to 3 minutes, which would burn about 8 calories. But hey, every little bit helps!

2. (c) Thirty minutes in front of the computer burns about 48 calories. You burn a bit more if you're filing papers or doing general office work.

3. (g) Some people can burn anything when they cook, but everyone can burn calories—about 87 calories per half-hour.

4. (i) The number of calories you burn while gardening depends on the tasks you're doing. Ordinary planting and pruning burns about 157 calories per half-hour. Weeding burns about 160 calories. And if you're digging dirt, spreading mulch or laying sod, you can burn about 175 calories in 30 minutes.

5. (h) Pushing a cart around the supermarket doesn't burn quite as many calories as taking a brisk walk, but it's not a bad way to get some exercise. Pop your toddler in the baby seat for a little extra resistance and you'll burn about 122 calories as you walk the aisles.

6. (j) Rearranging the furniture is a great way to give yourself fresh perspective. It's not a bad indoor workout either. It burns about 218 calories per half-hour, more than low-impact aerobics or disco dancing (191 calories each).

7. (a) You burn calories even when you sleep, about 22 every half-hour. If you get a full 8 hours a night, that's a total of 352 calories. Not bad for a night's work.

8. (e) Here's a good excuse to clean the dust bunnies out from under the bed. Vacuuming burns about 82 calories a half-hour. If you actually move the furniture out of the way before you vacuum, you'll burn even more.

9. (d) Doing the dishes by hand has its benefits. It burns about 74 calories per half-hour. We're not sure how many more you burn if you dry the dishes too.

10. (b) Couch potatoes, take heart. You burn about 26 calories just by sitting around watching a half-hour sitcom on the tube.

8-10 correct: Counterintelligence
4-7 correct: Counterculture
1-3 correct: Counterfeit

27. Smells Like . . .

1. (c) Cindy Adams, who definitely has a nose for news, is the longtime gossip columnist for the *New York Post*.

2. (i) Uninhibited, Cher's signature fragrance, arrived in the late 1980s and departed soon after. Look long enough and you'll find perfume collectors and Cher fans trading bottles of the precious elixir on the Internet.

3. (a) Patti LaBelle's Girlfriend was introduced in 1988. The singer also promoted another fragrance, called Patti LaBelle, in 1996.

4. (b) Lopez's first fragrance, Glow by JLo, was intended for women aged 15 to 25. Still, a more "mature" fragrance launched in 2003, is aimed at women over 25.

5. (e) Introduced in 1998, Moi was sold exclusively at Bloomingdale's stores, which also sold Kermit the Frog's Amphibia cologne for men.

6. (g) Actress and nature lover Stephanie Powers launched her Rare Orchid fragrance line on QVC. The scent supposedly replicates the aroma of orchids without harming any flowers.

7. (f) Redolent with honeysuckle, pineapple, peaches and orange blossoms, Now & Forever, launched in 2001 on

QVC, is just another part of Joan Rivers' successful home shopping product line. She also hawks clothing and jewelry on TV.

8. (d) Isabella Rossellini's Manifesto fragrance was introduced in 2001. Touted as a "floral, green musky scent," it contains a bushel of aromas, from jasmine and rose to basil and white pepper.

9. (j) Elizabeth Taylor's White Diamonds is the most successful celebrity fragrance of all time. Taylor has also marketed fragrances called Passion, Gardenia, Diamonds and Sapphires, Diamonds and Emeralds, Diamonds and Rubies, and Black Pearls.

10. (h) Shocking was created for Mae West in 1937 by designer Elsa Schiaparelli. The torso-shaped bottle is said to have been made in the proportions of West's anatomy.

8-10 correct: Sweet smell of success

4-7 correct: On the scent trail

1-3 correct: Sniff, sniff

28. Title Characters

1. (b) Madonna played the "real" Susan in the 1985 film *Desperately Seeking Susan*. Rosanna Arquette played a housewife named Roberta, who gets bopped on the head, suffers amnesia, and thinks she might be Susan.

2. (b) Bette Davis played Jane, the aging and somewhat demented former child star in *Whatever Happened to Baby Jane?*. Joan Crawford played her sister, Blanche, a former actress crippled in a car wreck. By 1962, Joan and Bette were virtual caricatures of their former glamorous selves. They made the most of it, camping it up in this cult classic.

3. (a) Anne Baxter played Eve, the seemingly innocent yet conniving ingénue in *All About Eve*. Bette Davis played

Margo Channing, an aging Broadway star who's taken in by Eve's act. The 1950 film won the Academy Award for Best Picture.

4. (b) Vanessa Redgrave played Julia, a member of an anti-Fascist movement in 1930s Europe, in the 1977 film *Julia*. The movie is based on Lillian Hellman's autobiographical book *Pentimento*. Jane Fonda portrayed Lillian Hellman.

5. (a) Bette Davis played Charlotte Hollis in the 1965 film *Hush Hush Sweet Charlotte*. Accused of killing her beau dozens of years earlier, the slightly loopy Charlotte has holed up in her old family home. When the state plans to tear down the house, she calls her cousin Miriam, played by Olivia de Havilland, to help. But Miriam tries to have her committed instead.

6. (b) A young and lovely Janet Leigh played Eileen Sherwood, a struggling actress, in the 1955 movie musical *My Sister Eileen*. Betty Garrett played her clever sister Ruth, a would-be writer who falls for an equally clever (and young and lovely) Jack Lemmon.

7. (b) Natalie Wood played the young Louise Hovick, who grew up to be stripper Gypsy Rose Lee, in the 1962 movie musical *Gypsy*. Rosalind Russell played her overbearing mother, "Mama Rose" Hovick.

8. (a) Julie Andrews was the original Millie Dillmount in *Thoroughly Modern Millie* (which was a 1967 film before it became a Broadway musical). Mary Tyler Moore played Miss Dorothy Brown, her best pal.

9. (b) Shelley Winters played Helen and Debbie Reynolds played her friend Adelle in 1971's *What's the Matter with Helen?*. After their sons are convicted of murder, they leave town and go to Hollywood to start a talent school for kids. But they're pursued by a stalker who won't let them forget the past. This movie was a late entry in the "two heavy-weight actresses-one weird film" genre, but it holds its own with the best of 'em.

10. (b) Meg Tilly played Agnes, a nun who becomes pregnant and loses the baby under mysterious circumstances, in the 1985 movie version of *Agnes of God*. Anne Bancroft played the mother superior who wants the whole situation to go away and Jane Fonda played a psychiatrist insistent on finding out what really happened.

8-10 correct: Name in lights

4-7 correct: Second billing

1-3 correct: Lost in a crowd scene

29. Birds Do It

1. (b) Female hamsters reach sexual maturity at 2 months of age. Unless you're planning to build a hamster farm, it's best to keep males and females separated. A pregnant female takes just 16 days to give birth to a litter of five to ten babies.

2. (b) A male iguana has two penises. Lots of snakes and reptiles do. But they only use one at a time for mating.

3. (a) A female whooping crane won't ovulate until her male mate dances for her—jumping around and flapping his wings in some sort of attractive way. When whooping cranes (an endangered species) are bred in captivity, human volunteers do the dancing to prepare the females for artificial insemination.

4. (a) A male octopus has one specialized tentacle, with an end that he uses to insert sperm into the female. After he mates, the end of the arm falls off and he can't mate again.

5. (b) Most whiptail lizards are parthenogenic females. That means they can reproduce without the need for male sperm. All of their offspring are female.

6. (c) Both males and females are necessary to make baby sea bass, but sometimes a school has too many of one gender.

When that happens, some of the fish restore the balance by changing from female to male or vice versa. If the balance shifts the other way, the fish just change back.

7. (b) After a female seahorse produces her eggs, she deposits them in the male's pouch, where they are fertilized and carried to maturity.

8. (c) Just imagine, if you were an elephant you'd be pregnant for 22 months. Then you'd give birth to a 3-foot-tall, 200-pound baby. Nine months doesn't seem bad at all, does it?

9. (c) Male proboscis monkeys can grow noses that are 8 inches long. To the females, longer is better, when it comes to noses.

10. (a) Yes, farmers with stopwatches confirm that it takes a bull just 5 seconds to mate with a cow. That's about long enough to say "Was it good for you?"

8-10 correct: Animal magnetism

4-7 correct: Animal instincts

1-3 correct: Animal crackers

30. She Said What?

1. (g) Comedienne Gilda Radner was the first performer chosen for the original cast of *Saturday Night Live*. Her memorable characters included Emily Litella and Roseanne Roseannadanna, but she was speaking as herself when she said, "I base my fashion taste on what doesn't itch."

2. (e) Mystery writer Agatha Christie knew what she was talking about when she said, "An archaeologist is the best husband a woman can have; the older she gets, the more interested he is in her." Her husband was archaeologist Max Mallowan.

3. (a) Bella Abzug, a former U.S. congresswoman from New York City, once said she was "born yelling." After a career as a lawyer, the flamboyant feminist entered politics at age 50. In her 1972 book, *Bella!*, she wrote, "The test for whether or not you can hold a job should not be the arrangement of your chromosomes."

4. (d) Cher has said, "The trouble with some women is that they get all excited about nothing—and then marry him." She doesn't fall into that category, however. She's had numerous high-profile romances, but she's only been married twice—to Sonny Bono and to Gregg Allman.

5. (c) Feminist writer Rita Mae Brown noted, "If the world were a logical place, men would ride side saddle," in her 1983 novel *Sudden Death*. Brown is best known for "co-writing" a series of mystery novels with her cat Sneaky Pie.

6. (j) Virginia Woolf observed, "Why are women . . . so much more interesting to men than men are to women?" in her book *A Room of One's Own*. She points out the number of books written about women by men and says, "If woman had no existence save in the fiction written by men, one would imagine her a person of the utmost importance."

7. (h) First Lady Eleanor Roosevelt wrote four books, including the 1937 memoir *This is My Story*. In it, she said, "Nobody can make you feel inferior without your consent." The comment rang true with so many women it has even been used as a bumper sticker motto by NOW.

8. (i) When she turned 80 in 1979, the colorful actress Gloria Swanson told *The New York Times*, "I've given my memoirs far more thought than any of my marriages. You can't divorce a book." Swanson had been married six times. She's best known for her portrayal of a demented screen star in *Sunset Boulevard*.

9. (f) Anne Morrow Lindbergh, who died in 2001 at age 94, wrote a number of fiction and nonfiction works. The well-traveled author and aviator once said, "My passport photo is

one of the most remarkable photographs I have ever seen—
no retouching, no shadows, no flattery—just stark me."

10. (b) Outspoken folk singer Joan Baez once began a sentence by saying, "In my humble opinion . . . ." Then she paused, laughed and said, "I've never had a humble opinion in my life. If you're going to have one, why bother to be humble about it?"

8-10 correct: Say hallelujah
4-7 correct: Say anything
1-3 correct: You don't say

31. Kiss Me, Kate

1. (b) In *Desk Set*, Kate played the head of a TV network research library. Spencer Tracy played an efficiency expert who's sent to replace Kate and her staff with computers (perish the thought!). This was 1957, when the idea of a computerized workplace was revolutionary and when a smart cookie like Katharine Hepburn could easily out-think a computer.

2. (b) *Guess Who's Coming to Dinner*, made in 1968, was the last film Kate and Spencer Tracy made together. He died shortly after filming was completed and she said that she never watched the completed film because it would have made her too sad.

3. True. Kate and John Wayne starred in *Rooster Cogburn* in 1975. Pairing those two screen legends was supposed to be a huge success, but the movie never quite lived up to the hype.

4. (a) In *The Lion in Winter* (1968), Kate portrayed Eleanor of Aquitaine. Her husband, Henry II of England, was played by Peter O'Toole. Her son, Richard I, was portrayed by Anthony Hopkins.

5. (c) Back in the 1930s, it was still a bit of a scandal for women to wear slacks in public. Kate tried to buck convention, but, in the beginning at least, it just annoyed people. Legend has it that when the movie studio stole the slacks from her dressing room, she walked around in her underwear until they were returned.

6. False. Katharine Hepburn and Audrey Hepburn were not related. Kate was born in Hartford, Connecticut. Audrey was born in Belgium and her baptismal name was Edda Kathleen van Heemstra Hepburn-Ruston.

7. (b) Believe it or not, this film does exist. It's called *Dragon Seed*, and it was based on a story by Pearl S. Buck.

8. (a) Kate's role as the missionary Rose Sayer in *The African Queen* (1951) is one of her best-known. She said she patterned the portrayal on First Lady Eleanor Roosevelt.

9. True. In *Suddenly, Last Summer* (1959), Kate played the villainous Mrs. Venable, whose son dies mysteriously while on vacation with her niece Catherine, played by Elizabeth Taylor. Catherine nearly goes insane with grief and guilt, and Mrs. Venable's solution to the problem is to set her up for a lobotomy.

10. (b) After a string of movie flops in the late 1930s, Kate took the role of Tracy Lord in the 1938 Broadway production of *The Philadelphia Story*. When the play became a hit, she wisely bought the film rights to it, starred in the 1940 film, and enjoyed a Hollywood comeback.

8-10 correct: Oscar winner

4-7 correct: Nominee

1-3 correct: Box-office poison

32. Color Full

1. (e) Starting sometime around the 1890s, houses of prostitution would identify themselves with red lights burning in their windows. Usually these were gas-lamps or electric lights with red-colored shades over them. It seems that the expression "red-light district" originated in the United States, but the use of red lights in brothels was just as common in Europe.

2. (i) For centuries, Buddhist monks have been identified by their orange robes. The fabric is colored in a dye made from the bark of the jackfruit tree.

3. (c) Laa-Laa, the yellow one, is one of two female Teletubbies from the children's TV series. The show's creators, Anne Wood and Andrew Davenport, describe Laa-Laa as "the happiest and silliest Teletubby." The other female is Po, the red Teletubby. Dipsy, the green one, and Tinky Winky, the purple one, are male.

4. (b) Shakespeare may have been the first person to write about jealousy as the "green-eyed monster." He referred to it in *Othello* and *The Merchant of Venice*. It's also possible that the expression was used before Shakespeare's time. He probably didn't invent it, but he did document it for the ages.

5. (j) Viagra, the little blue pill that treats male sexual dysfunction, was introduced in April 1998. In that month alone, doctors wrote an estimated 600,000 prescriptions for the drug.

6. (a) In early *Peanuts* comics, black-haired Violet was one of Charlie Brown's critical classmates. She also appears in the animated film, *A Charlie Brown Christmas*.

7. (h) In the 1940s, Frederick Mellinger was a ladies' undergarment salesman on New York's Lower East Side. At the time, women's "unmentionables" came in one color— white. Anything else was considered immodest—even immoral. When he started selling black lingerie, Frederick couldn't even convince newspapers to run his ads. They

said black lingerie was pornographic. So, he moved his business to Hollywood, where nubile young actresses were happy to buy his sexy lingerie. And Frederick's of Hollywood was born.

8. (d) Mrs. White is the character of the maid in the board game Clue. Her fellow characters include snooty Mrs. Peacock, sultry Miss Scarlet, pompous Colonel Mustard, clueless Professor Plum and sinister Mr. Green.

9. (f) When she turned 65 in 1970, Maggie Kuhn had to retire from her job. (At the time, 65 was the mandatory retirement age in the United States.) But she wasn't ready to fade away quietly. She formed a senior citizens' advocacy and political action group, dubbed the "Gray Panthers" by a New York talk-show producer (à la the Black Panthers militant civil rights group). Kuhn remained at the helm of the Gray Panthers until she died in 1995 at the age of 90.

10. (g) Rapper/singer Pink, known for her fuchsia-colored hair, grew up as Alecia Moore in the Philadelphia suburbs. Her albums include *Can't Take Me Home* and *M!ssundaztood*.

8-10 correct: Full spectrum
4-7 correct: Primary colors
1-3 correct: Color blind

33. More Likely

1. Men. A study by the Centers for Disease Control showed that women who married and divorced are less likely to marry a second time. Divorced men, on the other hand, seem to miss married life. They're considerably more likely to remarry after divorce.

2. Women. According to a 1999 study published in the *New England Journal of Medicine*, women were twice as likely as men to contract gonorrhea and chlamydia after one sexual encounter.

3. Women. *The Wall Street Journal* reported that at any given time 44% of women are on a diet, compared with 29% of men.

4. Men. Only 8% of men are color blind—about 9 million all together—but they make up 95% of all the color-blind people in the United States.

5. Men. A nationwide United States survey conducted by Response Insurance found that 58% of men admitted to driving faster than the posted speed limit, versus 48% of women.

6. Men. Yes, this is a trick question. Women don't have prostates. (Just wanted to be sure you were paying attention.)

7. Women. The American Council on Education reports that since 1990 white and Hispanic women in the United States have earned more bachelor's degrees than white and Hispanic men. Black women earned more bachelor's degrees than black men for the first time in 1994.

8. Women. A 1999 survey by the San Francisco-based Global Futures Foundation found that women are more likely to recycle household items. Women are also more likely to buy "environmentally friendly" products.

9. Men. But not by much. In the United States, 25.7% of adult men smoke and 21% of adult women do, according to 2000 figures from the National Center for Health Statistics.

10. Men. Statistics from the World Health Organization show a huge disparity in the suicide rates of men and women in the United States. And the gap widens as people age, with suicide most prevalent among men aged 75 and over.

8-10 correct: Most likely
4-7 correct: Somewhat likely
1-3 correct: Unlikely

34. Nobel Women

1. (a) Marie Sklodowska Curie shared the 1903 Nobel Prize in physics with her husband Pierre Curie and Henri Bequerel for their studies of radioactivity.

2. (b) Introduced in 1968, the Nobel Prize in economics is the newest Nobel Prize category. As of 2003, the economics prize has not been awarded to a woman.

3. (b) Toni Morrison, whose literary works include *Tar Baby* and *Beloved*, won the Nobel Prize in literature in 1993. She was the second American woman to do so.

4. (a) Although she was given the 1991 Nobel Peace Prize for her efforts to bring free democratic elections to Burma, political activist Aung San Suu Kyi could not accept the award in person. She was under house arrest in Burma at the time.

5. (b) Jody Williams is the founder of the International Campaign to Ban Landmines (ICBL). Its greatest achievement, and the one that earned it the Nobel Peace Prize, was the signing of an international treaty to ban antipersonnel landmines in 1997.

6. (a) In 1938, Pearl S. Buck became the first American woman to win the Nobel Prize in literature. Raised in China, she wrote several novels about Chinese life, including *The Good Earth*, which received the Pulitzer Prize in 1932.

7. (a) American geneticist Barbara McClintock proved the existence of "mobile genetic elements," better known as "jumping genes." Although her research was done mainly on corn plants, her theory is now being used in cancer research. It may help explain how cancers grow and spread.

8. (a) Known as Mother Teresa of Calcutta, she founded the religious order of The Missionaries of Charity in India, where she worked to feed and house the poor. She was awarded the Nobel Peace Prize in 1979.

9. (c) Marie Curie, the first woman to win a Nobel prize, was also the only woman to win two Nobel Prizes in two different categories. In addition to her Nobel Prize in physics, awarded in 1903, she won the 1911 Nobel Prize in chemistry for discovering and isolating the elements radium and polonium.

10. (b) Gertrude Belle Elion, an American chemist, won the 1991 Nobel Prize in physiology or medicine along with two collaborators. She is best known for developing Purinethol, a drug used to fight leukemia. She also helped create Imuran, a drug used to aid in kidney transplants, and acyclovir (better known as Zovirax), a herpes medication.

8-10 correct: Pure Nobel-ity
4-7 correct: A Nobel effort
1-3 correct: No bells

35. Women's Timeline

1. (c) In 1892, the first issue of *Vogue* magazine was published in New York. Its cover price was 10 cents.

2. (g) New Zealand was the first nation in the world to allow women both to vote and to stand for election. Women there were granted full voting rights in 1893.

3. (e) In 1914, President Woodrow Wilson signed a proclamation designating the second Sunday in May as Mother's Day in the United States. Anna Jarvis, a teacher from West Virginia, originally put forward the idea.

4. (b) Jeannette Rankin, a former social worker, became the first female member of the U.S. Congress in 1917. The representative from Montana served from 1917 to 1919 and again from 1941 to 1943, and was the only member of the U.S. House of Representatives to vote against U.S. involvement in both world wars.

5. (h) Although some states (including Montana) had granted women the right to vote before 1920, the 19th amendment to the Constitution granted women throughout the United States full voting rights. Also in 1920, women in Albania and Czechoslovakia gained full voting rights.

6. (d) Published in 1931, *The Joy of Cooking*, by Irma S. Rombauer and Marion Rombauer Becker, is one of the most successful cookbooks in history.

7. (j) In 1941, the first female "superhero," Wonder Woman, was introduced in All Star Comics No. 8. The character was created by psychologist William Moulton Marston.

8. (a) "Born" in 1958, the Barbie doll was named for the creator's daughter, Barbara.

9. (i) And women in the United States thought they waited a long time for the right to vote! Women in Switzerland were granted full voting rights in 1971—more than 50 years after the 19th amendment to the U.S. Constitution was ratified.

10. (f) The prefix Ms., used to designate a woman without indicating her marital status, originated with feminists in the late 19th century and became widely used by women's libbers in the 1970s. In 1972, New York congresswoman Bella Abzug introduced a bill that required the U.S. Government Printing Office to accept Ms. as a prefix on all government documents. It took effect in 1973.

8-10 correct: Right on time

4-7 correct: Just in time

1-3 correct: Out of time

36. Mostly Martha

1. Martha Graham. Lean and lithe, Graham began dancing at age 22 and founded her own dance company by the time she was 33. She led the modern dance movement as a dancer and choreographer. She died in 1991 at the age of 97.

2. Martha Stewart. One of the most successful business-women of all time, Stewart's reputation was tarnished in 2002 when she was indicted in an insider-stock-trading scandal. Before she began her career as an expert in home-making, cooking, decorating and other domestic issues, Stewart worked as a stockbroker.

3. Martha Washington. George Washington's wife was a 28-year-old widow named Martha Dandridge Custis, who came to the marriage with two children and a great deal of money and property (inherited upon the death of her first husband). She is buried beside George Washington at their Virginia home, Mount Vernon. They had no children together.

4. Martha Jefferson. The wife of Thomas Jefferson was said to be beautiful, smart and talented. She also, by some reports, was an heiress. The Jeffersons were married for just 10 years before Martha, then in her early 30s, died. They had five children together, including a daughter named—what else?—Martha.

5. Martha Coolidge. Another Martha with presidential con-nections, director Martha Coolidge is distantly related to former U.S. President Calvin Coolidge. She has directed several feature films, including *Rambling Rose*, *Valley Girl* and *Lost in Yonkers*.

6. Martha Reeves. Motown stars Martha Reeves and the Vandellas are known for 1960s hits such as "Heat Wave," "Dancing in the Street," "Jimmy Mack" and "Nowhere to Run."

7. Martha Raye. A vaudeville performer, comedienne and singer, Raye referred to herself as "Big Mouth." She was

awarded the Jean Hersholt Humanitarian Award by the Academy of Motion Picture Arts and Sciences in 1969 for her work entertaining U.S. troops during World War II, the Korean War and the Vietnam War.

8. Martha Quinn. One of the five original on-air veejays at the 1981 launch of MTV, Quinn outlasted most of her Music Television colleagues and went on to appear in movies such as *Chopper Chicks in Zombietown.*

9. "Martha My Dear." A jaunty little ditty clocking in at 2 minutes and 28 seconds, this song was written by Paul McCartney for Martha, his old English sheep dog. Find it on the Beatles' *White Album.*

10. Martha's Vineyard. No one is certain who the Martha of Martha's Vineyard really was. English explorer Bartholomew Gosnold is believed to have named the island in 1602. Depending on which source you consult, Martha may have been his daughter, his sister, his mother-in-law, or none of the above.

8-10 correct: Marthaholic
4-7 correct: Marthaphile
1-3 correct: Marthaphobe

37. First Women

1. (i) Not all is clear with regard to Bridgett Bishop. It seems she was a woman in her 50s or 60s, possibly a tavern keeper and probably fond of high living (which must have irritated her Puritan neighbors). It is certain, however, that in 1692 she became the first woman in Salem, Massachusetts, to be executed for the crime of witchcraft.

2. (c) Elizabeth Blackwell was rejected from twenty-nine medical schools before she was offered a place at Geneva Medical School in upstate New York. The male students

and professors sometimes made her school experience miserable, but she graduated in 1849 and became the first woman licensed to practice medicine in the United States.

3. (d) Louise Brown, the world's first "test-tube baby"—conceived by in vitro fertilization—was born on July 25, 1978 in Manchester, England. Four years later, her sister Natalie, another IVF baby, was born. Natalie is also the first "test tube baby" to become a mother. Her child was conceived naturally.

4. (j) At the 1976 Summer Olympics in Montreal, 14-year-old Nadia Comaneci of Romania became the first Olympic athlete to score a perfect "10" in competition. She did it seven times all together—four times on the uneven bars and three on the balance beam.

5. (e) In 1926, American Gertrude Ederle swam across the English Channel from France to England in 14 hours, 39 minutes and 24 seconds. Her time was more than 2 hours better than the previous record, held by a man. She was 19 at the time.

6. (a) Race car driver Janet Guthrie ranked third in NASCAR's Rookie of the Year standings in 1977, the same year she broke the gender barrier at the Indianapolis 500. Though engine trouble forced her out of the race in 1977, she finished 9th at Indy in 1978.

7. (h) Mary Kies of Connecticut, who invented a system for weaving straw with silk, was the first woman to receive a U.S. patent. She filed her registration in 1809.

8. (b) In 1869, Arabella Mansfield was the first American woman to pass the bar, but she never practiced law. The Iowa-born educator went back to her job as an English professor at Iowa Wesleyan College. She later became dean of the school of art and music at DePauw University.

9. (g) Twenty-six-year-old Valentina Tereshkova was the first woman to journey into space. In 1963, the Russian cos-

monaut made 48 orbits around the Earth in Vostok 6. The trip took 3 days.

10. (f) Not only was Victoria Woodhull the first woman to run for president of the United States—which she did as an Equal Rights Party candidate in 1872—she was also the first female stockbroker on Wall Street.

8-10 correct: First prize
4-7 correct: If at first you don't succeed . . .
1-3 correct: Who's on first?

38. Chick Flicks

1. *You've Got Mail*, starring Meg Ryan and Tom Hanks, was a remake of *The Shop Around the Corner*, starring James Stewart and Maureen Sullavan. *The Shop Around the Corner* had been adapted one other time, for the 1949 musical *In the Good Old Summertime*, starring Judy Garland and Van Johnson.

2. Mayim Bialik, also known for her starring role in TV's *Blossom*, played the character who grew up to be Bette Midler.

3. (c) *That Touch of Mink* paired Cary Grant and Doris Day as a bachelor businessman and a secretary.

4. Thelma Dickinson was portrayed by Geena Davis. (Call yourself a chick-flick champ if you knew Thelma's last name.)

5. Louise Sawyer was portrayed by Susan Sarandon. (See above.) Both Davis and Sarandon were nominated for Best Actress Oscars for their performances.

6. In *When Harry Met Sally*, Harry (Billy Crystal) met Sally (Meg Ryan) at the University of Chicago. She gave him a ride to New York.

7. (b) Deborah Kerr and Cary Grant were all set to meet at the Empire State Building when . . . oh come on, if we told you we'd ruin the ending.

8. False. But they starred together in the chick flicks *Pretty Woman* and *Runaway Bride*.

9. (c) 2002's *Two Weeks Notice* marked the first time that Sandra Bullock and Hugh Grant starred together in a film.

10. *Terms of Endearment* was the 1983 sobfest in which Shirley Maclaine played mom to a dying Debra Winger. It won an Oscar for Best Picture and one for Shirley and co-star Jack Nicholson as well.

8-10 correct: Hot and buttered

4-7 correct: Air-popped

1-3 correct: Burnt kernels

39. I Love to Tell the Story

1. (d) Rosalynn and Jimmy Carter grew up together in Plains, Georgia. When he was elected president of the United States, she became the "First Lady from Plains."

2. (j) Born Anna Marie Duke (which explains the title of her memoir), Patty Duke became the youngest actress to win an Oscar—for her role as Helen Keller in *The Miracle Worker*. Her long battle with manic-depressive illness is detailed in *Call Me Anna* and a later book, *A Brilliant Madness*.

3. (a) Best known as Ginger Spice, the red-headed member of the Spice Girls, Halliwell wrote *If Only* in 1999 and followed it up with a second memoir, *Geri—Just for the Record*, in 2002. Who knew she had so much to share?

4. (h) Hellman, author of such plays as *The Children's Hour* and *The Little Foxes*, won a 1969 National Book Award for *An Unfinished Woman*, the first volume of her memoirs. Two more volumes followed: *Pentimento* and *Scoundrel Time*.

5. (b) A nationally known recording artist by age 11, Brenda Lee was just 16 when she scored her first #1 pop hit, "I'm Sorry," in 1960. Little Miss Dynamite's other hits include "Break it to Me Gently" and "Rockin' Around the Christmas Tree."

6. (g) Her memoir, *Coal Miner's Daughter*, documented her rise from poor Kentucky girl to Nashville superstar. *Still Woman Enough* focuses on Loretta Lynn's professional career, marriage and family life.

7. (c) Perhaps you remember Whitewater, the land-deal scandal that threatened to bring down Bill and Hillary Clinton? Susan McDougal knew more about that deal than almost anyone else. But on the witness stand she became "the woman who wouldn't talk." She refused to give testimony the prosecution needed, and she went to jail because of it.

8. (i) Queen Noor of Jordan was an American-born Princeton grad named Lisa Halaby. While working for Royal Jordanian Airlines, she met and married Jordan's King Hussein. No doubt the course of her life was quite unexpected, as the title of this book implies.

9. (e) Actress/infomercial queen Somers had a harrowing childhood growing up in an alcoholic and abusive household—and she documents it all in *Keeping Secrets*.

10. (f) 1940s star Esther Williams spent her Hollywood career under water—literally—starring in musical extravaganzas that featured synchronized swimming with her as the centerpiece. Thus the former Olympic swimmer became the "million-dollar mermaid."

8-10 correct: Greatest story ever told

4-7 correct: Storybook romance

1-3 correct: Tell me another one

40. The Cinderella Syndrome

1. (c) We have Charles Perrault to thank for compiling a collection of fairy tales, including Cinderella, Little Red Riding Hood and Sleeping Beauty. His 1697 book adds a few touches to the Cinderella story that were uniquely his—the glass slipper, the pumpkin coach and the fairy godmother among them.

2. (a) The oldest known Cinderella tale comes from China and dates back to the 9th century.

3. (b) Anyone who was conscious before 1950 remembers a time when we didn't have Disney's *Cinderella*. Hard to imagine!

4. (b) Goofy comedian Jerry Lewis starred in the 1960 film *Cinderfella*, a Cinderella story in reverse.

5. (a) Yes, Bobby was a boy, but he's the one with the Cinderella complex. He convinces himself that his stepmother is evil, just like Cinderella's. And his suspicions are confirmed when Mrs. Brady asks him to sweep ashes out of the fireplace. Luckily, everything is resolved by the end of the episode.

6. (b) In the Cinderella story most commonly told, when the clock strikes midnight her lovely coach will turn back into a pumpkin and her gown will turn to rags. The midnight deadline was another facet of the story added by Charles Perrault.

7. (b) DJ Spinderella (known to her family as Dee Dee Roper) was the third member of the rap trio Salt-N-Pepa, which also featured Cheryl "Salt" James and Sandra "Pepa" Denton. She was immortalized in their song "Spinderella Ain't a Fella (She's a Girl DJ)."

8. (a) Broadway musical legends Richard Rodgers and Oscar Hammerstein II wrote a musical Cinderella especially for television in 1957. Julie Andrews was the star. When it was remade in 1965, Lesley Ann Warren played Cinderella.

9. (c) In the 1997 version of Rodgers & Hammerstein's *Cinderella*, featuring a multi-racial cast, Brandy starred as Cinderella, with Whitney Houston as her Fairy Godmother.

10. (a) "Bibbidi-Bobbidi-Boo," the Fairy Godmother's song in Disney's *Cinderella*, was nominated for an Academy Award in 1950. "A Dream Is a Wish Your Heart Makes" was also featured in the Disney film. "Impossible" is the Fairy Godmother's song from Rodgers & Hammerstein's *Cinderella*.

8-10 correct: Perfect fit
4-7 correct: Tight across the instep
1-3 correct: This glass slipper gives me bunions!

41. Person or Place

1. Place. Angora cats and Angora goats were bred in Angora, Turkey (now known as Ankara). It's possible that the long, silky cat hair was used as wool once upon a time. The goats certainly were bred for their long, silky coats, used to make mohair.

2. Place. The style of tying a necktie or scarf so that its broad ends lie flat on top of each other comes from the annual horse races at Ascot in England. Men who attended Ascot in the 1900s wore ties in the "ascot" style.

3. Place. In 1946, the U.S. military was conducting nuclear tests in the Bikini Atoll, a small island chain in the Pacific. At the same time, French designer Louis Réard was preparing to introduce a revolutionary two-piece bathing suit in Paris. Réard called his up-to-the-minute and explosive design the "bikini." (Good thing they weren't testing in Guam.)

4. Place. The word "damask" comes from Damascus, the capital of Syria. It's a richly patterned cloth made from cotton, linen or wool.

5. Place. There are several explanations for the origin of blue jeans, but it's pretty clear that the word denim comes from the French words *serge de Nimes*. Serge is a fabric with diagonal ribs (look closely at a pair of jeans and you'll see). Nimes is a city in southern France where heavyweight cotton serge was produced in the 17th century.

6. Person. Actually, the fedora was named for the title character in a play by Victorien Sardou. The French playwright wrote the part for Sarah Bernhardt in 1882. When she appeared on stage wearing a soft felt, wide-brimmed hat, she started a fashion trend.

7. Person. From the "too perfect to be true" department, the leotard was named for a French trapeze artist called Jules Léotard. He was famous for wearing tight-fitting ensembles in his act.

8. Person. In the 1960s, everyone from the Beatles to Johnny Carson wore Nehru jackets, but India's Prime Minister Jawaharlal Nehru is the man who made them popular. The Nehru was a structured but slim-fitting jacket with a short, rounded stand-up collar instead of traditional lapels.

9. Person. Lord Raglan, a 19th-century British noble, rode into battle during the Crimean War wearing a loose-fitting overcoat with sleeves that started at the neck rather than the shoulders. He wasn't the most successful soldier (he died of cholera shortly after his troops were routed at Sevastopol), but his fashion sense was right on. Raglan sleeves are still popular today.

10. Place. The tailless men's dinner jacket was named for Tuxedo Park, New York, where it was introduced in 1886. Traditionally, men wore tailcoats and black tie to formal dinners. The heir to the Lorillard tobacco fortune decided to buck the trend in a formal coat without tails, which he wore, on its debut night, with a scarlet vest.

8-10 correct: Fashion forward
4-7 correct: Fashion conscious
1-3 correct: Fashion victim

42. Chocolate Covered

1. (c) That whitish coating is called bloom. It's caused by moisture and high humidity.

2. False. Dark chocolate contains almost three times as much caffeine as milk chocolate. The trade-off is that dark chocolate contains less fat and cholesterol.

3. (a) Peter Paul Halijian of New Haven, Connecticut, founded the Peter Paul candy company. It introduced the Mounds bar—coconut wrapped in dark chocolate—in 1921. Almond Joy—coconut and an almond covered in milk chocolate—followed in 1947.

4. False. People in the United States eat about 12 pounds of chocolate per person per year. That's a lot, but it's nothing compared to Switzerland, where they consume more than 22 pounds per person per year.

5. (b) The Aztecs of Mexico and Central America are credited with introducing chocolate to the world. The word chocolate comes from an Aztec word meaning "bitter water." Aztecs drank cocoa beans ground up with spices—including chiles—and mixed with water, but no sugar. Sweetening the mixture was a European idea.

6. True. You always knew it was true, but medical research has proved it, at least in North America. Forty percent of women say that they crave chocolate (more when they are menstruating), compared with 15% of men.

7. (a) Fact is, "German" chocolate cake didn't come from Germany. The original recipe, which uses a coconut and pecan frosting, called for German's Sweet Chocolate. Samuel German is the man who developed that sweet baking chocolate. The recipe was first published in a Texas newspaper in 1957.

8. (a) Airy, white angel food cake has been around in the United States since the 1870s. Whipped egg whites give it that light texture. Moist, chocolaty devil's food cake, which

is often iced with chocolate frosting, originated in the early 1900s.

9. True. Cocoa butter is a vegetable fat, so it does not contain cholesterol (only animal fats do). That doesn't mean chocolate is a cholesterol-free food. Milk contains cholesterol; therefore milk chocolate does too.

10. (c) Sky Bar has been made by the New England Confectionery Company, or NECCO, since 1938. It's a molded chocolate bar with four separate compartments filled with fudge, peanut, caramel and vanilla. Sorry, no raspberry.

8-10 correct: Chocoholic

4-7 correct: Cocoa Puff

1-3 correct: Plain vanilla

43. Me, Me, Me

1. Margaret Mead. An American anthropologist and former curator at the American Museum of Natural History in New York, Mead is best known for her 1928 book, *Coming of Age in Samoa*.

2. Ethel Merman. This Broadway belter was famous for singing show-stopping numbers in *Anything Goes*, *Annie Get Your Gun*, *Gypsy* and many other American musicals.

3. Valeria Messalina. Vindictive, greedy and sex-mad, Messalina had no trouble making a fool of the hapless Emperor Claudius. One legend claimed that she defeated Rome's best-known prostitute in a contest to see who could bed more men in succession. Eventually her husband got wise and had her executed.

4. Dr. Jennifer Melfi. Lorraine Bracco's character on the TV series *The Sopranos* was in the unenviable position of being the psychologist to a mob boss. This wasn't the first time Bracco portrayed a woman with Mafia connections. She played a mob wife in the film *Goodfellas*.

5. Medusa. Originator of the "bad hair day," Medusa's head was covered with snakes. It's said that one look from her could turn a man to stone. That's why ancient Greek soldiers often carried a depiction of Medusa on their battle shields.

6. Catherine de Medici. Great-granddaughter of Lorenzo "the Magnificent" de Medici, Catherine was born in 1519 into one of Renaissance Europe's most powerful families. In 1533 she married Henry II of France. After his death, three of her sons ruled France—and she ruled her sons.

7. Dame Nellie Melba. Born Helen Porter Mitchell in 1861, she adopted the name Melba as a tribute to the city of Melbourne in her native Australia. Melba was one of the most sought-after opera singers of her day. The Peach Melba dessert was named for her.

8. Medea. The ancient Greek playwright Euripides created one of the juiciest female roles of all time. Medea was a sorceress married to Jason (who led the Argonauts and captured the Golden Fleece). When he threw her over for a younger woman, she took revenge by killing the new bride with a poisoned cloak, then killing her own sons to punish her husband.

9. Ethel Mertz. Lucy Ricardo's partner in crime on *I Love Lucy*, Ethel—portrayed by blond, blue-eyed and not-at-all-frumpy Vivian Vance—was always up for a caper even if she claimed otherwise. Give yourself extra credit if you knew her full name: Ethel Louise Roberta Mae Potter Mertz.

10. Golda Meir. Born in Russia in 1898, she emigrated to the United States and became a teacher in Milwaukee. By 1921, she had moved to Palestine (which became the state of Israel in 1948) and become active in politics. She served as prime minister of Israel from 1969 to 1974.

8-10 correct: It's all about me
4-7 correct: It's mostly about me
1-3 correct: Who, me?

44. Shop 'til You Drop

1. (b) At 5.3 million square feet, the West Edmonton Mall in Alberta, Canada, is the world's largest shopping mall. In addition to hundreds of stores and restaurants, it houses an amusement park, a water park, an 18-hole mini golf course, an NHL-size skating rink, and aquarium-style attractions featuring penguins, dolphins, sharks and other sea creatures.

2. (b) Macy's Herald Square store in New York City is the world's largest department store.

3. (c) In 2000, the highest number of grocery coupons distributed offered cents-off on household cleaners. Condiments, gravies and sauces were second and frozen foods third. By the way, did you know that September is National Coupon Month?

4. (a) Discount retailer Kmart was known for its Blue Light specials. They were unadvertised in-store sales and promotions that could be announced at any time during the business day.

5. (c) In 2002, Americans spent more than $10 billion— $10.4 billion to be exact—on dog and cat food, according to a study by Packaged Facts. The Pet Food Institute estimates that there were 61 million pet dogs and 76 million pet cats in the United States that year.

6. (b) Andy Warhol arrived in New York in 1949, fresh from receiving a fine arts degree from Carnegie Institute of Technology in Pittsburgh. He started working as an illustrator and specialized in drawings of shoes for magazines, including *Harper's Bazaar*, *Vogue* and *Glamour*. In the 1950s, he worked for the upscale retailer I. Miller Shoes, illustrating its catalog.

7. (c) BOGO stands for "Buy One, Get One" as in "buy one item at regular price, get one free."

8. (b) In 1922, Filene's in Boston became the first department store to issue charge cards to customers.

9. (b) When her husband died, seamstress Lena Bryant had to support herself and her young son. She began by sewing wedding gowns, until she discovered an underserved market—pregnant women. They rarely left their homes in the 1900s, partly because they did not have fashionable maternity clothes to wear. Bryant found her niche and eventually expanded her business to include "plus-size" clothing that she sold through a catalog she called Lane Bryant.

10. (b) In 2002, the typical American household accounted for seventy-three trips to the grocery store. That's down from 1999, when a family's "primary shopper" went to the supermarket eighty-three times during the year.

8-10 correct: Super shopper

4-7 correct: Mall rat

1-3 correct: Card denied

45. Butterfly Kisses

1. (b) Monarch butterflies summer in the northern United States and migrate to warmer places in Mexico or southern California for the winter. They generally fly at about 8 miles per hour, but they're expert gliders and can travel as much as 125 miles in a single day with the help of a strong tailwind. Along the way, the Monarchs stop to "refuel" on nectar, which builds up their fat reserves. Some arrive in Mexico weighing five times more than when they left their summer homes.

2. (a) Most butterflies get their energy by sucking up the sugary nectar from flowers, but they still require salts and minerals to maintain their body functions. So, they settle into mud puddles and suck up the mineral-rich water in a process called "puddling." The salts and minerals are absorbed into the butterfly's body and the water is squirted out its anus.

3. (b) Farfalle, the pasta known in the United States as "bow ties," is known in Italy as butterfly pasta. The Italian word for butterfly is *farfalla*.

4. (c) The sex act between male and female Monarch butterflies can take as long as 16 hours. (It's not uncommon for butterflies to spend an entire night mating.) The male passes a sperm "packet" to the female. It contains sperm to fertilize her eggs as well as nutrients to help her produce more eggs.

5. (b) Butterflies have two pairs of wings—four total.

6. (a) With a wingspan that measures about 11 inches, the Queen Alexandra's Birdwing butterfly, found mainly in the rain forests of New Guinea, is the world's largest butterfly. It's also among the world's rarest butterflies. The Pygmy Blue, found in the southern United States, is the world's smallest butterfly. Its wingspan is just 1/2 inch.

7. (b) Skippers, the fastest flying butterflies, can reach speeds of about 30 miles per hour. Most butterflies travel at about one-third that speed.

8. (c) After an adult butterfly emerges from its cocoon, or chrysalis, it has reached its full adult size and doesn't grow any more.

9. (a) A butterfly's wings are transparent. It's the powdery scales covering the wings that give them color. No two butterflies have precisely the same markings. They even vary from wing to wing on the same butterfly. As the butterfly ages, its scales may fall off or be scraped off by contact with plants and animals.

10. (c) Provided that it isn't eaten by birds or other predators, the Mourning Cloak butterfly can live for about 10 months. Generally, butterflies live for about 2 weeks, but some die off in as little as 2 days.

8-10 correct: Butterfly
4-7 correct: Chrysalis
1-3 correct: Larva

46. Miss Thing

1. (e) Representing Ohio, Halle Berry was named Miss Teen All American in 1985. The following year she was first-runner up to Miss USA.

2. (j) Like her character on the TV series *Designing Women*, Delta Burke was a beauty queen with a fine collection of tiaras. Her most prestigious title was Miss Florida 1974, but before that she held other titles, including Miss Florida Flame, Miss Veteran's Day and Miss Orlando Action Princess.

3. (g) She won't reveal her age, but Zsa Zsa Gabor does admit to holding the title of Miss Hungary sometime in the 1930s.

4. (i) Before her Hollywood debut, Kim Novak spent 1953 as Miss Deepfreeze, the spokesmodel for refrigerators made by Thor Appliances.

5. (h) America's Junior Miss 1962 was Diane Sawyer, who went on to be a TV weathercaster and a press aide to Richard Nixon, before becoming one of the highest-paid women on television.

6. (d) Growing up in northern Pennsylvania, Sharon Stone was named the Saegertown Spring Festival Queen and Miss Crawford County 1976.

7. (b) California native Tiffani-Amber Thiessen won the title of Miss Junior America in 1987. She starred in the TV series *Saved by the Bell* and *Beverly Hills 90210*.

8. (a) Winning the Miss New York competition sent Vanessa Williams to the 1984 Miss America pageant, where she became the first woman of color to win the title.

9. (c) She also won the Miss Black Tennessee title, but we prefer to think of Oprah Winfrey as Miss Fire Prevention 1971.

10. (f) Before she started kicking butt on the big screen in films such as the James Bond flick *Tomorrow Never Dies*, kung fu expert Michelle Yeoh held the title of Miss Malaysia 1983.

8-10 correct: Pageant queen
4-7 correct: First runner-up
1-3 correct: Miss Congeniality

47. Old Testament Women

1. Delilah. The irresistible Philistine talked Samson into revealing that the secret of his strength was his hair; then she had it cut off. Men have fretted about losing their hair ever since.

2. Miriam. When their mother left the baby Moses by the river for the Pharaoh's daughter to find, Miriam watched until she was sure that Moses was in safe hands. She was one of his primary supporters throughout her life. The one time she spoke against him, God punished her with leprosy, which Moses' prayers healed.

3. Ruth. The Book of Ruth is important to Bible scholars because it outlines the genealogy of King David. Ruth was from Moab, but married a man from Bethlehem. When he died, she went with her mother-in-law, Naomi, back to Bethlehem, where she married Boaz and began the line that would produce David.

4. Rachel and Leah. These two sisters gave birth to the sons that would lead the twelve tribes of Israel. Rachel was the one Jacob wanted, and he worked 7 years for her father to win her hand. Lifting her veil at the wedding, he found that the father had given him Leah instead. So he worked another 7 years to marry Rachel.

5. Jael. In the lesser-known story of Jael, she offers the Canaanite general Sisera refuge in her tent and murders him in the night. She was not the most hospitable woman in biblical history.

6. Hannah. A prophetess in her own right, Hannah was the mother of the prophet Samuel.

7. Eve. As punishment for yielding to temptation and eating the forbidden fruit, God burdened Eve with the pain of childbirth. Even so, he allowed her to outlive Adam.

8. Rahab. Before Joshua fought the battle of Jericho, he sent spies into town to check out the situation. Rahab, a local woman, hid them. In exchange for her kindness and trust, Joshua spared her and her family from harm during the attack.

9. Esther. The noble Queen Esther preserved the lives of the Jewish people when her husband, King Ahasuerus, threatened to have them all killed. For her quick thought and bravery she is celebrated at the Jewish feast of Purim.

10. Deborah. Though she was wise and skillful, Deborah was a little too proud to be completely noble. To punish her, God took away her gift of prophecy.

8-10 correct: Sunday-school superstar

4-7 correct: Sunday-school regular

1-3 correct: Never on Sunday

48. O' Baby

1. (d) Best known as the vocalist with Jimmy Dorsey's band in the early 1940s, Helen O'Connell had hits that included "All of Me" and "Tangerine." In the 1950s, she briefly co-hosted *The Today Show* and starred in her own television program.

2. (c) Savannah-born Flannery O'Connor reflected her devout Catholic upbringing in her two novels, *Wise Blood*

and *The Violent Bear it Away*, and her many short stories. Crippled by lupus, she died in 1964 at the age of 39.

3. (i) Recognizable by her shaved head and enormous blue eyes, Irish singer Sinead O'Connor scored a #1 hit in 1990 with the Prince song "Nothing Compares 2 U." But when she destroyed a photo of the Pope during a *Saturday Night Live* performance, she was shunned by critics and fans. In 1999 she was ordained as a priest by a Roman Catholic sect, and renamed herself Mother Bernadette Marie.

4. (j) Comedienne Rosie O'Donnell's career has included a recurring guest spot on 1980s sitcom *Gimme a Break*, and the roles of smart-mouthed Doris Murphy in *A League of Their Own* and Rizzo in the Broadway revival of *Grease*. Her natural likeability made her 1990s daytime talk show a success almost from the start.

5. (h) In 1959, American Atheists founder Madalyn Murray O'Hair and her son filed suit against the Baltimore school district, challenging the practice of mandatory prayer in schools. The case went to the U.S. Supreme Court, which ruled in her favor in 1963, and in 1964 *Life* magazine called her "the most hated woman in America." O'Hair and two of her children disappeared under suspicious circumstances in 1995. Their dismembered bodies were found in 2001, when a former American Atheists employee confessed to their murders.

6. (g) Scarlett O'Hara, the spoiled, selfish and spirited heroine of *Gone With the Wind*, is among the most recognizable characters from fiction and movies.

7. (b) Wisconsin-born Georgia O'Keeffe headed to Chicago and later to New York to make her way as a painter, and much of her early work focuses on urban cityscapes. But her heart was always in the wide-open spaces, and she's best known for the dazzling, hyper-realistic flower and still-life paintings she created at her home in New Mexico. She spent the last 40 years of her life on her ranch near Santa Fe, and died in New Mexico at the age of 98.

8. (e) Legend has it that the great Chicago Fire of 1871 started when Mrs. O'Leary's cow kicked over a lantern and set her barn alight. There was a Mrs. Catherine O'Leary, and she did keep cows in a barn on DeKoven Street, where the fire originated. Other than that, there's no conclusive proof that Mrs. O'Leary or her cow perpetrated the incident. It is true, however, that the Chicago Fire Academy now stands near the site of Mrs. O'Leary's barn on DeKoven Street.

9. (a) For her performance in *Paper Moon* in 1973, Tatum O'Neal became the youngest person ever to win an Oscar. She was 10 when she made the movie. She went on to strike a blow for Title IX and athletic girls everywhere when she played Amanda Whurlitzer, the star Little League pitcher in 1976's *The Bad News Bears*.

10. (f) Formed in Limerick, Ireland, in 1990, the Cranberries blended Celtic flavor into pop tunes and had their first U.S. hit with "Linger" in 1993. Dolores O'Riordan is their sweet-voiced lead singer.

> **8-10 correct: O'verpowering**
> **4-7 correct: O'kay**
> **1-3 correct: O'blivious**

49. The Beauty Treatment

1. (a) Many people in ancient Egypt painted their fingernails and toenails, but only the queens and kings painted their nails red. Commoners used pale colors.

2. (b) Max Factor was a Russian immigrant who arrived in Hollywood in the 1900s. He took one look at the exaggerated make-up being used by movie make-up artists and knew he had found his life's work. His make-up innovations, especially "Pan-Cake" foundation, helped actors achieve a more natural look on screen.

3. (b) Maybelline's breakthrough

product was a cake mascara introduced in 1917. At first it was sold only by mail-order. In 1932, Maybelline mascara became available in variety stores. Cost of a cake back then? Just 10 cents.

4. (b) It all goes back to the color wheel you learned about in art class. Red and green are opposites on the color wheel. So, make-up artists sometimes apply green-tinted "corrective" foundation to take the red out of one's skin.

5. (c) Door-to-door book salesman David McConnell founded Avon. He named the company after Stratford-upon-Avon, William Shakespeare's hometown.

6. (a) Starting in 1956, Clairol advertised its hair color with the slogan "Does she or doesn't she?" It was created to dispel the notion that only hussies colored their hair. Now you could wonder about the roots of any woman on the street! The second part of the slogan—"Only her hairdresser knows for sure"—sent women rushing to their beauty salons to "do" it.

7. (c) George Bunting, a pharmacist in Baltimore, created Noxzema as a cream to soothe sunburn. Around 1915, before it was sold in stores across the United States, he used to hawk it on the beaches of the Maryland shore. When a customer raved about how the cream soothed his eczema, the name was changed from Dr. Bunting's Sunburn Remedy to Noxzema—the cream that "knocks eczema."

8. (c) Cosmetics start to lose their potency, and to collect bacteria, as soon as they're opened. So, to protect yourself from infection, it's a good idea to replace your powder eye shadow every 2 years. Replace your liquid eye shadow and liner after 1 year, and change mascara after 6 months.

9. (b) Mary Kay Cosmetics, founded by Mary Kay Ash in 1963, awards some of its top salespeople pink Cadillacs.

10. (a) Polish émigré Helena Rubinstein entered the beauty business with a recipe for skin cream, but that was just the beginning of her amazing career. After opening salons in London and Paris, she moved to New York and became a

beauty supplier of choice to fashionable women. She introduced waterproof mascara in 1939, letting women around the world feel free to tear up whenever they chose.

8-10 correct: Classic beauty
4-7 correct: Inner beauty
1-3 correct: Makeover candidate

50. She's a Buckeye

1. Gloria Steinem. The women's rights activist and founding editor of *Ms.* magazine was born in Toledo. Told on her 50th birthday that she didn't look her age, she replied, "This is what 50 looks like." Good for her!

2. Dorothy Dandridge. The first black woman to be nominated for a best-actress Oscar was born in Cleveland. Sexy and stunning, she began her career as a nightclub singer and later starred with Harry Belafonte in *Carmen Jones*, and with Sidney Poitier and Sammy Davis, Jr. in *Porgy and Bess*.

3. Chrissie Hynde. Though she has lived in England for years, musician and animal rights activist Hynde was born in Cleveland.

4. Jerrie Mock. A resident of Bexley, she flew her single-engine Cessna 180 "Spirit of Columbus" around the world in 1964. She also was the first woman to fly across the Pacific in a single-engine plane, and she set nine world speed records. People called her "the flying housewife." (How flattering.)

5. Annie Oakley. Though she made her international reputation with the Buffalo Bill Show, this "cowgirl" was born in Darke County, Ohio, in 1860. That's also where she learned to shoot, by hunting game to feed her family.

6. Erma Bombeck. The syndicated columnist and author of *The Grass Is Always Greener Over the Septic Tank* began her career as a reporter for the Dayton *Journal-Herald*.

7. Cathy Guisewite. Born in Dayton but raised in Michigan, she became the ultimate single woman's cartoonist when her comic strip "Cathy" debuted in 1976. Today the strip appears in 1,400 newspapers around the world.

8. Berenice Abbott. Best known for her photographs of New York's buildings and people, Abbott was born in Springfield, Ohio.

9. Phyllis Diller. Known for her feather-trimmed frocks, bleached blonde hair, and fictional husband named "Fang," this lady from Lima is also an accomplished concert pianist.

10. Theda Bara. When this silent movie actress was cast as a vampire in the 1915 film *A Fool There Was*, she became famous for her exotic, heavily made-up "vamp" look. Her movie studio promotional "biography" said she was the child of a French artist and an Arabian princess. In fact, she was a tailor's daughter from Cincinnati.

8-10 correct: Buckeye bulls-eye

4-7 correct: Buckeye belle

1-3 correct: Passing the buck

51. Signature Songs

1. (c) Welsh belter Shirley Bassey performed the title songs for three James Bond films, including *Diamonds are Forever* and *Moonraker*. She's most closely associated with the theme from *Goldfinger*, which hit #8 on the U.S. charts in 1965.

2. (h) Perky actress Doris Day sang "Que Sera Sera" (Whatever will be will be) in the 1955 Alfred Hitchcock film *The Man Who Knew Too Much*. She began her career as a big-band singer with Les Brown's Band of Renown, and she had other hits, including 1944's "Sentimental Journey." But "Que Sera Sera" became her signature song.

3. (f) Disco diva Gloria Gaynor struck a chord with everyone who'd loved and lost in the 1970s. Her 1979 anthem "I Will Survive" was played so often the grooves wore out. Thank goodness someone invented CDs. Now Gloria can go on forever. (Did you think she'd crumble? No!)

4. (j) As a teenager in the 1930s, sultry Lena Horne danced in the chorus of Harlem's famous Cotton Club. By her 20s, she became the first black actress in Hollywood to secure a long-term studio contract. She sang "Stormy Weather" in the 1943 film of the same name. It has remained her signature tune.

5. (a) No one "sold" a song quite like Miss Peggy Lee. She could croon, she could belt. She could be gentle or rough. "Fever," which she wrote in 1958 with her guitarist-husband Dave Barbour, is the sexy song for which she's known best. (Unless you happen to be a Disney fan. If so, you know her best for providing the voice of "Peg" in *Lady and the Tramp*.)

6. (g) French cabaret singer Edith Piaf embodied all the smoky mystery and heartache of Paris in the 1930s. Growing up as a street urchin, she used her wits, talent and a few affairs with well-connected men to launch her career. The dreamy "La Vie en Rose," which she wrote in 1945, became her best-known song.

7. (e) In 1972, the time was right for a female anthem, and Australia's Helen Reddy supplied it, storming onto the world stage with her Grammy-winning hit "I Am Woman." Her other hits included "Delta Dawn," "Angie Baby" and "Ain't No Way to Treat a Lady."

8. (d) Success was fast and furious for Jeannie C. Riley, a Nashville secretary who recorded "Harper Valley P.T.A." in 1968. The sassy story-song described how a spunky young mother took on—and beat—the hypocritical establishment biddies of her small-town P.T.A. Despite winning a

Grammy and selling more than 10 million copies of the single, Jeannie never saw success like that again.

9. (b) It seems natural that Washington, D.C.-born Kate Smith is forever linked with one of the most patriotic songs in American history. In 1943, the iron-lunged singer performed Irving Berlin's "God Bless America" in the film *This Is the Army*. In the midst of World War II, the song and the singer became immediate hits. Smith performed it for generations afterward.

10. (i) When Tammy Wynette's "Stand By Your Man" was released in 1968, it became the biggest-selling single by a female recording artist in country music history. Known for her tumultuous love life, including five marriages and some ugly incidents within them, Tammy became a poster girl for suffering wives.

8-10 correct: Original recording
4-7 correct: Cover version
1-3 correct: Strictly karaoke

52. Queen of the Nile

1. (b) Cleopatra was about 18 when she became queen of Egypt in 51 B.C. She was the oldest living child of Ptolemy XII. Her two older sisters, Cleopatra and Berenice, were already dead. Her younger siblings included a sister named Arsinoe and two brothers, both named Ptolemy.

2. (a) Cleopatra's first husband—and co-ruler—was her brother, Ptolemy XIII. She was 18 and he was 10 when they married. (Egyptian kings and queens usually ruled jointly and often they were brother and sister.) After Ptolemy XIII died, Cleopatra married her other brother, Ptolemy XIV. She was about 22 at the time and he was 12.

3. (a) Kohl was history's first eyeliner. Ancient Egyptian men and women used the paste—made from a metal called antimony, mixed with burnt almonds, copper and clay—to outline their eyes. Besides being a beauty treatment, kohl was supposed to protect the wearer from the "evil eye."

4. (b) Cleopatra grew up speaking Greek. Everyone in the Egyptian royal court did. Only ordinary folks spoke Egyptian, and most nobles couldn't be bothered to learn it. But Cleopatra did learn Egyptian and several other languages, including Hebrew and Arabic, which helped make her popular among her people.

5. (c) The Roman historian Plutarch said, "Her actual beauty was not in itself so remarkable; it was the impact of her spirit that was irresistible." Modern historians tend to agree with the part about her physical beauty. The images of Cleopatra found on coins shows her as an ordinary-looking woman with a rather big nose.

6. (a) Cleopatra's legendary love affair with Julius Caesar began when she was 21 and he was 52. Although she was married to Ptolemy XIII, she gave birth to Caesar's son, whom she named Ptolemy Caesar.

7. (c) When Caesar visited Egypt, he wanted to meet with Cleopatra and Ptolemy XIII, but the brother-sister/husband-wife were warring at the time. To travel safely through the land her brother occupied, Cleopatra was transported rolled up in a carpet. It's said Caesar was so impressed by her clever disguise that he fell in love on the spot.

8. (a) After her affair with Caesar ended, Cleopatra began a passionate romance with the Roman politician Mark Antony. They had three children together, including the twins Alexander Helios (the Sun) and Cleopatra Selene (the Moon).

9. (c) Cleopatra committed suicide after Mark Antony's death, although the story of her being bitten by a poisonous snake may simply be a colorful legend.

10. (c) Cleopatra was buried with Mark Antony in Alexandria, though her mausoleum has never been found. Archaeologists think the burial site is now underwater in the harbor at Alexandria.

8-10 correct: Ruling class
4-7 correct: Friend of the pharaohs
1-3 correct: Queen of denial

53. In Your Dreams

1. In your dreams. The 1998 National Sleep Foundation poll found that women surveyed slept an average of 6 hours and 41 minutes a night. Sixteen percent said they slept fewer than 6 hours a night, even though adults generally require 8 hours of sleep per night. No wonder so many women are tired!

2. In the light of day. Pregnant women sleep best during the second trimester of pregnancy, when the baby moves into a position that doesn't press on the bladder. During the third trimester, the baby's position shifts again and women are likely to experience more sleepless nights.

3. In the light of day. More women than men suffer from restless legs syndrome (RLS), that uncontrollable pins-and-needles feeling that leads to twitching or kicking when your legs are at rest. About 15% of pregnant women develop RLS during their third trimester.

4. In the light of day. Sleep-eating is a sleep disorder similar to sleep-walking and sleep-talking, and we can't think of anything more unfair! Doctors call this Nocturnal Sleep-Related Eating Disorder. Sufferers have been known to

make their way to the fridge and chow down, even though they appear to be asleep. In the morning, they don't remember a thing!

5. In your dreams. More women than men report instances of insomnia—chronic difficulty falling asleep or sleeping through the night.

6. In your dreams. Regular exercise can be a healthy way to adapt your body to a regular sleep cycle, but don't work out at bedtime. That burst of adrenaline you feel after a workout can make you too energized to sleep. It's best to exercise at least 6 hours before you go to sleep.

7. In your dreams. Adults need about 8 hours of sleep per night; babies need about 10. Trouble is, babies tend to grab their shut-eye during little naps throughout the day, making it impossible for the adults in their lives to sleep a full 8 hours at night.

8. In your dreams. Even if you never snored before in your life (yes, we believe you), you may snore when you're pregnant. During pregnancy, especially in the third trimester, your nasal passages can swell, making it difficult to breathe and causing you to snore.

9. In the light of day. Women have more trouble sleeping during menstruation. The bloating, headaches and cramps that can come with your period may cause sleepless nights.

10. In your dreams. Keep your bedroom temperature hovering at or below 70°F. A cool-ish room with good air circulation is the best environment for sweet dreams.

8-10 correct: Life is a dream
4-7 correct: Sweet dreams
1-3 correct: Bad dreams

54. A Price Above Rubies

1. (a) The name "amethyst" comes from the Greek for "not intoxicated." Ancient Greeks believed that people who drank from amethyst cups never got tipsy. No wonder purple amethyst was said to be the favorite stone of Bacchus, the god of wine!

2. (c) Tanzanite, named for the African nation of Tanzania, where it was discovered in 1962, is a brilliant blue gem. Tiffany & Co., the New York jeweler, named the stone, and introduced it to the jewelry market in 1968.

3. (c) When England's Prince Charles proposed to Lady Diana Spencer in 1981, he presented her with an 18-carat sapphire ring surrounded by diamonds. Diana's sister-in-law, Sarah Ferguson, received a ruby-and-diamond engagement ring from Prince Andrew.

4. (b) Most of the world's emeralds come from Colombia in South America.

5. (b) Documents from ancient Greece say that engravers and others who did exacting work relaxed their eyes by gazing at emeralds. There's some medical validity to this—green is said to be the most restful color.

6. (a) Jet, a very hard form of coal, was the principal gem used in "mourning jewelry" during the 19th century. After England's Queen Victoria lost her husband Prince Albert, she went into a period of mourning that lasted 40 years. During that time, she always wore jewelry set with coal-black pieces of jet to symbolize her grief. Thus, jet became known as the "jewel of widows."

7. (b) In the 19th century, opals were considered unlucky. One of the more famous "fatal" opals belonged to Alfonso XII, king of Spain. The king's mother, sister and sister-in-law all died after wearing that opal. To prove the curse was a fraud, the king wore the opal—then *he* died! To rid the family of the unlucky opal, his queen, María Cristina, gave

the gem as an offering to the Virgin of Almudena, a patron saint of Madrid.

8. (c) Powdered lapis lazuli mixed with oil was an ingredient in the brilliant blue paint that monks in the Middle Ages used to decorate illuminated manuscripts.

9. (b) Even though it looks like a stone, amber is a "vegetable" product. It is fossilized resin from pine trees that lived more than 50 million years ago.

10. (a) Pigeon's-blood rubies from Burma have traditionally been among the world's most valuable. Their glowing red color was supposed to resemble the blood of a freshly killed pigeon. The second most valuable rubies are the slightly darker ones called rabbit's blood.

8-10 correct: A brilliant mind
4-7 correct: Sparkling personality
1-3 correct: Needs polishing

55. This Is a Bust

1. (a) Breasts contain fat and glandular tissue. The larger your breasts, the more fat they contain. Glandular tissue keeps the breast firm. So, after menopause, when your mammary glands shrink, your breasts begin to sag.

2. (b) Montgomery's glands are the small bumps on the areola around the nipple. They were named for William Montgomery, an Irish obstetrician of the 19th century.

3. (c) The science of mammography developed over time, beginning with the discovery of the X-ray in the 1890s. After that, X-rays were used to detect tumors throughout the body, but the first machine made specifically to scan the breast was introduced in 1966.

4. True. During the first trimester of pregnancy a woman's nipples and areolae darken.

5. (c) As of 2000, the most common bra size in the United States is 36 C, up from 34 B. It's not clear if this is due to a growing number of women opting for breast enhancement surgery, a general "fattening" of the population, or some combination of the two.

6. (c) When large-breasted women complain about back pain, they're not kidding. The average D cup breast weighs 8 pounds. (Multiply by two for the full frontal effect!)

7. (a) The Wonderbra, which lifts the breasts and creates "cleavage" where none existed, was designed by Louise Poirier for the Canadian company Canadelle. The design was licensed to the British firm Gossard in 1964 and made a little splash in Britain. When Playtex took over the license in 1994, Wonderbras burst into the United States, selling at a rate of one every 15 seconds!

8. False. Breast size has nothing to do with milk production. It's a simple case of supply and demand. The more your baby nurses, the more milk your breasts will produce.

9. (b) French designer Jean-Paul Gaultier created the cone-shaped bras for Madonna's Blonde Ambition tour (immortalized in her film *Truth or Dare*). In 2001, a black-and-fuchsia model sold for $21,150 to Chile's Museum of Fashion and Textiles.

10. (c) To find your bra size, measure around your upper rib cage and add 4 or 5 to the measurement to get an even number. Then measure around your breasts at their fullest point (usually over the nipples). If the difference between the two measurements is less than an inch, you're an AA cup; 1 inch is an A cup; 2 inches is B, and so on.

8-10 correct: Your cups runneth over
4-7 correct: Standing firm
1-3 correct: Boob job

56. Gentlemen Prefer Blondes

1. Reese Witherspoon. After 2001's *Legally Blonde* was a surprise box-office success, Witherspoon signed a $15 million contract to star in the film's 2003 sequel, *Red, White & Blonde*.

2. Deborah Harry. New Jersey girl Harry worked as a beautician, a Playboy bunny and a waitress before hitting it big as the lead singer in the 1970s punk band Blondie. With her boyfriend Chris Stein, she wrote most of the band's songs. She also released four solo albums, including 1989's *Def, Dumb & Blonde*.

3. Marlene Dietrich. In the film *Blonde Venus*, Dietrich starred as a married lounge singer having an affair with a wealthy playboy, played by Cary Grant. She drifts into prostitution to raise money for her sick husband's operation and to support her child. Racy stuff for 1932. It got past the censors when producers claimed Dietrich might have been messing around, but she wasn't enjoying it.

4. Blondie. In the comic strip created by Chic Young in 1930, the title character, Blondie (maiden name: Boopadoop), was a flighty flapper whose boyfriend was playboy rich-kid Dagwood Bumstead. Their comic-strip marriage took place in February 1933, whereupon hapless Dagwood was disinherited by his billionaire father (for marrying a gold digger) and forced to earn his own living.

5. Suzanne Somers. Before *Three's Company*, before Thighmaster, Somers portrayed the silent, ethereal object of desire known as "Blonde in T-bird" in the 1973 movie *American Graffiti*.

6. Carly Fiorina. At age 44, Fiorina became the CEO of Hewlett-Packard, one of the world's prominent computer manufacturers. She was a primary force behind the merger of Hewlett-Packard and Compaq.

7. Blonde Bomber. Skating for the San Francisco Bay Bombers in the 1960s, Joan Weston was known as the Queen of the Roller Derby. At one time she was the highest-paid woman in professional sports. In 1988 she helped found the American Roller Derby League. She died of Creutzfeldt-Jakob Disease, a rare condition related to mad cow disease, in 1997.

8. Liz Smith. Texas-born Smith is one of America's best-known gossip columnists. Her memoir, *Natural Blonde*, recounts her growing-up years and her career, with a few Hollywood insider tidbits thrown in.

9. Anita Loos. Author and screenwriter Loos wrote *Gentlemen Prefer Blondes*, the tale of jazz-age party girl Lorelei Lee in 1925. (She followed it with *Gentlemen Marry Brunettes*.) Her book was made into a film in 1928 and was later adapted for Broadway, but its greatest success was the 1953 movie musical version starring Marilyn Monroe and Jane Russell.

10. "Big Blonde." Dorothy Parker's O. Henry Prize-winning short story, "Big Blonde," is a witty, incisive look at the burden of blondeness. Are blondes really dumb, or does society just expect them to act that way? Sounds like a subject for a women's lib-era theorist, but Parker tackled it in 1929!

8-10 correct: Natural blonde
4-7 correct: Bottle blonde
1-3 correct: Your roots are showing

57. Fashionable Women

1. (b) London's Mary Quant was the epitome of Swingin' Sixties design, and her boutique in Chelsea was where the "in crowd" went for their fashions. Quant not only introduced the miniskirt in 1964; she also wore one to meet the queen of England in 1966.

2. (b) With her pixie haircut and boyish figure, 91-pound Lesley Hornby personified the look of the 1960s. Suddenly, voluptuous curves à la Marilyn Monroe and Ann-Margret were out. Thin was in. As Twiggy, Hornby became an internationally recognized face of fashion. She was only 15 when she started modeling and about 19 when she officially "retired."

3. (c) She was the senior fashion editor of *Vogue*, then she turned her talents to designing wedding gowns and opened her first couture salon in 1990. Since then Vera Wang has designed wedding wear for such celebrity brides as Sharon Stone, Kate Hudson and Sarah Michelle Gellar.

4. (c) Beverly Johnson's accessible, girl-next-door beauty made her an inspired choice for the cover of *Vogue*'s August 1974 "American-look" issue. At the time, editors worried that putting a black woman on the cover would push the boundaries of how *Vogue* readers defined beauty. They should have given readers more credit. The issue was a top seller that year.

5. (a) In the 1980s, Norma Kamali merged fashion and comfort, designing dramatic clothing—with enormous, exaggerated shoulders—in brightly colored sweatshirt fleece.

6. (c) English designer Katharine Hamnett is as well known for her political statements as for her fashions. Her "Choose Life" collection debuted in 1983 (other slogans included "Stop Acid Rain" and "Preserve the Rainforests"). When George Michael and Andrew Ridgely of Wham! wore them in the 1984 video for "Wake Me Up Before You Go Go" the shirts flew out of the stores.

7. (a) Laura Ashley and her husband started designing their own countrified fabrics and making prairie-style dresses from them in the 1950s. Cotton covered with tiny flowers and trimmed in ruffles and lace was Laura Ashley's style. The fashion press called it "milkmaidism,"

but it caught on in the crunchy-granola 1960s and remains alive and well to this day.

8. (a) Early in her career, Donna Karan designed sportswear for Anne Klein. After Klein died in 1974, Karan took over the Anne Klein label with her college friend, designer Louis Dell'Olio. She started her own label in 1984.

9. (c) Diane von Fürstenberg scored a hit with her form-fitting, polyester wrap dresses in the 1970s. She said you could wear them to the office, the shops or the disco—and she should know. Perpetually clad in her own designs, she was a walking advertisement for her company.

10. (b) You can recognize Gloria Vanderbilt jeans by the swan embroidered on the tiny fifth pocket. The American heiress was a major force in the designer jeans market of the late 1970s, and she has since slapped her swan on everything from perfume to eyeglasses.

8-10 correct: Haute couture

4-7 correct: Ready-to-wear

1-3 correct: One size fits all

58. Double Your Pleasure

1. Abigail Adams. Wife of the second U.S. president (John Adams) and mother of the sixth (John Quincy Adams), Abigail Adams was smart, sensible and not afraid to express her opinion. The hundreds of letters that Abigail and John exchanged have helped historians piece together a detailed and personalized picture of life in early America.

2. Bonnie Blair. Blair set a new 500-meter speed skating world record at her Olympic debut in 1988. The record stood until 1994, when Blair herself topped it. In three Olympic appearances she won six medals, including five gold—a record for American women.

3. Coco Chanel. Gabrielle "Coco" Chanel was famous for her stylish, yet comfortable, haute couture designs, like the classic Chanel suit. We're not sure what happened to perfume formulas one through four, but Chanel No. 5 wasn't a bad move either.

4. Dorothea Dix. In the mid-19th century, Dix's campaign for the care of the mentally ill was groundbreaking at a time when people who should have been hospitalized and treated were often imprisoned and punished for their behavior. When she started, there were just thirteen mental hospitals in the United States. By the time she retired in 1880, there were 123. She helped found and direct thirty-two of them.

5. Fannie Farmer. When she wrote *The Boston Cooking-School Cook Book* in 1896, Farmer became the first cookbook author to standardize measurements for ingredients. Suddenly, American cooks were measuring level teaspoons instead of adding "a pinch of this and a dash of that" to their recipes.

6. Germaine Greer. Australian writer, feminist and social critic Greer published *The Female Eunuch* in 1970. Among her suggestions for equality between the sexes was putting an end to marriage and monogamy. For some reason, this didn't catch on.

7. Hedda Hopper. In the glory days of Hollywood, two women battled for supremacy as Tinseltown's top gossip columnist. One was Louella Parsons and the other was Hedda Hopper—known as "the Hat" for her over-the-top headgear. Hopper wrote a syndicated gossip column from the 1930s until her death in 1966.

8. Joan Jett. Rocker Joan Larkin changed her name to Joan Jett sometime in the 1970s. She gained fame as a 15-year-old member of the Runaways—a 1970s female jailbait quintet. Her first solo success came with the 1982 #1 hit "I Love Rock 'n' Roll." In 2001, she performed a cover version of "Love Is All Around," the theme to *The Mary Tyler Moore Show*.

9. Krystyne Kolorful. Canadian stripper Krystyne Kolorful (possibly not her real name) has tattoos covering 95% of her body, making her the world's most tattooed woman, according to the *2003 Guinness Book of World Records*.

10. Lillie Langtry. Beautiful, charming and virtually inescapable, Langtry was, at any given time, a Victorian London socialite, an actress, and a spokesmodel for everything from face powder to bustles. She hobnobbed with everyone from Oscar Wilde to Teddy Roosevelt. Trouble was, she was a married woman who virtually abandoned her husband and might well have carried on an affair with King Edward VII. This Lillie was no shrinking violet!

8-10 correct: Double good

4-7 correct: Double dipping

1-3 correct: Double trouble

59. Rose Fever

1. (c) The hybrid rose Hot Cocoa was introduced in 2002. It's not exactly brown—more a brick-hued orange—but that was close enough to earn its name.

2. (c) Valentine's Day is the #1 holiday for cut-flower purchases, according to the Society of American Florists. They estimate that 54% of flowers sold for Valentine's Day are roses, and 69% of those are red.

3. (c) Get out your tape measure. The Society of American Florists says that a "long-stemmed" rose measures 18 inches or longer from end to end.

4. (a) Rose petals—a lot of them—are pressed to extract pure rose oil for perfumes. It takes about 60,000 roses to yield enough petals to produce 1 ounce of pure essential oil.

5. (b) The Dolly Parton rose is vivid orange-red. Parton is among the dozens of famous women who have had rose varieties or cultivars named for them. Others include Barbra Streisand (mauve) and Judy Garland (yellow, orange and red).

6. (a) There are several explanations for how tea roses got their name, but everyone seems to agree that it has to do with their scent. Some say that the flowers naturally have an aroma similar to tea. Others say that the first tea roses were imported from China on cargo ships that carried tea. Packed together for months, the roses absorbed some of the tea scent.

7. (a) If you're a rose gardener, especially in the southern United States, you know about thrips. They're tiny flying insects that use their jaws to scrape long brown trails on the surface of rose petals.

8. (c) Cutting flower stems when they're submerged in water helps to prevent air bubbles from forming in the stems. Air can block the stem and prevent it from taking up water. Cutting stems on an angle also helps to improve the flow of water to the flower. To keep your cut flowers looking perky, place them in a vase of clean, fresh water and trim the stems every 2 or 3 days.

9. (c) Rose hips are the tart, bright red "fruits" of the rose left on the stem after the flower blooms. They are loaded with vitamin C. Use them to brew tea, or sprinkle them into salads, sauces and breads the same way you would use cranberries.

10. (a) The correct name for a cabbage rose is centifolia. The word means "hundred leaves," which is a perfect description of these plump flowers with row upon row of petals. In full bloom, they look as round and full as a head of cabbage, which is how they got their name.

8-10 correct: Bountiful bouquet
4-7 correct: Single stem
1-3 correct: Just thorns

60. M . . . M . . . Good

1. Maureen McCormick. McCormick had already done commercials and guest roles on TV when she was cast as Marcia, the oldest of the Brady girls. She's a talented singer, and in an "uncredited vocal" she provided the voice for Mattel's talking Chatty Cathy doll in 1970.

2. Maria Montessori. The first Italian woman to receive a medical degree, Montessori educated "special-needs" and learning-disabled children in the 1900s. Her classes were loosely structured and allowed children to pursue what interested them. Once the schools were proven successful, the Montessori method spread throughout the world.

3. Maureen McGovern. Now she's a well-known cabaret singer, but McGovern was an unknown when she recorded "The Morning After" from the 1972 disaster flick *The Poseidon Adventure*. The song won an Oscar, and McGovern hit #1 on the pop charts with it in 1973.

4. Mary Magdalene. The New Testament says that Mary Magdalene was healed by Jesus, became his disciple, witnessed his death and was the first person to whom he appeared after his resurrection. Although she's often depicted as a reformed prostitute, some scholars dispute this interpretation. Fragments of a lesser-known Gospel have been attributed to her.

5. Marianne Moore. Hard to believe that a woman too shy to submit her work for publication (a poet friend published them for her) would become a world-renowned poet famous for the three-cornered hat she used to wear around New York's Greenwich Village. Witty and thoroughly contemporary, Moore favored such "unpoetic" subjects as baseball and horseracing. Her *Collected Poems*, published in 1951, won the Pulitzer Prize for Poetry.

6. Maria Mitchell. One of the first modern female astronomers, Mitchell made her name with the discovery

of "comet Mitchell" in 1847, for which she won a gold medal from the king of Denmark. She later became Vassar College's first female professor of astronomy, and she was the first woman elected to the American Academy of Arts and Sciences.

7. Melina Mercouri. As an actress, Mercouri played a spirited prostitute in 1960's *Never on Sunday*. A passionate advocate of all things Greek, she was expelled from that country during a political coup in the 1960s. She returned in 1974 and started a career in politics. As Greece's minister of culture, she lobbied for the "Elgin Marbles," a group of friezes that are said to have been removed from the Parthenon by British archaeologists, to be returned to Greece.

8. Melba Moore. A dynamic singer and actress, Moore was a member of the original Broadway cast of *Hair*. For her work in the musical *Purlie*, she won a Tony as Best Supporting Actress—the first black actress to do so.

9. Molly Malone. On Grafton Street in Dublin stands a statue of "sweet Molly Malone," the beautiful but tragic fishmonger from the  Irish folk tune. As the song goes, "She pushed her wheelbarrow/Through streets broad and narrow/Crying 'Cockles and mussels, alive, alive, oh!'"

10. Maria Muldaur. Folk/blues singer Muldaur hit the top 10 in 1973 with "Midnight at the Oasis," a breathy, thinly veiled song about sex that was pretty racy for Top 40 radio of the time.

8-10 correct: M . . . m . . . miraculous
4-7 correct: M . . . m . . . marvelous
1-3 correct: M . . . m . . . maybe next time

61. Did She Really?

1. Really. The wife of Feodor Vassilyev, an 18th-century Russian peasant, gave birth to 16 pairs of twins, seven sets of triplets and four sets of quadruplets, according to the *2003 Guinness Book of World Records*. After an achievement like that, you'd think they would have mentioned her by name!

2. Not really. She wasn't 60. She was 63! Tamae Watanabe of Yokohama, Japan, climbed Mt. Everest, the world's highest mountain, in May 2002. Before her, the oldest woman to reach the summit of Everest was a mere 50 years old.

3. Not really. In 1999, Tori Murden, a 36-year-old woman from Louisville, Kentucky, became the first woman and the first American to row across the Atlantic. Her 81-day journey covered almost 3,000 miles, from the Canary Islands to Guadeloupe.

4. Really. It's rare, but it can happen. In 2003, a Croatian woman who slept with two men at the same time became pregnant by both of them. She gave birth to fraternal twins 9 months later and DNA tests showed the kids had different fathers.

5. Not really. When Benazir Bhutto took office as prime minister of Pakistan in 1988, she became the first woman in modern history to lead a predominantly Muslim country. Two years later, she was ousted on charges of political corruption. Although she reclaimed the office in 1993, she was ousted again in 1996.

6. Really. In October 1901, Annie Edson Taylor figured that a stunt like going over Niagara Falls in a barrel would bring her fame and fortune. The 63-year-old widow needed both. So she designed a contraption to keep her safe and plunged down Horseshoe Falls on the Canadian side of Niagara. She survived, which was more than could be said for the fourteen people who tried the stunt after her. But she never saw the payoff she'd hoped for.

7. Really. Yes, Christine Martin from the United Kingdom sat in a tub of maggots for 90 minutes. Why? To raise money for a trip to Nepal organized by a medical research charity. If it makes a difference, she was wearing a swimsuit during her maggot bath.

8. Not really. Belinda Soszyn of Australia ran up the 1,576 steps of New York's Empire State Building in 12 minutes and 19 seconds. That's pretty impressive, but it's far behind her fellow Aussie Paul Crake, who did it in 9 minutes and 53 seconds. (We'll take the elevator, thanks.)

9. Really. *The Diary of Anne Frank*, the memoir written by a teenage girl in Amsterdam during the Holocaust, is the world's best-selling diary. It has sold more than 25 million copies and has been published in fifty-five languages. Although Anne was killed in a concentration camp during World War II, her father Otto survived to publish her book.

10. Really. In 1972, Vesna Vulovic was working aboard a Boeing DC-9 jet when it exploded in midair over Czechoslovakia Republic. She fell 33,333 feet without a parachute and survived.

8-10 correct: Really good
4-7 correct: Really promising
1-3 correct: Really not

62. Initially

1. Daughters of the American Revolution. Chartered by an Act of Congress in 1896, the DAR is composed of female descendants of people who aided in achieving American independence during the Revolutionary War.

2. Young Women's Christian Association. The YWCA started in London in 1855. The first ones in the United States opened in 1858 in New York and 1859 in Boston. Today

the Y offers health and cultural programs for women of all faiths. It's also the nation's largest non-profit provider of shelter, violence prevention and child-care services.

3. Girl Scouts of America. Juliette Gordon Low founded the GSA in 1912 with a troop in Savannah, Georgia.

4. National Organization for Women. Founded in 1966, NOW is the biggest women's activist organization in the United States. It champions the causes of equal rights, sexual harassment and violence prevention, reproductive freedom and lesbian rights.

5. Equal Rights Amendment. One of NOW's pet causes (see above), ERA would make it unconstitutional to discriminate based on gender. It also would guarantee equal pay for equal work. Right now women typically earn 76 cents for every 1 dollar earned by men in the same type of employment. Originally proposed to Congress in the 1920s, ERA has never been ratified.

6. Hormone Replacement Therapy. Until recently, supplements of the hormone estrogen with progestin were prescribed to alleviate various symptoms of menopause. However, a Women's Health Initiative survey of more than 16,000 women, concluded in 2003, has since found that the positive effects of HRT are so minimal as to be insignificant.

7. Women's Army Corps. During World War II, the newly formed Women's Army Corps performed essential non-combat jobs for the U.S. military. "WACs" were communications specialists, cooks, aerial photograph analysts, codebreakers and even auto mechanics.

8. Mothers Against Drunk Driving. After her daughter was killed by a drunk driver in 1980, Candace Lightner of California formed MADD (originally called Mothers Against Drunk Drivers). MADD lobbies against laws that let DUI offenders keep their driver's licenses after repeated arrests (the driver who killed Lightner's daughter had four prior convictions).

9. League of Women Voters. Founded in 1920 by Carrie Chapman Catt, the LWV was an outgrowth of the women's suffrage movement. It was created to help women understand the U.S. political system. Today the non-partisan organization aids in voter registration and education, and lobbies for causes such as campaign finance reform.

10. Women's Christian Temperance Union. Formed in 1873 to fight the abuse of alcohol and its negative effects on the community, the WCTU campaigned for total abstinence from alcohol, tobacco and drugs with "pray-ins" at local saloons. It's still alive today as the oldest voluntary, non-sectarian women's organization in continuous existence.

8-10 correct: UR A QT

4-7 correct: UR OK

1-3 correct: L8R 4 U

63. Bay State Babes

1. (a) Emily Dickinson, the famously reclusive poet, was known as the "Belle of Amherst." She lived almost her entire life in her family's home there. Though she wrote dozens of poems, only seven were published during her lifetime. Six volumes were published after her death.

2. (b) In 1837, Mary Lyon, a teacher from Buckland, opened the Mount Holyoke Female Seminary (now Mount Holyoke College) to offer women an advanced education comparable to what was available to men. In 1870, a bequest by Sophia Smith of Hatfield, who amassed a fortune from wise investments, allowed the establishment of Smith College for women.

3. (c) Nancy Kerrigan was born and raised in Woburn, not far from Boston. After winning an Olympic bronze medal in 1992, she was the frontrunner to take the gold in 1994 until rival skater Tonya Harding paid a couple of thugs to

attack her. Despite a severe knee injury, Kerrigan won a silver medal at the 1994 Winter Olympics in Lillehammer, Norway.

4. (c) Donna Summer started out life as Adrian Donna Gaines in Boston. She made her professional debut at age 19 at a Boston club called the Psychedelic Supermarket, and burst onto the disco scene in 1975 with the 17-minute seduction song "Love to Love You Baby."

5. (a) Paula Cole's 1998 song "I Don't Want to Wait" has been used as the theme for the TV series *Dawson's Creek*.

6. (c) Architect Eleanor Raymond was way ahead of her time when she designed the first solar-powered house in 1948. Known as the Dover Sun House, and designed in partnership with Dr. Maria Telkes of MIT, it was the first occupied solar-powered house in the United States.

7. (c) When Massachusetts Governor Paul Cellucci resigned his post to become the U.S. ambassador to Canada, his job fell to Lieutenant Governor Jane M. Swift. Interestingly, Swift was pregnant at the time. Thus, not only did she become the nation's youngest female governor at age 36, she also became the first governor to give birth while in office.

8. (c) Interviewer extraordinaire Barbara Walters joined *The Today Show* in 1961 and worked there for 15 years, including a stint as the show's first official female co-host. She left to co-anchor the *ABC Evening News*.

9. (b) Anne Whitney is counted among the leading female sculptors of the 19th century, but that didn't stop unenlightened Boston town fathers from revoking one of her commissions when they learned she was a woman. Her most famous pieces include a statue of Samuel Adams, now in the U.S. Capitol, and statues of Adams and Leif Ericsson in Boston.

10. (a) At 5 feet 8 inches school teacher Deborah Sampson (or Samson) towered over the women of the 1700s. She could easily pass for a man, and she did when she joined up to

fight in the Revolutionary War as "Robert Shurtliff."
Known for her bravery, she was shot in the thigh and
removed the musket ball herself (lest a doctor discover her
secret). In 1983, she was designated the Official Heroine
of Massachusetts.

> *8-10 correct: Mass appeal*
>
> *4-7 correct: Mass market*
>
> *1-3 correct: Mass hysteria*

64. Power of Three

1. The women on *Friends*. Monica Geller, Phoebe Buffay and
   Rachel Green are played by Courteney Cox, Lisa Kudrow
   and Jennifer Aniston respectively.

2. The Dixie Chicks. Natalie Maines and sisters Martie
   Maguire and Emily Robison are the Grammy Award-win-
   ning country music trio known as the Dixie Chicks. For
   each #1 single, #1 album, gold and platinum album the
   Chicks have little chicken feet tattooed on their own feet.
   So far each Chick has nine tattoos.

3. Women who played Catwoman on TV. The *Batman* TV
   series of the 1960s had a lot of standout villains, but
   Catwoman was in a class by herself. Lee Meriwether,
   Eartha Kitt and Julie Newmar all played the role. Michelle
   Pfeiffer played Batman's feline nemesis in the movies.

4. The Brontë sisters. Charlotte Brontë was the author of the
   19th-century novel *Jane Eyre*. Her sister Emily wrote
   Wuthering Heights. A third sister, Anne, was also an author.
   Their brother Patrick was a talented painter who became
   an opium addict.

5. Chess champions. The Polgar sisters might be the closest
   things that the chess-playing community has to pin-up
   girls. Born in Hungary, Zsuzsa (also known as Susan),

Zsofia and Judit Polgar are so skilled that they insist on competing in men's tournaments instead of the less prestigious women's tournaments. Both Zsuzsa and Judit have achieved vaunted grandmaster status. Judit reached the grandmaster level at age 15 years, 4 months and 27 days. At the time, she was the youngest player ever to do so.

6. The Andrews Sisters. The music of the 1930s wouldn't have been the same without the Andrews Sisters, the first all-female group to hit platinum (with "Bei Mir Bist du Schoen" in 1938). Their other hits included "Don't Sit Under the Apple Tree," "Rum and Coca Cola" and "Boogie Woogie Bugle Boy."

7. The Three Fates. In ancient Greek mythology, the three Fates were goddesses who watched over births and determined the newborn's life path.

8. Anton Chekhov's *Three Sisters*. Olga, Masha and Irina are the title characters of Chekhov's 1901 play, generally considered to be his finest work.

9. The only three women to win the tennis Grand Slam in a calendar year. Wimbledon, the French Open, Australian Open and U.S. Open are the four tournaments that make up the professional tennis "Grand Slam." Maureen Connolly won all four in 1953. Margaret Court did it in 1970 and Steffi Graf in 1988. Graf also won all four in a row a second time, but not in the same year. So did Martina Navratilova and Serena Williams.

10. *Time* magazine's Persons of the Year for 2002. Cynthia Cooper, Coleen Rowley and Sherron Watkins were the "whistle blowers" who called attention to mismanagement and misdeeds at WorldCom, the FBI and Enron, respectively.

8-10 correct: Three cheers
4-7 correct: Three-dimensional
1-3 correct: Three-ring circus

65. The Sopranos

1. (d) While it's unlikely that the Druid priestess of Bellini's *Norma* was a real person, her beloved Pollione was probably based on a real Roman politician.

2. (c) The story of Tosca came from a French drama written by Victorien Sardou especially for the actress Sarah Bernhardt. Several composers fought for the right to use the play as the basis for an opera libretto, but Puccini won out in the end.

3. (e) Donizetti's opera *Lucia di Lammermoor* was based on a novel by Sir Walter Scott and was inspired by a real event that took place in Scotland in 1669. The real Lucia was a woman named Janet Dalrymple, whose father forced her to marry a man she didn't love and who wound up killing her husband.

4. (g) The character of Violetta in *La Traviata* ("The Misguided Girl") was based on the real French courtesan Marie Duplessis. French playwright Alexandre Dumas the younger immortalized her in the play *Camille*, which was the basis for Verdi's *La Traviata*. Marie died in Paris in 1846 at age 22.

5. (a) The Egyptian-themed *Aïda*, by Verdi, premiered at a lavish new opera house in Cairo on Christmas Eve 1871.

6. (j) Bizet's *Carmen* is one of the world's most recognizable operas. Even people who don't know a legato from a staccato can identify the Toreador Song. The title role may be played by a soprano or by a woman with a slightly lower vocal range—a mezzosoprano or an alto.

7. (b) Puccini was inspired to create *Girl of the Golden West* after he saw a U.S. melodrama by the same name in 1905. In some productions, Minnie arrives on horseback to save Dick from being hanged in the last act.

8. (f) The title *La Gioconda* means "The Joyful Woman" in Italian. Odd, since the heroine of Ponchielli's opera is miserable throughout the whole thing. The story is based on a 19th-century play by French writer Victor Hugo.

9. (h) Composer Richard Strauss used the tale of *Salome*, written by Oscar Wilde, as the libretto for his one-act opera. The opera is loosely based on a Bible story, although in the biblical version Salome is not murdered. In some stagings the role of Salome is split between a soprano and a ballerina who performs Salome's seductive "dance of the seven veils."

10. (i) Like his *Girl of the Golden West*, Puccini's *Madame Butterfly* was inspired by his visit to the United States in the early 1900s. The tragic tale was based on an American short story.

8-10 correct: Bravissima!
4-7 correct: Mixed reviews
1-3 correct: Off-key

66. I Do, I Do

1. Best man. The groom's right-hand man makes the first toast to the happy couple at the wedding reception. These days it's common for the maid of honor to offer the second toast.

2. Maid of honor. In addition to helping the bride dress for the occasion, the maid (or matron) of honor holds the bride's bouquet at the ceremony.

3. Head usher. Before a traditional wedding ceremony, the ushers escort female family guests to their seats. This may include the grandmothers, aunts, stepmothers and other women who are not part of the bridal party. The most responsible of the group may be designated as the head usher. He takes the bride's and groom's mothers to their seats unless one of the other ushers is the brother of the bride or groom. In that case, the son usually escorts his mother.

4. Groom. Emily Post says that the bride's engagement and wedding rings may be purchased by the groom or his family. The man himself usually takes care of this.

5. Bride. Most brides choose and pay for their own wedding gowns, although the bride's family may pick up the tab.

6. Bridesmaids. Any or all of the bridesmaids may organize a bridal shower before the wedding.

7. Groom's family. Traditionally, the groom's family pays for the honeymoon trip, although it's not uncommon for the wedding couple to take on these expenses.

8. Best man. If the wedding party includes a ring bearer, and if he's a responsible kid, he may hold the bride's ring during the ceremony. But most couples prefer the safer option of letting the best man keep the bride's ring until it's needed.

9. Father of the bride. In Christian weddings it's traditional for the father of the bride to walk his daughter up the aisle. In Jewish weddings, the bride's parents both walk with her.

10. Mother of the bride. The first person to greet guests in the receiving line is the mother of the bride, followed by the groom's mother and then the bride and groom. Fathers of the bride and groom aren't usually part of the receiving line, but if they're included they stand immediately to the left of their spouses.

8-10 correct: I do

4-7 correct: I might

1-3 correct: I don't

67. Swingin' Girls of Song

1. Rosemary. The immortal "Love Grows (Where My Rosemary Goes)" came from Edison Lighthouse in 1970. They never made it quite that big again, but we thank them for leaving us Rosemary.

2. Mary. The Association sang "Along Comes Mary" in 1965. If you never understood the lyrics to this one, there's a reason. They're too trippy to be believed. " . . . the gassed/And flaccid kids are flung across the stars" indeed!

3. Renee. "Walk Away Renee" by the Left Banke (note irreverent 1960s spelling) was a top hit of 1966. If the weepy lyrics about lost love don't get you, the flute solo in the middle definitely will.

4. Donna. "Donna the Prima Donna" was a hit for Dion in 1963. Just another romantic boy left broken-hearted by a superficial girl who "wants to be just like Zsa Zsa Gabor, even though she's the girl next door." Sigh.

5. Rhonda. "Help Me Rhonda," a Beach Boys hit from 1965, demonstrated once again the resilience of the male heart. Boy's fiancée leaves him flat. He needs a new girl to help him forget about her. It seems to be working. We never hear the fiancée's name, but Rhonda's name is repeated about forty-five times (we lost count!).

6. Sue. Poor Dion just did not pick the right girls (see question 4). Before he messed with "Donna the Prima Donna," he tangled with "Runaround Sue" in 1961. Some boys don't learn.

7. Judy. We're not sure what kind of a disguise glasses could be, but they worked for Judy. John Fred and his Playboy Band had a hit with "Judy in Disguise" in 1968. The lyrics don't make much sense, but the pause before "with glasses" was too cute to resist.

8. Maria. R.B. Greaves sang "Take a Letter Maria" in 1969. (It only sounded like Tom Jones.) Hard-working husband comes home to find his wife "in the arms of another man." Could it be because he spent too much time working . . . in the office . . . with Maria?

9. Caroline. No one turned knees to jelly like Neil Diamond, and "Sweet Caroline" was his big song of 1969. How many women that year would gladly have changed their names?

10. Jennifer. As if his 1968 song "Jennifer Juniper" weren't adorable enough, Donovan sings the last verse in French! Jennifer was the most popular name for girls born in the United States during the 1970s. Some attribute this to the popularity of Ali MacGraw's character Jennifer in *Love Story*, but we think a lot of moms-to-be were Donovan fans.

8-10 correct: Miniskirts forever

4-7 correct: Go-go boots in the closet

1-3 correct: Lost love beads

68. Olympians

1. (b) Though she didn't win a medal, England's Princess Anne competed with the British Olympic equestrian team at the 1976 Montreal Olympics. She was thrown from her horse and suffered a mild concussion. She remounted and finished the event—jumping seventeen more fences—but she doesn't remember anything that happened after her fall!

2. (h) Germany's Birgit Fisher became the first woman in any sport to win two Olympic golds 20 years apart. Her first was in canoeing at the 1980 Moscow Olympics. The latest was in 2000 at Sydney. All told, she paddled her way to seven Olympic gold medals and three silver.

3. (j) At age 19, at the 1956 Olympics, Australia's Dawn Fraser snagged her first 100-meter freestyle gold medal. She came back for the next two Olympics and took gold in the 100 meters both times. During the 1964 Olympics she also took a flag from the Imperial Palace in Tokyo, which got her banned from swimming for four years. Ouch.

4. (g) Thirty-four-year-old Daina Gudzineviciute of Lithuania earned a gold medal in trap shooting at the 2000 Sydney Olympics. It was only the second gold medal earned by any athlete in Lithuania's history.

5. (i) Norway's Sonja Henie was 12 when she skated at the 1924 Chamonix Olympics. She didn't medal then, but she won three consecutive figure-skating gold medals at the Olympics—in 1928, 1932 and 1936. No other female figure skater has accomplished that feat. And Henie did it all before her 25th birthday.

6. (c) At the 2002 Winter Olympic Games, they called Janica Kostleic the "Croatian Sensation." The 20-year-old became the first alpine skier to win four Olympic medals in 1 year, and in the process she earned the first-ever Olympic medal for Croatia.

7. (a) Catriona LeMay Doan is the fastest woman on ice. The Canadian speed skater set an Olympic record for the 500 meters with her gold-medal performance at the 1998 Nagano Olympics, then came back to defend her title at the 2002 Salt Lake City Olympics. Whoosh!

8. (d) Elegant, fleet-footed Merlene Ottey won eight track and field medals over five Olympics—1980, 1984, 1992, 1996 and 2000. Seven of them were for individual performances. The eighth was the silver medal she earned as part of Jamaica's 400-meter relay team. She was 40 when she won that one.

9. (f) At the 2000 Sydney Olympics, Naoko Takahashi became the first Japanese woman to win a gold medal in Olympic track and field. She also set a new Olympic record for the women's marathon, finishing in 2 hours, 23 minutes and 14 seconds. The second-place finisher, Lidia Simon of Romania, was just 8 seconds behind her!

10. (e) Never a cheerful crowd pleaser, the Soviet Union's Ludmilla Turischeva was all business when it came to gymnastics. Her dramatic, formal routines

earned her nine Olympic medals at the 1968, 1972 and 1976 Olympics. She even beat her sprightly teammate Olga Korbut to win the all-around gold in 1972.

8-10 correct: **Going for gold**
4-7 correct: **Polishing the silver**
1-3 correct: **Barely bronze**

69. She's Got Spirit

1. Rah, rah, rah. Sandra Bullock, class of 1982, was a cheerleader for the Generals of Washington-Lee High School in Arlington, Virginia.

2. Ha, ha, ha. First Lady Laura Welch Bush graduated in 1964 from Midland Lee High School in Midland, Texas. She wasn't a cheerleader, but oddly enough, her husband, George W. Bush, was a cheerleader during his prep school days at Phillips Andover Academy.

3. Ha, ha, ha. When she was a student at Harborfields High School in Greenlawn, New York, Mariah Carey wasn't damaging her pipes by screaming on the sidelines. She spent her after-school hours taking voice lessons.

4. Ha, ha, ha. At Maine South High School in Park Ridge, Illinois, Hillary Rodham Clinton, class of 1965, was a student council officer and a member of the National Honor Society, but she left the pompom shaking to her classmates.

5. Rah, rah, rah. *Ally McBeal* star Calista Flockhart, class of 1983, cheered for the Renegades at Shawnee High School in Medford, New Jersey.

6. Ha, ha, ha. Growing up in the Bronx, New York, Jennifer Lopez attended the all-girls Holy Family Catholic High School. No cheerleading duties for "Jenny from the Block."

7. Rah, rah, rah. Madonna was a cheerleader at Adams High School in Rochester, Michigan, and there are photos to prove it.

8. Ha, ha, ha. In 1985, all-American actress Julia Roberts graduated from Campbell High School in Smyrna, Georgia. Hard as it is to believe, she insists that she wasn't popular, didn't date much, and definitely was not a cheerleader.

9. Rah, rah, rah. Before she devoted her life to dramatics, Meryl Streep, class of 1967, was a cheerleader at Bernards High School in Bernardsville, New Jersey.

10. Rah, rah, rah. Can't you just picture perky actress Renee Zellweger cheering for the Tigers of Katy High School in Katy, Texas? The class of 1987 grad was also on the gymnastics team.

8-10 correct: Varsity

4-7 correct: Junior varsity

1-3 correct: Cheering from the bleachers

70. It's Me, Margaret

1. Margaret Mitchell. Former Atlanta newspaper reporter Mitchell was so shy about her fiction writing only two people were aware that she was working on a novel—her husband and a friend who virtually dared Margaret to submit her manuscript to a publisher. She did—then tried to get it back! Good thing she couldn't. *Gone With the Wind* sold more than a million copies in its first year and won the 1936 Pulitzer Prize.

2. Margaret Sanger. A trained nurse, Sanger became a crusader for birth control and women's rights in the early 20th century. She started a birth-control magazine called *The Woman Rebel* in 1914, founded the first birth-control clinic in the United States in 1916 and became the first president of the International Planned Parenthood Federation.

3. Margaret Thatcher. The first female British prime minister, Thatcher won three consecutive terms. Her political success notwithstanding, the staunch conservative was not ter-

ribly popular. The woman they called the "Iron Lady" even dodged a 1984 assassination attempt.

4. Margaret O'Houlihan or Houlihan. When Sally Kellerman portrayed her in the 1970 film version of *M*A*S*H*, her name was Margaret "Hot Lips" O'Houlihan. On television in 1972, Hot Lips, played by Loretta Swit, was renamed Houlihan. *M*A*S*H* trivia experts claim that Hot Lips was inspired by a real Korean War combat nurse known as Hotlips Hammerly. No word on whether she was a Margaret too.

5. Margaret Hamilton. Taking on the dual role of Miss Gulch and the Wicked Witch of the West in the 1939 movie *The Wizard of Oz* made Hamilton an object of fear for generations of children. Years later, those kids hardly recognized her as the kind-faced shopkeeper Cora who hawked Folgers Coffee in commercials.

6. Margaret Cho. Born in San Francisco to Korean parents, Cho has been performing stand-up comedy since she was 16. Her live shows *I'm the One That I Want* and *The Notorious C.H.O.* have been made into movies.

7. Margaret Truman. Daughter of U.S. President Harry S. Truman, Margaret Truman had a successful singing career and worked as a TV and radio host. She wrote her first mystery novel, *Murder in the White House*, in 1980. It inspired a series of Washington, D.C.-based whodunits.

8. Margaret Chase Smith. This lady from Maine served in Washington for 32 years—four terms as a U.S. congress-woman and four as a U.S. senator. She was the first member of the Senate to publicly denounce Senator Joseph McCarthy's Communist "witch hunts" of the 1950s. In 1964 she lost to Barry Goldwater in the Republican party presidential primary.

9. Margaret Bourke-White. During World War II, *Life* magazine photographer Bourke-White became the first female correspondent to cover active war zones. Her photos of Nazi concentration camps, apartheid in South Africa and rural poverty in the United States documented the horrors of war and human suffering.

10. Margaret O'Brien. Born Angela Maxine O'Brien in 1937, she changed her name after her first big role in *Journey for Margaret*, when she was just 5 years old. Her work in *Meet Me in St. Louis* earned her an Oscar as the "Outstanding Child Actress" of her day. She also originated the role of Mary Lennox in the 1949 film *The Secret Garden*.

8-10 correct: Princess Margaret
4-7 correct: Square Peg
1-3 correct: Wake up Maggie

71. Holy Women

1. (a) After spending much of her life as an invalid, Mary Baker Eddy became convinced that the cause of disease and illness was mental rather than physical. She believed that reading from the Bible helped to heal her. Thus members of the First Church of Christ, Scientist, which she founded in 1879, seek spiritual rather than medical help for their ailments.

2. (c) Mother Seton, a convert to Catholicism, founded the first American Catholic sisterhood, the Sisters of Charity. She was canonized in 1975, the first American-born saint.

3. (b) Betty Bone Schiess was a member of the so-called "Philadelphia Eleven," the first group of women to be ordained as Episcopal priests.

4. (c) Khadijah was the first wife of the prophet Muhammad, and she's generally considered to be the first convert to the religion of Islam. She was a 40-year-old widow when they married. He was 25.

5. (b) Among the first to use the media for evangelism, Aimee Semple McPherson broadcast prayer meetings from Los Angeles in the 1930s and gained a national reputation. Even a mysterious kidnapping attempt—generally considered a publicity stunt—didn't diminish "Sister" Aimee's following.

6. (c) Mother Ann Lee founded a Shaker colony in upstate New York in 1776. Possibly believing herself to be the second incarnation of Jesus, Mother Ann preached persuasively and passionately. But her insistence that all members of the sect maintain a celibate lifestyle ensured that the Shaker movement would remain relatively small.

7. (b) Sally J. Priesand was ordained as a Reform rabbi at Cincinnati's Hebrew Union College in 1972. Priesand was not the first female rabbi in the modern world, however. That is generally considered to be Regina Jonas, who was ordained in Berlin in 1935 and died in the Auschwitz concentration camp.

8. (a) Samding Dorji Phagmo is the only female head of a Tibetan Buddhist monastery and is considered to be a "living Buddha," a title given to those who have shown outstanding knowledge of and devotion to the practice of Buddhism. The tradition of a female head of the Samding monastery dates back to the 13th century.

9. (b) St. Frances Xavier Cabrini, also known as Mother Cabrini, is considered to be the first American saint. Although she became a U.S. citizen near the end of her life, and her Missionary Sisters of the Sacred Heart worked with Italian immigrants in the United States, she was born in Italy.

10. (a) Rabi'a al Adawiyya is a female saint in the sect of Sufism, a mystical branch of Islam. She was born in the city of Basra (now part of Iraq) around 713. As a young woman she was captured and sold into slavery. Her devotion to the Divine eventually led her to freedom and earned her a reputation as a holy woman of pure spirit.

8-10 correct: Spiritual leader
4-7 correct: Faithful follower
1-3 correct: Disbelief

72. Just Marilyn

1. False. Marilyn was born a brunette, as early photos confirm.

2. (c) Marilyn played Sugar Cane, star vocalist with an all-girl band, in *Some Like it Hot.*

3. True. Though it is airbrushed out of some photos, the mole on her chin was real.

4. (c) When Marilyn stepped over a subway grate in *The Seven-Year Itch*, allowing her dress to blow up above her knees, men in movie audiences went wild. But that was nothing compared with the chaos that occurred when she filmed the scene in New York City.

5. True. Marilyn was pictured in the first-ever *Playboy*, in December 1953. The photos came from a nudie calendar shoot she had done in the 1940s. *Playboy* founder Hugh Hefner owns the burial vault next to hers at Westwood Memorial Park in Los Angeles.

6. (a) Yankee star Joe DiMaggio married Marilyn in January 1954. Even though they remained friendly throughout her life—and DiMaggio regularly placed roses on her grave—they divorced less than a year after the wedding.

7. True. But not in the way you'd think. Early in her career, Marilyn had a chin implant to change the shape of her jaw line. Some people speculate that she had work done on her nose as well, but those who claim she had breast implants are probably just jealous.

8. (a) Arthur Miller, who wrote *Death of a Salesman* and *The Crucible*, was Marilyn's third husband. She even converted to Judaism to marry him. He wrote the screenplay for *The Misfits* for her, but they were divorced before the movie was finished.

9. True. It's hard to imagine that the woman who became the world's most recognizable actress was never even nominated for an Oscar, but it's true. She did, however, win a Golden Globe Award as Best Actress in a Comedy

for *Some Like it Hot*. She also received good reviews for her dramatic roles, especially in *Bus Stop*.

10. (b) *The Misfits*, which came out in 1961, was Marilyn's last completed film. She died in 1962, leaving *Something's Got to Give* unfinished.

8-10 correct: Screen legend

4-7 correct: Cameo role

1-3 correct: Bit player

73. Lone Star Women

1. (c) Pearl was Janis Joplin's nickname. It was also the title of her 1971 #1 album, which featured her famous rendition of "Me and Bobby McGee." Sadly, Joplin didn't live to enjoy her success. She died of a heroin overdose shortly before the album was released.

2. (a) Mildred "Babe" Didrikson once said she wanted to be the greatest athlete who ever lived. In the 1930s and 1940s she lived up to her dream as an AAU and Olympic track and field and basketball star. An expert golfer, she blazed through amateur tournaments and was a co-founder of the Ladies Professional Golf Association (LPGA).

3. (a) Before she became known as Granny on *The Beverly Hillbillies*, Irene Ryan appeared in a bunch of unmemorable films in the 1940s and 1950s, including *The WAC from Walla Walla* and *Bonzo Goes to College*.

4. (c) Texas governor Ann Richards raised her national profile by delivering the keynote address at the 1988 Democratic National Convention. But Texans were already familiar with her energy and outspokenness. What would you expect from a woman who attended Baylor University on a debate scholarship and then became a junior high social studies teacher before entering politics?

5. (b) Fort Worth *Star-Telegram* columnist Molly Ivins has always had a fondness for the bizarre. Her first job was in

the complaint department at the Houston *Chronicle,* and she was soon promoted to sewer editor. All of which led her to a career covering Texas politics and its attendant peculiarities. Her books include *Bushwacked: Life in George W. Bush's America, Molly Ivins Can't Say That, Can She?* and *Shrub: The Short but Happy Political Life of George W. Bush.*

6. (c) Selena, the Latina singer who met an untimely death 2 weeks before her 24th birthday, helped introduce Tejano music to a broader audience and fueled the growth of Latin music in general. Tejano, named for Texans with Mexican roots, is a blend of Spanish traditional music with polka or waltz rhythms. Shortly after her death, Selena became the first artist ever to have five Spanish-language albums on the *Billboard* Top 200 at one time.

7. (b) Kate Jackson was born in Birmingham, Alabama. Her co-stars on the original *Charlie's Angels* TV series both were Texas girls. Farrah Fawcett was born in Corpus Christi and Jaclyn Smith hails from Houston.

8. (b) Sandra Day O'Connor is best known as the first woman appointed to the U.S. Supreme Court. Yet the Texas-born attorney began her professional career in Arizona, where she was a state senator from 1969 to 1975. She also was a county judge and later a judge on the Arizona State Court of Appeals.

9. (c) Though her work is highly regarded, Katherine Anne Porter was hardly prolific. *Ship of Fools* is the only complete novel she wrote, along with just four short-story collections, in more than 30 years.

10. (a) Joan Crawford was born Lucille LeSueur in San Antonio in 1904. The movie icon, who won an Oscar for her role as Mildred Pierce, became infamous after her adopted daughter Christina exposed Joan's not-so-idyllic life in the best-seller *Mommie Dearest.*

*8-10 correct: **Deep in the Heart of Texas***
*4-7 correct: **Yellow Rose of Texas***
*1-3 correct: **All My Exes Live in Texas***

74. Mind Your Manners

1. Perfect taste. If the table is set with all the utensils for the meal from beginning to end, the dessert fork and spoon will be placed horizontally above the dinner plate.

2. Perfect taste. If asparagus is served al dente—slightly firm to the bite—and the sauce is only drizzled on the tips, feel free to pick it up and eat it tip to end in small bites. If it's marinated or covered in sauce, use your knife and fork.

3. Recipe for disaster. Unless you're three and your mom is cutting your meat, eat steak and other meats by cutting one small piece at a time. Using a knife and fork "continental style" means holding the knife in your right hand and the fork in your left. Dining "American style" means that you put down the knife and switch the fork to your right hand to eat. Either is proper.

4. Recipe for disaster. Wait staff should always serve diners from the left and clear from the right. If you're dining in someone's home, pass plates of food to your right so that the person next to you will be served from the left.

5. Recipe for disaster. Cover your mouth delicately when you burp at the table, and always excuse yourself—quietly. Same goes for sneezing and coughing at the table. (And don't even think about using your napkin as a handkerchief!)

6. Perfect taste. A couple generally is not seated side-by-side at formal dinner parties. The host and hostess sit at opposite ends of the table. The male guest of honor sits at the hostess's right. The female guest of honor sits at the host's right. The rest of the guests are seated alternately by gender.

7. Perfect taste. There's nothing wrong with serving salad after the main course. You'll find it done in Europe quite often, and many fancy restaurants have adopted the fashion.

8. Recipe for disaster. When the soup is served, spoon up a small amount, moving the spoon away from you. Touch it to your lips. If it's too hot to eat, wait patiently until it cools. Never blow on it! Ditto for hot tea or coffee served

at dessert. Stir in your milk and sugar and let the drink cool gradually.

9. Recipe for disaster. Besides being gross, swallowing bone or gristle is a good way to make yourself sick. Emily Post says if you bite into something you shouldn't swallow remove it from your mouth as inconspicuously as possible using your fork. Then place it at the side of your plate.

10. Perfect taste. Red wine and white wine are properly served in different types of glasses. A red wine glass has a relatively short stem and a rounded bowl, so that the warmth of your hand reaches the wine when you hold the glass. A white wine glass has a more vertical shape and a longer stem, to keep the wine cool.

8-10 correct: Perfect guest

4-7 correct: Well-mannered

1-3 correct: Elbows off the table!

75. Notorious

1. (a) Bonnie Parker and Clyde Barrow—the legendary Bonnie and Clyde—headed a gang that robbed banks in Texas and throughout the southern United States. They died together in a shoot-out with police in 1934.

2. (c) In 1892, Lizzie Borden's father and stepmother were found hacked to death in their Fall River, Massachusetts, home. The 32-year-old Lizzie was accused of the murder, but eventually acquitted. To this day, no one is certain who committed the crime. The old Borden house is now a bed and breakfast.

3. (c) Radical feminist Valerie Solanas shot and wounded Andy Warhol in 1968. It was ostensibly the start of her campaign to "destroy the male sex." Fortunately, Warhol recovered. Solanas served 3 years in jail for assault, and later spent time in mental health facilities.

4. (b) In 2002, actress Winona Ryder was found guilty of theft and vandalism after shoplifting $5,500 worth of merchandise from a Saks Fifth Avenue store in Beverly Hills. She was sentenced to 3 years' probation and 480 hours of community service.

5. (a) During the French Revolution, Charlotte Corday was on the side of the monarchy. Jean-Paul Marat was leading a bloody rebellion against them. Pretending to be sympathetic to Marat's cause, Corday arranged a meeting with him, promising that, with her help, he could "render a great service to France." He asked her to come into the room while he was taking a bath. Little did he know she was carrying a knife, which she used to stab him then and there. She was sentenced to die on the guillotine for the crime.

6. (a) Mary Mallon was a cook in New York City in the early 20th century. Even though she knew she was a carrier of typhoid, she kept working in restaurants and public kitchens, and infecting thousands of people with the disease. Eventually Typhoid Mary was captured and institutionalized.

7. (c) At the start of the Swingin' Sixties in London, Christine Keeler was a call girl having an affair with John Profumo, the British secretary of state for war. At the same time, she was in a relationship with Yevgeny Ivanov, a Russian naval attaché accused of spying on Great Britain. Pillow talk led to accusations that Profumo breached national security. He resigned. The Russian attaché was recalled to Moscow and never heard from again. Keeler is now a ordinary citizen living in London.

8. (b) The mysterious Mata Hari was a Dutch woman named Margaretha Geertruida Zelle. After living with her husband, a soldier named MacLeod, in Indonesia, she moved to Paris and began a career as a dancer with a sideline in seduction and espionage. In 1917, she was convicted of spying for Germany. She was executed by firing squad.

9. (b) Members of Charles Manson's "Family" in the 1960s, Patricia Krenwinkel, Susan Atkins and Leslie Van Houten were convicted of murder and sentenced to death. Their sentences were changed to life imprisonment in 1972, after the U.S. Supreme Court ruled that capital punishment was unconstitutional.

10. (b) Mary Read and Anne Bonney were pirates during the 18th century. Known for their bloodthirsty ways and expert swordsmanship, they often dressed as men. But when they finally were captured and tried in court, they both "pleaded their bellies" (claimed to be pregnant) to avoid being hanged.

8-10 correct: Crime fighter

4-7 correct: Innocent bystander

1-3 correct: Accomplice

76. Heart Throbs

1. (j) Frankie Avalon was a 1950s teen idol and star of those beach-party movies with Annette Funicello. He started his career as a musician, playing trumpet in a Philadelphia rock-and-roll band with his pal Bobby Rydell. Between 1958 and 1960, Frankie had seven top-10 hits. "Venus" hit #1 in 1959.

2. (d) When it comes to *The Partridge Family*, you had to be there (and preferably under age 12) to understand. True, most of them didn't sing or play instruments, but that really is David Cassidy performing "I Think I Love You." And that really was 4 million copies of the record sold in 1970.

3. (a) In 1973, the DeFranco Family had the year's top-selling single with "Heartbeat is a Love Beat." More than 2.5 million copies were sold. Lead singer Tony DeFranco was just 14 years old at the time. The group was managed by the publishers of *Tiger Beat* and *Fave* magazines, which certainly didn't hurt its chances for media exposure.

4. (e) Leif Garrett started his singing career doing covers of oldies hits like "Runaround Sue" and "Surfin' U.S.A." Despite his teenybopper appeal, his only top-10 hit was 1979's "I Was Made for Dancing."

5. (c) The Bee Gees' younger, cuter brother, Andy Gibb made a name for himself in 1977 with two #1 hits: "I Just Want to be Your Everything" and "(Love Is) Thicker than Water." In 1978, he hit #1 again with "Shadow Dancing." Sadly, by the 1980s he had a serious drug problem. In 1985, he was in rehab. And in 1988 he died from a heart ailment.

6. (b) Rick Nelson, son of TV's Ozzie and Harriet, suffered from the fact that he was too cute to be taken seriously as a musician. Truth was, Rick fell into rock and roll by singing on his parents' sitcom. But he made the most of it, with dozens of top-10 singles between 1958 and 1961, including "Hello, Mary Lou," which was #9 in 1961.

7. (f) Among the manufactured pop acts of the 1980s, Boston's New Kids on the Block set teenybopper hearts racing the fastest. Donnie Wahlberg, Danny Wood, Joe McIntyre and brothers Jordan and Jonathan Knight had a #1 pop album with *Hangin' Tough* in 1988, including the #1 hit "I'll be Loving You (Forever)."

8. (i) Donny Osmond joined the singing Osmond brothers in 1963, when he was just 5. Six years later, he was recording as a solo artist. "Sweet and Innocent" hit #7 in 1971, and "Puppy Love" was #3 in 1972. Impossibly clean-cut though they may have been, the Osmonds were for real musically. In 1972, they earned more gold records in a single year than any group in history.

9. (h) Bobby Sherman was a regular on TV's *Shindig!* from 1962 to 1964. But he reached true heart-throb status as Jeremy Bolt on the TV series *Here Come the Brides* in the late 1960s. In the meantime, Bobby was hitting the top 10 from 1969 to 1971 with songs like "Easy Come, Easy Go" and "Julie, Do Ya Love Me?"

10. (g) Rick Springfield was a teen sensation in his native Australia before he hit it big playing Dr. Noah Drake on TV's *General Hospital*. His first Australian #1 hit was 1972's "Speak to the Sky." His first U.S. #1 single was "Jessie's Girl" in 1981.

8-10 correct: Fan club president

4-7 correct: Autograph collector

1-3 correct: My mom gave away my records

77. You Jane

1. Jane Austen. *Emma*, perhaps the most popular of Austen's six novels, was published in 1815, 2 years before her death at age 42. The tale of a good-hearted but meddlesome young woman has been made into numerous films and TV movies and was the basis for the 1995 film *Clueless*.

2. Jane Wyatt. All-American actress Jane Wyatt is best known for her portrayals of two famous mothers, Margaret Anderson on TV's *Father Knows Best* (for which she won three Emmy awards) and Mr. Spock's mother on the original *Star Trek* TV series and in the film *Star Trek IV: The Voyage Home*.

3. Jane Addams. The Hull-House Settlement, which Addams founded in 1889, provided day-care services, employment assistance and other help for newly arrived immigrants in Chicago. Addams also supported the founding of the American Civil Liberties Union (ACLU) and the National Association for the Advancement of Colored People (NAACP). She won the Nobel Peace Prize for her work with the Women's International League for Peace and Freedom.

4. Jane Jetson. Wife of George and mother of Judy and Elroy, Jane Jetson was the original cartoon mom of the future. *The Jetsons* premiered on television in 1962, with Penny Singleton, who played Blondie on TV, doing Jane Jetson's voice. If *The Jetsons* was before your time, you still might be interested to know that Don Messick, who voiced Astro, the Jetsons' dog, also provided the voice for Scooby Doo.

5. Jane Alexander. Patrician actress Alexander won a Tony Award for *The Great White Hope* and an Emmy Award for the TV movie *Playing for Time*. Her most challenging performance, however, came in 1993 when President Bill Clinton asked her to head the National Endowment for the Arts. She led the organization for 4 years.

6. Lady Jane Grey. When England's Protestant king Edward VI died in 1553, his Catholic sister Mary was set to inherit the throne. But the Protestant ruling class didn't want a Catholic queen, so they installed Edward's first cousin once removed, Lady Jane Grey, on the throne instead. Queen Jane ruled for just 9 days, until Mary seized power and had Jane executed.

7. Jane Campion. As of 2002, New Zealand's Jane Campion (*The Piano*, 1993) was one of just two women ever nominated for a Best Director Oscar. The other is Italy's Lina Wertmuller (*Seven Beauties*, 1976). Neither won the Academy Award.

8. Jane Eyre. The heroine of Charlotte Brontë's 1847 novel of the same name, Jane Eyre is orphaned in childhood and later works for the moody, mercurial Mr. Rochester as a governess. They fall in love and plan to marry, until Jane discovers that Mr. R. is hiding some dark and troubling secrets. Hmm . . . .

9. Jane Porter. Tarzan's Jane Porter (who knew she had a last name?) is the daughter of Professor Archimedes Q. Porter of Baltimore, Maryland. In 1912's *Tarzan of the Apes*, the first of Edgar Rice Burroughs' Tarzan stories, Tarzan follows Jane back to America but doesn't win her love. Readers hated the ending, but Burroughs was no fool. He used it as an opportunity to write a sequel to bring the two together.

10. Jane E. Brody. *New York Times* personal health columnist Jane E. Brody is the author of seven books, including *Jane Brody's Nutrition Book* and *You Can Fight Cancer and Win*.

8-10 correct: Sweet Jane

4-7 correct: Plain Jane

1-3 correct: Calamity Jane

78. Easy as Pie

1. (a) Grasshopper pie is a 1950s-vintage "ice-box pie." The chocolate cookie crust is filled with a mixture of whipped cream, gelatin and green crème de menthe liqueur. After the pie is assembled, it's chilled to set the filling.

2. (b) Key lime pie is named for the tart, yellowish Key limes that grow in the Florida Keys. The first Key lime pies were made in the 1850s, and they've been a specialty in South Florida ever since.

3. True. Shoofly pie, which is probably a Pennsylvania Dutch creation, is filled with molasses and brown sugar. Legend says that it earned its name because the pie was so sweet you had to shoo the flies away from it.

4. (c) Shepherd's pie is a savory pie. Traditionally, it has a crispy potato "crust" filled with minced lamb. It's said that frugal cooks invented this pie as a way to use up the leftovers from their Sunday roasts.

5. (c) Raisins are used as the filling for funeral pie, which is customarily served after a funeral to make a bereaved family's grief a little less bitter. The tradition comes from Germany and was introduced to the United States in Amish and Mennonite communities.

6. False. Boston cream pie isn't even a pie really. It's a round cake filled with custard and topped with a chocolate glaze. The chocolate is what separates Boston cream pie from similar cream-filled cakes. Chefs at Boston's Parker House hotel introduced that innovation.

7. (b) The meringue used to top lemon meringue pie is made from egg whites beaten with granulated sugar.

8. (c) Just about any apple can be used to make apple pie, except Red Delicious. Those sweet apples aren't tart enough to give the pie its flavor, and they turn mushy when baked.

9. False. Pies came to the United States from Europe, where cooks baked anything from apples to "four and twenty blackbirds" in a pastry shell. In medieval times, poultry pies were served with leg bones sticking out as "handles" for guests to serve themselves.

10. (a) Sinfully sweet Mississippi mud pie got its name from the oozing chocolate filling that's as thick as mud. It's a picturesque name, but it's misleading. The recipe didn't come from Mississippi. It was the work of a chef from someplace up north.

8-10 correct: Pie in the sky

4-7 correct: Pie-eyed

1-3 correct: Eating humble pie

79. We Love Lucy

1. Lucille McGillicuddy. Diehard fans know that her middle name was Esmerelda. Lucy investigated her Scottish roots in an episode that featured a dream sequence, a dragon, and Ricky as Scotty MacTavish MacDougal MacCardo.

2. Jamestown, New York. Lucy mentioned this in several episodes (sometimes calling it West Jamestown). Lucille Ball really did grow up there, and it's where you'll find the Lucy-Desi Museum today.

3. True. In the last episode, called "The Ricardos Dedicate a Statue," Lucille Ball and Desi Arnaz's children, Lucie Arnaz and Desi Arnaz, Jr., appeared in a crowd scene. Contrary to popular belief, Desi Arnaz, Jr., did not portray Little Ricky on the show.

4. The Tropicana. When Ricky eventually bought the club, he renamed it Club Babalu.

5. Mrs. Trumbull. Kindly neighbor Mrs. Trumbull, played by actress Elizabeth Patterson, babysat for Little Ricky when the Ricardos were in New York. Give yourself par-

tial credit if you said "Lucy's Mother." After all, she was the one who traveled to California with them to take care of the baby. She also stayed behind in New York with him when the Ricardos and their best friends, the Mertzes, went to Europe.

6. True. The instrumental theme to *I Love Lucy* does have words, but they're used only once on the show. In the episode called "Lucy's Last Birthday," in which Lucy thought her friends had forgotten her birthday, Ricky serenaded her with them.

7. Italy. The episode is called "Lucy's Italian Movie." After she was cast in an Italian film called *Bitter Grapes*, Lucy decided to prepare for the role by joining a group of women in a vineyard, crushing grapes for wine.

8. Her nose. Don't worry; it was made of putty. After accidentally smashing William Holden in the face with a pie at the Brown Derby restaurant, Lucy panicked when she found Holden back at her Hollywood apartment visiting Ricky. She disguised herself with a putty nose, then set it on fire when she lit a cigarette.

9. True. Lucy and Desi had a string of Hollywood heavyweights on the show. Several big names, including John Wayne and Rock Hudson, appeared on the episodes that took place when the Ricardos went to Hollywood. Bob Hope appeared in the first episode of the show's last season. He and Lucy performed a baseball-themed musical number called "Nobody Loves the Ump."

10. Vitameatavegamin. This so-called health tonic, containing vitamins, meat, vegetables and minerals, also contained 23% alcohol. Lucy got so tipsy on the stuff during rehearsals, her TV debut as the Vitameatvegamin girl was a fiasco.

8-10 correct: Prime time
4-7 correct: In syndication
1-3 correct: Off the air

80. Comic Relief

1. (c) The wacky, green-skinned witch Broom-Hilda first flew onto the funny pages in 1970.

2. (g) When she made her comic-book debut in 1967, Barbara Gordon was the chief librarian at the Gotham City Library. She was also the daughter of Police Commissioner Gordon, Batman's ally. In later years, Barbara became a U.S. congresswoman, but she always retained her identity as the crime-fighting Batgirl.

3. (i) By day, Jean Grey was a student and later an actress. As Marvel Girl, she was an original member of the comic-book X-Men, a band of crime-fighting mutants who made their first appearance in 1963. Endowed with telepathic powers, Marvel Girl was forever battling the dark side of her personality that threatened to turn her toward evil. When she saw she would lose the fight, she blew herself up.

4. (e) Vixen, one of the few black female comic-book characters, is a former fashion model named Mari McCabe. The African totem she wears around her neck endows her with animal powers—the strength of an elephant, the ferocity of a lioness, the dexterity of a chimp. She made her Action Comics debut in 1981.

5. (b) In the comic strip drawn by Mell Lazarus, Miss Peach is a teacher at the Kelly School (named in honor of Walt Kelly, who created the Pogo comic strip). Like her bratty students, Miss Peach has a head that's way too big for her body. Unlike them, she's got a "peachy" disposition.

6. (j) Most of the time, Diana Prince was a major in the U.S. Army, stationed at the Pentagon. That is until she turned into Wonder Woman, the best-known female superhero of all time. Her famous bracelets, which could deflect bullets, were made from a rare (and, alas, fictional) metal known as Feminium.

7. (f) When she's not using her superpowers, Invisible Girl is Sue Richards, a Connecticut wife and mother. Sue got her

powers of invisibility when she was blasted by cosmic radiation during a space flight with her husband Reed, her brother Johnny and their friend Ben. The blast turned Reed into Mr. Fantastic. Johnny became the Human Torch and Ben turned into The Thing. Together they fight crime as the Fantastic Four.

8. (a) Brenda Starr, the flame-haired comic-strip beauty, is a star reporter. When she debuted in the *Chicago Tribune* in 1940, Brenda Starr was one of just a handful of comic-strip characters created by women. Dale Messick wrote and drew the strip for about 30 years.

9. (d) Nurse Tommie Thompson is the red-headed girl in Apartment 3G. Her roommates are the blonde LuAnn Powers, a wealthy young widow, and brunette secretary Margo Magee. These three bachelorettes have lived together in the comics since May 1961.

10. (h) Winnie Winkle joined the steno pool in 1920. Back then she was known as "Winnie Winkle the Breadwinner," one of the first working girls in comics. She was the sole support for her parents and her younger brother, but she still had plenty of time for romantic entanglements. She married in the 1930s and was left widowed and pregnant during World War II, which struck a chord with many women of the day. In later years, Winnie became a fashion designer. She made her last newspaper appearance in 1996.

8-10 correct: Superhero

4-7 correct: Loyal sidekick

1-3 correct: Ordinary citizen

81. She Is Love

1. Jennifer Love Hewitt. While Jennifer is her real first name, family and friends call the petite actress Love. Playing Sarah on TV's *Party of Five* wasn't her first acting job, but it was the one that brought her fame and fortune. Since then, she's portrayed Audrey Hepburn in a TV movie and played Julie James in the horror flicks *I Know What You Did Last Summer* and *I Still Know What You Did Last Summer*.

2. Courtney Love. The unpredictable, irrepressible Courtney Love formed Hole in 1989. The band recorded three well-regarded albums over the next 10 years. In the mid-1990s she starred as Larry Flynt's AIDS-stricken wife Althea in *The People vs. Larry Flynt*.

3. (b) Darlene Love began her singing career with a 1960s girl group called the Blossoms, but she became music's best-kept secret by recording uncredited lead vocals on a bunch of hit songs, including "Da Doo Ron Ron." She's sung backup for everyone from the Beach Boys to Aretha Franklin. She also starred on Broadway in *Leader of the Pack*, and played Danny Glover's wife in the *Lethal Weapon* movies.

4. Christie Love. After a stint as a regular on *Laugh-In*, Teresa Graves starred in a TV series called *Get Christie Love*.

5. Lovey. From 1964 to 1967, actress Natalie Schafer portrayed the laughable, loveable Lovey Howell, wife of millionaire Thurston Howell III, on *Gilligan's Island*. Lovey counted her reign as Queen of the Harvard Pitted Prune Bowl Parade among her accomplishments.

6. (c) Sarah Breedlove, known as Madam C.J. Walker, developed a method to "de-kink" black women's hair using a shampoo and pomade along with a "hot comb." Sold door-to-door at the beginning of the 20th century, Madam C.J. Walker's products were such a success she became the first black woman millionaire in the United States.

7. Linda Lovelace. How does the Catholic school-educated daughter of a police officer—whose high school nickname was "Miss Holy Holy Holy" because she was so chaste—wind up as America's most famous porno actress? It's a story too long to tell here. Linda Lovelace (real name: Boreman) starred in *Deep Throat* in 1972. By 1980, she was a born-again Christian. She died after a car accident in 2002.

8. Patty Loveless. Voted the 1996 Country Music Association female vocalist of the year, Patty Loveless was born Patty Ramey, the daughter of a Pikeville, Kentucky, coal miner. She adapted her last name from her first husband, Terry Lovelace.

9. Monie Love. Born in England, Monie Love (real name: Simone Johnson) hit it big in the United Kingdom with her 1980s hit "Grandpa's Party." Then she moved to the United States and rapped with Queen Latifah on "Ladies First," took a job as a DJ on a New York radio station and hosted MTV's *Lip Service*, where contestants lip-synched to popular songs.

10. (b) In 1942, at the age of 28, Nancy Harkness Love became the head of the WAFS, the Women's Auxiliary Ferrying Squadron, a corps of women designated to fly new military aircraft from factories to the army bases where the planes were put into action.

8-10 correct: True love

4-7 correct: Puppy love

1-3 correct: Lovelorn

82. More or Less

1. (a) We'll let you choose which one you should be drinking, but the fact is a glass of milk contains just a few more calories than a can of beer.

2. (b) They look similar, but a plantain has about twice the carbohydrates of a banana.

3. (a) You should be able to tell just by the taste—one table-spoon of salty caviar contains 240 mg of sodium, while a whole Entenmann's cheese Danish contains 200 mg. We don't recommend a steady diet of either, but we know which one we'd pick to snack on.

4. (a) A raw portion of shrimp contains about 173 mg of cholesterol—that's before you bread it, or fry it, or boil it and dip it in cocktail sauce. Four ounces of raw swordfish contains just 45 mg, although it does have slightly more fat and calories than the shrimp.

5. (a) Sorry to break it to you, but that little dish of chocolate ice cream contains about 9 g of fat, while two strips of bacon contain 5 g. Of course it's not nearly as much fun to eat bacon straight from the package while you're watching a good movie on TV.

6. (b) The orange wins, but it's awfully close. An orange contains 69.7 mg of vitamin C and a cup of fresh cantaloupe contains 67.5 mg. Vitamin C helps you fight colds, and it helps you fight wrinkles. It's used by the body to form the collagen that keeps skin supple.

7. (a) Believe it or not, baked beans beat broccoli for potassium content—752 mg versus 456 mg. Potassium helps keep your muscles—especially your heart—strong and resilient.

8. (b) Think Popeye. You know that spinach is loaded with iron—a good deal more than the cooked chick-peas. Iron keeps your blood healthy.

9. (a). Given the choice between raspber-ries and okra, we'd pick the raspberries every time (sorry, okra fans). Great to know that they also contain about twice the dietary fiber as okra. Dietary fiber aids in digestion.

10. (b). The yogurt wins by a mile. It contains 415 mg of calcium, compared with just 156 mg in the cottage cheese. That cottage cheese also contains about six times

as much sodium as the yogurt. Unless you can't live without curds, go for the yogurt.

> *8-10 correct: You know what you eat*
> *4-7 correct: You eat what you know*
> *1-3 correct: Oh no*

83. Shakespeare's Women

1. (b) Beatrice is about as close as Shakespeare comes to a free-thinking, positive female character. Nice to know she was his original creation and not an adaptation from myth or legend, as many of his characters were. She's happy, witty and in the end, despite her vow never to marry, she finds love with Benedick.

2. (d) *King Lear*, Shakespeare's highly regarded tragic play, came from an old English fable. Poor Cordelia has a hard time of it throughout. Her attempts to prove her loyalty to her father are misconstrued and she's banished from his kingdom. By the time everyone figures out her real intentions, she's been executed.

3. (f) The female lead in *Troilus and Cressida* was one of Shakespeare's least noble characters. As soon as Troilus falls for her and asks her to be faithful, she grows bored and cheats on him. The unhappy and cynical story was loosely based on Greek mythology.

4. (h) It's hard to say if *Othello* was a commentary on interracial love. Othello was black, Desdemona white, though historians say race relations weren't a big concern in Shakespeare's day. Besides, the issues these two had were due more to lack of communication and trust than to social mores. If ever a Shakespearian couple needed ye olde marriage counselor it was Desdemona and Othello.

5. (j) Young love can be beautiful, but in the case of *Romeo and Juliet,* it's doomed to tragedy. These two kids (Juliet is

just 14 and Romeo isn't much older) have to fight her family and his just to be together. In the end they both commit suicide. Strange the things some people find romantic.

6. (i) The title character in *The Taming of the Shrew*, Katharina is a nasty, opinionated woman. She's also the elder daughter of a wealthy man, who insists that she marry before her sweet younger sister is allowed to. Enter the nasty, gold-digging Petruchio, who marries Katharina for her money and sets out to break her spirit and "tame" her. (A shrew is a small rodent—how flattering!)

7. (a) One of Shakespeare's more tragic figures, ambitious Lady Macbeth convinces her husband to murder the Scottish king so he can inherit the throne. After the deed is done, she's so consumed with guilt she sees blood on her hands that she can't wash away. When she says "Out, damned spot!" she's not talking about the laundry.

8. (c) Hamlet says he loves Ophelia. Ophelia loves Hamlet. But, yet again, in typical Shakespearian tragic fashion, they're destined not to be together, and they're destined to die. (What is it about these tragedies anyway?)

9. (e) Titania is the queen of the fairies in *A Midsummer Night's Dream*. When she and her husband, Oberon, quarrel, it causes unrest in the love lives of the mortals in the play.

10. (g) Viola is a female character who spends all but one act of *Twelfth Night* dressed as a boy and working as a page for Duke Orsino, whom she secretly loves. In Shakespeare's day, all female roles were performed by boys. So the original production of *Twelfth Night* presented an interesting conundrum in which a boy played a girl playing a boy.

8-10 correct: As You Like It
4-7 correct: All's Well That Ends Well
1-3 correct: The Comedy of Errors

84. The Healers

1. (a) The Apgar Score, created by Dr. Virginia Apgar, detects health problems in newborns. Immediately after a birth, the physician checks a baby's Appearance, Pulse, Grimace (or facial reflexes), Activity (or muscle tone) and Respiration. A low Apgar score signals problems that need immediate attention.

2. (a) The International Red Cross, which provides assistance to people in need, was founded in Switzerland in 1864. After working with the organization in Europe during the 1870s, Massachusetts-born Clara Barton brought the idea home with her. She founded the American Red Cross in 1882.

3. (b) In the early 20th century, factory workers were exposed to toxic agents like lead dust, mercury and arsenic. Alice Hamilton's research into their harmful effects led to laws to protect workers and compensate them for illness incurred on the job. Ironically, Hamilton did her research in a U.S. government job for which she received no salary!

4. (c) In the 1960s, some pregnant women took the experimental drug thalidomide to curb morning sickness. But thalidomide also caused birth defects. When it was up for approval by the U.S. Food and Drug Administration, Dr. Frances Kathleen Oldham Kelsey refused to allow it. Drug manufacturers were furious, but ultimately, thalidomide was banned and Kelsey received the President's Medal for Distinguished Service for her resolve and good judgment.

5. (c) In 1990, Antonia Novello was appointed U.S. surgeon general. A pediatrician and medical school professor, she became the first woman, and the first Hispanic, to hold the position. During her tenure, she focused on the plights of women and children with AIDS and worked to raise awareness of domestic-violence issues.

6. (a) In 1925, Mary Breckinridge founded the Frontier Nursing Service, a network of traveling nurse-midwives in rural Kentucky. Before FNS, Leslie County, Kentucky, had

the highest death-in-childbirth rate in the United States simply because women didn't have access to medical care. After FNS, the county death-in-childbirth rate dropped to well below the national average.

7. (b) Elizabeth Kübler-Ross gained worldwide notoriety with the publication of her 1969 book *On Death and Dying*. She was one of the first mental-health professionals to call attention to the unique psychological needs of the elderly and terminally ill.

8. (b) If it weren't for Alice Evans, you might not have pasteurized milk in your fridge. Working for the U.S. Department of Agriculture, Evans isolated the organism that causes brucellosis, a cattle disease that can be passed to humans through contaminated milk. Pasteurization kills the brucellosis organism. Thus Evans's work led to the creation of mandatory pasteurization laws in the United States.

9. (a) In 1960, 1 year after she was named dean of the Yale University School of Nursing, Florence Wald visited a hospice for terminally ill patients in England. She returned determined to implement the same type of care in the United States. In the 1970s, she helped to found Hospice Incorporated, the first hospice in the United States.

10. (b) Blalock-Taussig surgery is also known as the "blue-baby operation." It corrects heart defects in newborn babies so that blood circulates properly from the heart to the lungs and back again. Dr. Helen Taussig and Dr. Alfred Blalock of Johns Hopkins University first performed it successfully in 1944.

8-10 correct: Medical miracle

4-7 correct: Healing touch

1-3 correct: Take two aspirin and call me in the morning

85. Flower Power

1. (c) Narcissus was a beautiful boy who was so fond of his own good looks that he ignored all the nymphs and goddesses who pursued him. (You know the type. Why do you think they're called narcissists?) He was punished for his behavior by falling in love with his reflection in a pool of water. He looked at himself for so long that he grew roots and turned into the narcissus flower.

2. Gardenia. Jazz singer Billie Holiday often performed with a fragrant white gardenia tucked in her hair.

3. False. Poinsettias, the red-leafed Christmas favorites, are not poisonous. Of course, that doesn't mean you should eat them. They don't taste particularly good, and their milky white sap can cause an allergic reaction on the skin.

4. (a) Gypsophila is more commonly known as baby's breath. The tiny white, delicately scented flowers often are used as "filler" in large bouquets. The botanical name comes from the Greek for "chalk-loving," and refers to the chalky soil in which the flowers grow.

5. Daisy. In the Henry James short story *Daisy Miller*, the title character is a spoiled ingénue from Schenectady, New York, visiting Europe for the first time. Her unsophisticated manner and ignorance of social mores cause scandals throughout her tour, alienate the man who loves her, and eventually cause her death from a mysterious continental ailment.

6. True. The chrysanthemum came from China, but it became revered in Japan. By the 8th century the chrysanthemum—*kiku* in Japanese—had become part of the official seal of the Japanese emperor. Japan also celebrates an annual Chrysanthemum Day.

7. (a) Dr. Johann Gottfried Zinn, a German medical professor, wrote the first description of zinnias in the 18th century. Thus, the brightly colored flower was named for him. When he wasn't studying flowers, Dr. Zinn was writing medical texts. His research on the human eye revealed a ligament that doctors now call Zinn's zonule.

8. Sunflower. Helios is the Greek god of the Sun. Helianthus is the botanical name for the sunflower. Giant yellow sunflowers are known for the way they turn their faces toward the sun.

9. (b) According to the U.S. Department of Agriculture, in 2002 lilies generated the second-highest sales in wholesale dollar value, with $57.5 million sold. They were a distant second to roses, which tallied $67.7 million. But they were way ahead of the #3 flower, tulips, with $26.3 million.

10. Iris. Most irises are bearded, which refers to the crinkly "beards" on their lower blossoms. Iris is the Greek goddess of the rainbow. The French royal *fleur de lis* symbol is derived from the iris.

> *8-10 correct: Hothouse flower*
> *4-7 correct: Garden variety*
> *1-3 correct: Wilted blossom*

86. Jersey Girls

1. (h) Carol Blazejowski, the woman they call "Blaze," was born in Elizabeth and was a basketball star at Montclair State, winning the Wade Trophy as college women's basketball player of the year in 1978. In 1994, she was inducted into the Basketball Hall of Fame and in 1997 she became the general manager of the WNBA New York Liberty.

2. (j) In 1977, "You Light Up My Life" topped the charts for 10 weeks and singer Debby Boone became a household name. Born in Hackensack, Boone is the daughter of 1950s teen idol Pat Boone. After winning two Grammy

Awards for "You Light Up My Life" and a third as the year's best new artist, she never reached those heady heights again.

3. (d) She wrote *Vogue's Book of Etiquette* in 1948, but Millicent Fenwick, the "pipe-smoking granny" congresswoman from New Jersey, was hardly a conventional gal. Beginning her political career on the Bernardsville School Board, she was elected to her first term in the U.S. Congress in 1974 at age 64. The four-term congresswoman also was the model for the character of Lacey Davenport in the *Doonesbury* comic strip.

4. (c) Lauryn Hill from South Orange formed the Fugees—short for refugees—with Wyclef Jean and Pras Michel in the 1990s. Her solo album, 1998's *The Miseducation of Lauryn Hill*, won five Grammys.

5. (g) Both Whitney Houston and her gospel-singer mom, Cissy, were born in Newark (Whitney's cousin, singer Dionne Warwick, hails from East Orange). Blessed with a beautiful face and "pipes" to match, Whitney burst onto the music scene in 1985, scoring #1 pop and R&B hits with "Saving All My Love For You" and "How Will I Know."

6. (i) Clara Louise Maass, a nurse from East Orange, literally gave up her life for science. In 1901, she volunteered to be bitten by a mosquito carrying yellow fever so doctors could track the disease's progress. When she survived her first infection, she was bitten again and died just 10 days later at age 25.

7. (f) Keshia Knight Pulliam from Newark was 4 in 1983 when she was cast as Rudy Huxtable, the youngest kid on *The Cosby Show*. In 1986 she became the youngest actress ever to receive an Emmy nomination. Since then, she's graduated from Spelman College and returned to TV to win celebrity editions of *The Weakest Link* and *Fear Factor*.

8. (e) One of Alfred Hitchcock's icy-blonde leading ladies, Newark-born Eva Marie Saint starred opposite Cary Grant in Hitchcock's *North by Northwest*. She won an Oscar for

her work in *On the Waterfront*, appeared in many movies of the 1950s and 1960s, and became known to TV audiences as Cybill Shepherd's mother in the series *Moonlighting*.

9. (a) New Jersey is the #2 blueberry-producing state in the United States, and we can thank Elizabeth Coleman White of New Lisbon for that. "Miss Lizzie," who grew up on her family's cranberry farm, pioneered crossbreeding studies that turned New Jersey's wild blueberries into a successful commercial crop.

10. (b) In 1993, Republican Christine Todd Whitman was elected New Jersey's 50th governor. She was the first woman to hold the post. Whitman, who grew up in Hunterdon County, served two terms as governor before becoming the head of the federal Environmental Protection Agency in George W. Bush's administration.

8-10 correct: Cruising "down the shore"
4-7 correct: Passing the Pine Barrens
1-3 correct: Stuck on the turnpike

87. You Should Be Dancing

1. (b) In French, *pas de deux* means "step for two." In a ballet, a *pas de deux* is usually danced by a man and a woman.

2. (a) The mambo, a sexy dance to an Afro-Caribbean beat, came from Cuba. It probably originated in the 1940s and made its way to the United States—along with "mambo king" bandleaders like Dámaso Pérez Prado and Tito Puente—by the 1950s.

3. (b) "Arm breaker" and "comb" are just two of the colorfully named jive dance moves. In the comb, the man takes his partner's hand behind his head and guides it down to his shoulder as if he's combing his hair. For the arm breaker, the woman's arm is bent behind her back and she "unwinds" until she's in a more normal (and comfortable) position.

4. (b) Although she was a dancer, Twyla Tharp is best known as a modern dance choreographer. She's worked with major dancers and companies throughout the world, and recently directed and choreographed *Movin' Out*, a Broadway show based on the music of Billy Joel.

5. (b) The Lindy Hop style of jitterbug dancing was named for Charles Lindbergh (a.k.a. Lucky Lindy), the pilot who made the first solo flight—or "hop"—across the Atlantic Ocean in 1927.

6. (c) When a ballerina is on *pointe*, she's dancing on the tips of her toes in specially padded "toe shoes." This really is a "don't try this at home" skill, and kids with prima ballerina dreams should be discouraged from attempting it at too early an age. It hurts and  can cause serious injury. In fact, it's so unnatural that ballet purists prefer dancing on *pointe* to be performed only by dancers portraying imaginary or fantasy characters.

7. (b) There's never any worry about what to do with your hands when you're country line dancing. Hook your thumbs in the waistband of your jeans and let your fingers rest on your hips.

8. (c) Believe it or not, the waltz caused a minor uproar in the 18th century. The idea of men and women dancing with their bodies pressed together was unheard of. Words like "indecent" and "lascivious" were used to describe it, and it was banned in some towns in the German countryside (where it originated). One critic said, "I can understand that mothers like the waltz, but I cannot understand that they let their daughters dance it."

9. (a) The hora, an Israeli folk dance, originated in Romania. It's performed in a closed circle. If a lot of people are dancing, circles are formed one inside the other.

10. (c) If you're square-dancing, you need a caller. Who else could tell you when it's time to allemande left, swing your partner, or do-si-do?

8-10 correct: Dancing queen
4-7 correct: Light on your feet
1-3 correct: Sit this one out

88. On the Scene

1. (e) In July 1994, 7-year-old Megan Kanka was raped and killed by a convicted sex offender living in her Hamilton Township, New Jersey, neighborhood. In Megan's memory, New Jersey enacted "Megan's Law," which requires communities to be notified when a convicted sex offender moves into town. A version of Megan's Law is now a federal statute as well.

2. (f) Alpha Delta Pi, the first college sorority in the United States, was founded at Wesleyan College in Macon, Georgia, in 1851. The "secret society" was started by Eugenia Tucker, who invited her "dearest and most admired" friends to join.

3. (a) In April 1887, just weeks after Kansas women received the right to vote in city elections, Susanna Madora Salter was elected mayor of Argonia, Kansas. The first female mayor in the United States was just 27 when she was elected, but she had a political pedigree. Her father had been the town's first mayor, and her father-in-law was a former Kansas lieutenant governor.

4. (d) Brownie Wise, a Detroit single mom, sold Tupperware in the late 1940s to pay her family's expenses. She was so successful that Earl Tupper, the company's founder, asked how she did it. Her secret was the Tupperware "party," where she demonstrated the revolutionary products. Wisely, Tupper hired Wise to head his company's Tupperware Home Parties division. Today, the company estimates that a Tupperware party takes place somewhere in the world every 2.5 seconds!

5. (b) In 1899, Mrs. John Howell Phillips of Chicago became the first woman in the United States to receive a driver's license.

6. (h) When Providence, Rhode Island, homemaker Katharine Gibbs was widowed unexpectedly in 1909, she learned stenography as a way to support herself. Figuring that other women in similar situations needed job training, she took what she'd learned and taught it to others. She opened the first Katharine Gibbs School in 1911, starting what would become the crème de la crème of secretarial training colleges.

7. (c) *Roe v. Wade*, the Supreme Court case that pioneered a woman's right to choose whether to terminate a pregnancy, originated in Dallas County, Texas, in 1970. "Jane Roe" was an alias used to represent a group of pregnant women seeking to overturn a Texas law that prohibited abortions unless the mother's life was endangered. Henry B. Wade was the district attorney in Dallas County.

8. (g) Coming home from work in Montgomery, Alabama, seamstress Rosa Parks took a seat in the "colored" section of a city bus and refused to give it up when a white man demanded it. Her act of defiance in the segregated South got her arrested. It also sparked the Montgomery Bus Boycott of 1955, which, more than a year later, led the U.S. Supreme Court to declare segregation on city buses to be unconstitutional.

9. (j) The first Million Mom March in support of gun control took place in Washington, D.C., on Mother's Day 2000. The turnout didn't quite reach a million. The official count of moms and others participating was closer to 750,000.

10. (i) The first Women's Rights Convention, organized by Lucretia Mott and Elizabeth Cady Stanton, was held in 1848 in Seneca Falls, New York. It addressed such issues as inequitable property laws and

educational opportunities for women, and, of course, the campaign for women's right to vote.

8-10 correct: Everything in its place
4-7 correct: Temporarily misplaced
1-3 correct: Out of place

89. Stamping Ground

1. Eleanor Roosevelt. Eleanor Roosevelt, wife of Franklin Delano Roosevelt, has become a highly respected American first lady. But in her day, she was sometimes considered to be too actively involved in liberal causes and too free with her opinions. Among her many accomplishments, she was the U.S. delegate to the United Nations from 1945 to 1953, and again in 1961. She was pictured on stamps in 1984 and 1998.

2. Edith Wharton. Known for her novels about upper-class life in America's "Gilded Age" at the turn of the last century, her works include *The House of Mirth* and *The Buccaneers.* She won the 1920 Pulitzer Prize for *The Age of Innocence*, and was featured on a stamp in 1980.

3. Betsy Ross. We'll probably never know if Betsy Ross really sewed the first stars-and-stripes flag of the United States. Some claim it's a fact and others say it's a folktale. It is true that the twice-widowed Betsy Ross, who was still only in her 20s, was a seamstress in Philadelphia in 1776. And it's true that she was honored with a stamp in 1952.

4. Ayn Rand. The unconventional author of *Atlas Shrugged* and *The Fountainhead* was the subject of a stamp in 1999.

5. Mary Cassatt. One of just two women to exhibit her paintings with the Impressionists in Paris, Mary Cassatt is known for her gentle portraits of mothers and children. The Pittsburgh-born painter was depicted on a 1988 stamp. Her painting "The Boating Party" appeared on a 1966 stamp, "Breakfast in Bed" was part of a 1998 series

featuring the work of American artists, and four more of her paintings were pictured on a 2003 stamp series.

6. Dinah Washington. Queen of the Blues Dinah Washington was also the queen of "living large" in her day. She had dozens of hit songs, diamonds, furs, cars . . . and seven husbands before her death at age 39. "What a Difference a Day Makes," released in 1959, was her biggest chart success. She was featured on a stamp in 1993.

7. Queen Isabella of Spain. She was the first woman to appear on a U.S. postage stamp, although she's just a background presence on an 1893 stamp commemorating Columbus's voyage to the New World.

8. Rose O'Neill. The artist herself isn't pictured on the 2001 stamp, but her pointy-headed Kewpies are. They debuted in *Woman's Home Companion* magazine in 1909 and became a craze, spawning a comic strip, children's books, dolls and household goods. There was even a Rose O'Neill Kewpie Shop on Madison Avenue in New York.

9. Patricia Roberts Harris. The first black woman to serve in a U.S. presidential cabinet position, Harris was appointed the secretary of housing and urban development (HUD) under Jimmy Carter in 1977, and later secretary of health, education and welfare (what we now call health and human services). She was honored with a stamp in 2000.

10. Moina Michael. Next time you buy a tiny paper poppy on Veterans' Day, think of Moina Michael. Inspired by the World War I-era poem "In Flanders Fields" ("In Flanders fields the poppies blow/Between the crosses row on row"), Michael came up with the idea of selling symbolic poppies to benefit disabled veterans and their families. A stamp honoring Michael and the poppy campaign was issued in 1948.

8-10 correct: First class
4-7 correct: Metered mail
1-3 correct: Postage due

90. Read the Label

1. (a) Ascorbic acid is the chemical name for vitamin C. It's used as a color stabilizer because it slows the fading effect that oxygen can have on certain processed foods. It's also used as a vitamin additive in beverages and breakfast cereals.

2. (b) Calcium thioglycolate is a chemical that dissolves hair protein and allows it to slip away from the skin's surface. It's commonly used in depilatories and it can cause rashes if it's left on the skin for too long.

3. (a) FD&C stands for Food, Drug & Cosmetic. It means that the artificial coloring agent is safe for use in all three types of products.

4. (c) Guar gum is made from guar beans, which come from India. It's used as a thickener for bottled sauces and dressings because it has about eight times more thickening power than cornstarch. Guar gum is also an emulsifier, which helps keep the oil and water in the dressing from separating.

5. (c) Poor sodium lauryl sulfate (SLS)! The foaming detergent ingredient used in shampoos and some toothpastes has been the subject of an Internet hoax in recent years. Despite urban myths to the contrary, SLS does not cause cancer. (The American Cancer Society and the FDA agree on this.) It has been known to cause skin rashes, it will irritate your eyes if you don't rinse it off immediately, and it can give you diarrhea if you swallow too much of it. That's all.

6. (b) You won't find seaweed listed on the label of your Ben & Jerry's, but there's probably some inside. Thickeners like carrageenan and alginate, which give ice cream its thick, creamy texture, are derived from seaweed.

7. (a) The original formulation of Coca-Cola included coca leaves—the same leaves that are used to manufacture cocaine. That ingredient was taken out of use around 1909.

8. (a) Propylene glycol keeps moisture in foods, but prevents excess moisture from forming on them. That's why it's used in marshmallows and shredded coconut and other foods that tend to "sweat" when they're kept in plastic bags. It does basically the same thing for car antifreeze, which keeps ice from forming inside machinery in cold weather. And it's used in various cosmetics and medicines. It's also used to make fake fog on stage and movie sets.

9. (b) Red is by far the most frequently used artificial food coloring, and the coloring known as Red No. 40 is the most commonly used additive. Yellow No. 5 is the second most commonly used coloring in food, medicine and make-up. It's also called tartrazine.

10. (b) Monosodium glutamate, better known as MSG, is a flavor enhancer designed to make food taste more intense. It also can produce an intense physical reaction in some people, bringing on headaches, nausea and even heart palpitations.

8-10 correct: Sealed for freshness
4-7 correct: Some settling may occur
1-3 correct: Contents under pressure

91. Valentine's Day

1. Valentine's Day is always celebrated on February 14. That date coincides with the ancient Roman fertility festival called Lupercalia. It's also the date that folks in medieval Europe believed birds chose their mates for the spring season. St. Valentine, a 3rd-century martyr, isn't especially associated with lovers, but February 14 was designated as his day of honor by the 5th-century pope Gelasius.

2. True. An A.C. Neilsen study found that more than $358.1 million in candy sales were made during "Valentine's Week" 2002. But that's because Valentine's Day candy

buyers are last-minute shoppers. For the top three candy holidays—Christmas, Easter and Halloween--—people stock up early and spend more on candy overall.

3. (c) Osculation is "the act of kissing," according to Webster's.

4. Women receive slightly more than half of the valentines sent on Valentine's Day. It's the second largest holiday for sending greeting cards (behind Christmas) and the second-largest holiday for greeting card purchases by men (behind Mother's Day).

5. X is the symbol used to indicate a kiss on a love letter or valentine card. The tradition comes from the days when people who were unable to write their names would sign documents with an X, then kiss it to prove their truthfulness.

6. (a) Conversation Hearts, the tiny colored candies with loving mottoes stamped on them, were created by the New England Confectionary Company (NECCO) in the 1860s. At the time they were called motto hearts. Today, NECCO manufactures about 8 billion Sweethearts® Conversation Hearts each year. They're sold for only 6 weeks a year—between January 1 and February 14.

7. Men planned to spend an average of $125.96 on their spouses or significant others for Valentine's Day 2003, according to a study by the National Retail Federation. The same survey found that women expected to spend an average of $38.22.

8. (b) The Society of American Florists says that most Valentine's Day flower purchases by women are for their mothers—a total of 23%. Fifteen percent of women buy Valentine's Day flowers for their husbands or significant others, and the same percentage buy flowers for themselves.

9. Higher. For Valentine's Day 2002, 130 million roses were sold in the United States. (Did you receive your fair share?)

10. (b) Esther Howland of Worcester, Massachusetts, made the first mass-produced valentine cards in the United States. She sold $5,000 worth of them in 1849, her first year of production.

8-10 correct: Heart's desire
4-7 correct: Hearts and flowers
1-3 correct: Miss Lonelyhearts

92. Which Häppened First?

1. (a) In 1975, 36-year-old Junko Tabei of Japan became the first woman to reach the summit of Mt. Everest. The 4 foot 9 inch climber led an all-female expedition to the top. As of this writing, women have never served on a U.S. Navy submarine. Close quarters on older subs, offering virtually no privacy, made it impossible for both genders to live and work side by side. The Virginia class of subs now in production may be outfitted to accommodate both genders.

2. (b) Marthe Distel, a French journalist, founded the Cordon Bleu cooking school in 1895. While most of its chef-teachers were men, the students included women. Ruth Wakefield of Massachusetts probably wasn't among them, but she left her mark on world cuisine by inventing the chocolate-chip cookie in the 1930s.

3. (a) In 1919, quiet Alice Hamilton shook up the staid society at Harvard Medical School by becoming its first female professor. Change came more slowly for women who wanted to attend Harvard Medical School. The school's first female graduates were in the class of 1949.

4. (b) Helen Magill White received a Ph.D. at Boston University in 1877, making her the first woman in the United States to earn the degree. Twenty years later, the first Boston Marathon was run, but it took until 1972

before women were officially allowed to compete in it. Nina Kuscsik led the women's field that year.

5. (b) Edith Houghton was the first female scout in Major League Baseball, working for the Philadelphia Phillies from 1946 to 1952. Houghton started playing baseball in 1922 at age 10. In fact, women played baseball as far back as the 1860s, when Vassar and Smith Colleges fielded intramural teams. But girls weren't allowed to play Little League Baseball until 1974.

6. (a) The first women to set foot at the South Pole were a group of geologists from Ohio State University, a biologist from New Zealand and a reporter from Detroit, who stepped off the plane together (so the group could all be "first") in 1969. The first woman to walk in space was Svetlana Savitskaya of the Soviet Union in July 1984.

7. (a) The first female FBI agents were hired in the 1920s but were kicked out by then-director J. Edgar Hoover in 1927. Just 2 months after Hoover died, in 1972, women were once again hired as FBI agents. The first two were Susan Lynn Roley, a former Marine, and Joanne B. Pierce, a former nun. Meanwhile, at the Kiwanis Club—a service organization dedicated to "improving the quality of life for children and families"—women were not accepted as members until 1987.

8. (b) In 1956, breastfeeding rates in the United States dropped by about 20%. A group of mothers in Illinois decided to reignite women's awareness of the health benefits of breastfeeding. Calling themselves the La Leche League (*leche* is Spanish for milk), they incorporated in 1958. The Pregnancy Discrimination Act, which prohibits employers from discriminating against women who are pregnant or who might become pregnant, was enacted by the U.S. Congress in 1978.

9. (a) The honorary position of Poet Laureate in the United States, started in the 1930s, is designed to raise the public interest in reading and writing poetry. Louise Bogan was the first woman to hold the title, from 1945 to 1946.

Although the title of Poet Laureate has existed in England since the 17th century, no woman has ever been chosen for the post.

10. (a) Mensa, founded in 1946, has always accepted female members. Its only qualification for membership is a score among the top 2% of the population on a standardized intelligence test. It took an act of Congress in 1975 to convince the U.S. Military Academy at West Point to accept women. The first female cadets graduated in 1980.

> *8-10 correct: Totally happening*
> *4-7 correct: What's happening?*
> *1-3 correct: How'd that happen?*

93. La La Ladies

1. k.d. lang. Born Kathryn Dawn Lang in Edmonton, Alberta, lang comes by her country roots naturally. She grew up in Consort, a prairie town of just 650 people. A vocal animal rights activist and lesbian, she had her biggest chart success with "Constant Craving" and is best known for posing "butch" with model Cindy Crawford on the cover of *Vanity Fair*. It was the magazine's third bestselling cover of all time.

2. Emma Lazarus. Engraved on a plaque at the Statue of Liberty, her poem, "The New Colossus," gave us the immortal lines, "Give me your tired, your poor,/Your huddled masses yearning to breathe free." Lazarus, the daughter of Russian-Jewish immigrants, wrote that beautiful tribute in 1883.

3. Lois Lane. In the *Superman* comics, mild-mannered reporter Clark Kent has the hots for Lois Lane, but she only has eyes for Superman.

4. Lucy Lawless. Amazon icon Lawless is a New Zealand native. After winning the title of Mrs. New Zealand in

1989, she acted in a couple of commercials, but it was her height (5 feet 10 ½ inches) and her physique that led producers to cast her in the TV movie *Hercules and the Amazon Women*. That role led to *Xena: Warrior Princess*.

5. Selma Lagerlöf. In 1909, Swedish author Lagerlöf became the first woman to win the Nobel Prize for literature. Her first and most highly regarded work was *Gösta Berlings Saga*, but she is also known for the beloved Swedish children's story *The Wonderful Adventures of Nils*.

6. Veronica Lake. While Lake was filming *Forty Little Mothers*, her cascading locks kept falling over one eye. Thus her legendary "peekaboo" hairstyle was born. At just over 5 feet tall, she was the perfect costar for Alan Ladd (known for his short stature). Together they starred in *The Glass Eye*, *The Blue Dahlia* and *This Gun for Hire*, among others.

7. Lady Caroline Lamb. A society woman with a taste for scandal, Lamb latched on to Lord Byron and refused to let go—even after he married her husband's cousin. Their passionate, public affair left her a bit unhinged by the time Byron died in 1824. In her novel *Glenarvon* she cast herself as the fictional heroine and Byron as the hero.

8. Wanda Landowska. No one since Bach did more for the harpsichord than Landowska. By the 20th century, few concert musicians played the baroque instrument. Landowska made the first modern recording of Bach's Goldberg Variations in 1933 and rekindled the world's love of harpsichord music.

9. Jessica Lange. Lange filled the "Fay Wray role" in a remake of *King Kong*, but her 1982 portrayal of actress Frances Farmer is what put her on Hollywood's radar. That year she won a Best Supporting Actress Oscar for *Tootsie*. She's been a Best Actress nominee five times, and she won for *Blue Sky* in 1994.

10. Angela Lansbury. These days, Lansbury is known as Jessica Fletcher, the mystery writer/detective on TV's *Murder, She Wrote*. But her many memorable roles include Semadar,

Delilah's older, nicer sister in *Samson and Delilah*; Laurence Harvey's sinister mother in *The Manchurian Candidate*; and Mrs. Potts, the kettle in Disney's *Beauty and the Beast*.

8-10 correct: Crème de La crème

4-7 correct: La vie en rose

1-3 correct: C'est La vie

94. When She Was Born . . .

1. (j) Dance-pop belter Taylor Dayne had a clutch of top-10 hits in the late 1980s and early 1990s, including "Tell It to My Heart," "With Every Beat of My Heart" and "Love Will Lead You Back." She started out life as Leslie Wunderman in Baldwin, New York.

2. (g) Singer, model and former *Baywatch* babe, Tara Leigh Patrick was named Carmen Electra by Prince, who also produced her first album in 1992.

3. (b) The plump, golden-voiced Cass Elliot—better known as Mama Cass of the Mamas and the Papas—was born Ellen Naomi Cohen in Baltimore, Maryland. Among her solo hits was the classic, "Dream a Little Dream of Me."

4. (d) E! Entertainment Television's *Fashion Emergency* is hosted by plus-size model Emme. Her family knows her better as Melissa Miller.

5. (c) You didn't believe Whoopi Goldberg was her real name, did you? Nope. Her mother named her Caryn Elaine Johnson. Born in New York City, little Caryn was performing on stage by the time she was 8 years old.

6. (h) Author Jamaica Kincaid was born Elaine Potter Richardson on the island of Antigua. In her writing, she's known for expressing her conflicted feelings about her family. Her works include *My Brother*, *The Autobiography of My Mother* and *Mr. Potter*.

7. (i) Thelma Catherine Ryan was born on the eve of St. Patrick's Day while her father was working the night shift. When he arrived home to find she'd been born, he called her his "St. Patrick's babe in the morn." He nicknamed her "Pat," which is how we know the former first lady and wife of Richard Nixon.

8. (e) When *Interview with the Vampire* author Anne Rice was born in 1941, her parents named her Howard Allen O'Brien after her father, Howard. Rice maintains that her mother gave the baby girl a traditionally male name to give her "an unusual advantage in the world." In fact, Rice was self-conscious about her name, and changed it to Anne on her first day of school. Rice is her married name.

9. (f) Early in her career, Mary Isabel Catherine Bernadette O'Brien was part of a folk trio called the Springfields. It was a name she carried with her, as Dusty Springfield, for the rest of her life. A huge pop star in England, she had hits in the United States with "I Only Want to Be With You" and "You Don't Have to Say You Love Me."

10. (a) Born into slavery in 1797, Isabella Baumfree attained her freedom in 1827. Preaching the causes of women's rights and abolition, she took the name Sojourner Truth. Despite the hardships of her life (including giving birth to thirteen children), she lived to a ripe old age. She's best remembered for her stunning "Ain't I a Woman?" speech, pointing out the societal double standards faced by black women.

8-10 correct: Nom de plume

4-7 correct: Incognito

1-3 correct: Alias

95. Lady Be Good

1. Lady of the Lake. In the legends of King Arthur, the Lady of the Lake presents Arthur with the magical sword Excalibur. She's also said to be the lover of the wizard Merlin and the foster mother of Sir Lancelot (also known as Lancelot du Lac, or Lancelot of the Lake).

2. "Lady Madonna." Written by Paul McCartney, "Lady Madonna" was the Beatles' first single of 1968. McCartney has said mothers, who manage to care for their children, run their households and "make ends meet," inspired the song.

3. Lady Bird. Claudia Alta Taylor Johnson has been known as "Lady Bird" since she was a little girl. The nickname comes from the British term for ladybug, which is also used in the southern United States. Her pet causes during and after her time as first lady are wildlife and the beautification of America. She founded the Lady Bird Johnson National Wildflower Research Center.

4. My Fair Lady. Based on the George Bernard Shaw play *Pygmalion*, the Broadway musical *My Fair Lady*, by Alan Jay Lerner and Frederick Loewe, debuted in 1956. Julie Andrews played Eliza Doolittle, a Cockney flower seller who is transformed into a refined lady by Professor Henry Higgins (played by Rex Harrison). The show's memorable score featured "I Could Have Danced All Night."

5. Pink Lady. This cocktail probably originated in the 1920s. The gin makes it potent. The grenadine makes it pink. And the egg white makes it frothy. Some people add apple brandy and lemon juice to the mix.

6. "Lay Lady Lay." Bob Dylan wrote his 1969 hit "Lay Lady Lay" to be used as the theme for the movie *Midnight Cowboy*. The song never made it into the film, possibly because the producers didn't like it and possibly because Dylan didn't deliver it on time—the stories vary. Instead, Dylan included it on his album *Nashville Skyline*.

7. Lady Slipper. Also known as the Lady's Slipper orchid, the Cypripedium genus is found through-out North America, although its forest habitats in many places are threatened by logging. The pink-and-white flower known as the Showy Lady Slipper (Cypripedium reginae) is the state flower of Minnesota.

8. Lady in Red. Gangster John Dillinger was killed by lawmen outside Chicago's Biograph Theater in 1934. Legend has it he was set up by Anna Sage, a brothel-keeper. When she accompanied him to the movies that night she was wearing an orange skirt that looked red in the theater's marquee lights. After the shooting she disappeared for a time, and became known simply as the "lady in red" (or the "woman in red").

9. Ladyfinger. These cakey biscuits are eaten plain or used to make various types of desserts.

10. *Lady Chatterley's Lover.* Oliver Mellors, a gamekeeper on the Chatterley estate, becomes Lady Chatterley's lover in D. H. Lawrence's controversial, sex-filled novel. The book was considered so obscene that only 1,000 copies were published privately in Italy in 1928 (no English or American publisher would touch it). The ban created big demand for the book, but it wasn't available through a commercial publisher until 1959—and even then the publisher was sued for obscenity.

8-10 correct: Ladylove
4-7 correct: Ladylike
1-3 correct: She's no lady

96. Pair Shaped

1. (e) Ice-skating partners Tai Babilonia and Randy Gardner were the United States' gold medal hopefuls at the 1980 Winter Olympics. An injury to Randy kept them out of medal competition, but they left a lasting impression on

the hearts of skating fans. The pair toured with a number of professional ice shows and remains active in skating.

2. (c) As principal dancers on *American Bandstand*, Justine Carrelli and Bob Clayton were the hottest couple on 1950s TV. They made personal appearances, were photographed for magazine covers and received thousands of fan letters each week. As teens, they were romantically involved. Today they're married to others.

3. (g) One of the great musical-comedy writing teams of all time, Betty Comden and Adolph Green wrote scripts, screenplays and lyrics for shows and movies such as *On the Town*, *Singin' in the Rain* and *Bells Are Ringing*. Among their best-known songs is the Frank Sinatra hit "New York, New York."

4. (i) Known as the pre-eminent couple of the Broadway stage, husband and wife Alfred Lunt and Lynn Fontanne starred together in numerous productions from the 1920s up to 1960. In fact, their contracts demanded that they work together rather than in separate plays. They were noted for their on-stage use of natural mannerisms, instead of formal dramatic gestures. Broadway's Lunt-Fontanne Theater is named for them.

5. (h) Husband-and-wife singing duo Steve Lawrence and Eydie Gorme have been performing great American standards and show tunes together for more than 40 years.

6. (j) Gynecologist William Masters and psychologist Virginia Johnson weren't married when they began their human sexual behavior research in the 1950s—and they weren't married when their collaboration ended in the 1990s—but they did marry during the time they worked together. They're best known for their 1966 book, *Human Sexual Response*.

7. (f) Carole King wrote the music. Her husband Gerry Goffin wrote the words. Together they were one of the hot songwriting teams of the 1960s. Their first hit was "Will You Love Me Tomorrow?" in 1961. They wrote for a wide range

of performers, from the Byrds to Herman's Hermits to the Monkees. They even wrote "The Loco-Motion" for Little Eva in 1962. She was their kids' babysitter at the time.

8. (b) Few movie dance teams are as beloved as Fred Astaire and Ginger Rogers. She was elegant and he was suave and lithe. Together they lit up the screen in *Top Hat* and *The Gay Divorcee*, among others.

9. (a) Ashford and Simpson started writing and producing songs for Motown in the 1960s. Romantic duets, like "Ain't No Mountain High Enough" and "You're All I Need to Get By," were their specialty. They married in 1974 and began performing and recording together. Their biggest hit together was 1985's "Solid."

10. (d) Ice-dancing pair Jayne Torvill and Christopher Dean won a gold medal for England at the 1984 Winter Olympics, with a perfect score on their performance to Ravel's *Bolero*. They retired from competitive skating for almost 10 years, then came back to earn a bronze medal at the 1994 Winter Olympics.

8-10 correct: Perfect pairing

4-7 correct: Matchmaker

1-3 correct: Better off single

97. Oh, You Beautiful Doll!

1. (b) Beautiful Crissy with the growing hair was a big hit in the late 1960s and early 1970s. When you turned the knob on her back, her long auburn hair grew longer. The original Crissy wore an orange lace mini dress. Later versions had other mod outfits. Crissy also had a group of "growing hair" pals, including her little sister Velvet.

2. (a) Dressy Bessy was a soft doll designed to help preschoolers learn to dress themselves. Her clothes had real buttons to button, buckles to fasten and laces to tie. For boys, there was Dapper Dan.

3. (c) Skipper was Barbie's little sister. She was introduced in 1964, about 6 years after Barbie came onto the toy scene. By that time, Barbie already had a boyfriend named Ken (introduced in 1961) and a pal named Midge (introduced in 1963). Barbie's cousin Francie arrived in 1966, followed by Stacey and Christie (Barbie's first black friend) in 1968 and PJ in 1969.

4. (c) When you pushed Heidi's belly button she waved to you. Like most dolls of the 1960s, Heidi had a group of "friends," including Jan from Japan.

5. (a) Cheerful Tearful went from a smiling face to a pouty puss when you raised and lowered her arm. The earliest versions of these Mattel dolls changed expression when you squeezed their tummies.

6. (b) The Flatsy might have been a weird concept for a doll, but she sure was popular. These posable figures from the early 1970s were almost two-dimensional. Most of them came packaged in picture-framed scenes. When you finished playing, you simply popped the doll into her frame.

7. (c) Battery-operated Dancerina did pirouettes when you pushed or pulled the button on her plastic tiara. Introduced in 1968, this chubby, sweet-faced ballerina came with a plastic phonograph record.

8. (a) Both Holly Hobbie and Rainbow Brite were introduced on greeting cards before the characters were licensed to doll manufacturers. Holly Hobbie was an American Greetings creation and Rainbow Brite came from Hallmark.

9. (c) Ginny, a dressable toddler doll, was made by Vogue Dolls starting in the 1920s. She reached the height of her popularity in the 1950s, when little girls loved to change her clothes and style her hair. The earliest dolls had movable arms and legs. Later models "walked" and turned their heads. Creator Jennie Graves named the doll for her daughter, Virginia.

10. (a) Gene Marshall, the glamorous fashion doll who debuted in 1995, was conceived by illustrator Mel Odom, who also created a complete persona for her. According to her "biography," Gene is an actress from Hollywood's golden age of the 1940s and 1950s. TV and movie costumers design her elegant outfits—from gowns to swimwear to period pieces such as an usherette's uniform.

8-10 correct: Living doll
4-7 correct: Kewpie doll
1-3 correct: Baby doll

98. Goddess Bless

1. (e) The Greek goddess Artemis was the goddess of the hunt and of wild animals. She was associated with the moon, while her twin brother, Apollo, was associated with the sun. This virgin goddess was ferociously jealous and reflected an interesting kind of androgyny. In some parts of ancient Greece, women who worshipped Artemis would dance in the moonlight wearing phalluses.

2. (j) Athena, the Greek goddess of wisdom, was also the goddess of war and strategy. She lent her name to the city of Athens.

3. (a) The Earth Mother, Demeter, was one of the key deities in ancient Greece. Everyone wanted a bountiful harvest, and Demeter had the power to determine how well the crops would produce. When she wasn't helping the farmers she was desperately trying to steal back her daughter, Persephone, who had been kidnapped by the god of the underworld. Even goddess-mothers have to watch out for their kids.

4. (g) Luck knew no class boundaries as far as the Roman goddess Fortuna was concerned. During her festival each

June slaves were allowed to celebrate her bounty, along with the rest of the population.

5. (f) The Norse goddess Freya was a wild woman known for her sexual appetites. This love goddess, who sometimes traveled in a chariot pulled by cats, could transform herself into a falcon to fly on her own. Friday was named for her.

6. (b) When the Buddha met Kishimo-jin she was an evil figure who terrorized children and was even known to eat them. But the Buddha taught her benevolence and she became children's great protectress. Shrines in ancient Japan depicted her as an Earth Mother suckling a baby.

7. (h) The Chinese goddess of mercy, Kwan-yin, was selfless as only a female deity could be. So concerned was she by the suffering in the world that she preferred to remain on Earth rather than reaching paradise in nirvana.

8. (i) In ancient Egyptian mythology, the sky goddess, Nut, married her brother, Geb, the Earth god. (Brother-sister bonding was okay in ancient Egypt. Most of the pharaohs married their sisters.) When the Sun god, Ra, found out about the wedding he was so angry about not being invited that he forbade Nut to have children. She managed to get around him and gave birth to five gods and goddesses, including Isis, the Egyptian mother goddess.

9. (c) Everyone in Hawaii knows Pele, the fire goddess who also controls the flow of lava from the island's volcanoes. Stay on her good side and everything's fine. Cross her, and devastation will follow.

10. (d) Vesta, the Roman hearth goddess, guarded the home and, in a broader sense, the entire Roman nation. Her most famous devotees were the young women known as Vestal Virgins.

8-10 correct: Divine

4-7 correct: Mere mortal

1-3 correct: Cosmic joke

99. Queen of Scots

1. (c) Mary was born on December 8, 1542 in Scotland, but she didn't live there long. By the time she was 5, she'd been sent to France to be educated and she didn't come back to Scotland until she was 19.

2. (a) Even though she didn't live in Scotland, Mary became its queen when she was just 6 days old, after her father died from battle wounds. While Mary was living in France, her mother, who was French, ruled Scotland on her behalf.

3. (c) This one's tricky, but the short answer is that Mary was betrothed to her first husband, Francois II of France (see below), when she was 5. In fact, that wasn't her first engagement. When she was just 1 year old, the political wheeler-dealers in Scotland and England had planned for her to marry Edward IV of England, her first cousin once removed. That engagement didn't last long.

4. (b) Mary's first husband was Francois II of France. When they married, she was 15. He was 14 and had not yet become the French king. One year later, Francois's father died and Francois became king, making Mary queen of France. A year after that, he died of an ear infection and the next year, Mary finally went home to rule Scotland.

5. (b) All together, by the time she was 25, Mary had had three husbands: Francois II of France; Henry, Lord Darnley; and James, Earl of Bothwell.

6. (b) Mary's only son, James, became the king of both Scotland and England. In Mary's day, England and Scotland were separate nations divided by religion and politics. But James was the rightful heir to both thrones.

7. (c) Historians say Mary stood about 6 feet tall, which was notably tall for women—and men—in the 16th century.

8. (b) The "casket letters" are one of the great historical mysteries surrounding Mary, Queen of Scots. They indicate she was involved in a plot to murder her second husband, Lord Darnley. The casket refers to a small locked box used to keep private papers, and the letters were love letters that Mary wrote to the Earl of Bothwell while she was married to Lord Darnley. Bothwell was implicated in Darnley's murder, but Mary's part in it was never proven.

9. (b) Mary was an athlete and extremely fond of golf, which originated in Scotland.

10. (a) After being imprisoned for 19 years, almost half her life, Mary was beheaded in 1587, at the age of 44. As a Catholic, Mary posed a threat to England's Protestant queen Elizabeth I. As long as she was alive, there was a chance Catholics would organize in her name to overthrow Elizabeth. Even so, it took Elizabeth years to order Mary's execution. When the day arrived, Mary wore a simple black cape, which she dropped to reveal a bright red dress. It took two blows to cut off her head, after which her body kept moving—until her favorite dog was found hidden under her dress, rustling her skirts.

8-10 correct: Queen

4-7 correct: Princess

1-3 correct: Commoner

100. Handy with a Needle

1. (b) Tatting is the craft of making lace by looping and knotting thread with a hand shuttle.

2. (b) Antimacassars are lacy doilies placed over the backs of chairs. We think of them as quaint decorative items, but they started out with a practical purpose. Victorian men used a kind of hair oil called Macassar, which left grease stains on the furniture. Carefully placed antimacassars protected the upholstery.

3. (a) Arachne was so proud of her weaving skill she challenged the goddess Athena to a contest. Big mistake. The competition was close, which just annoyed the goddess more. Ultimately, Athena turned Arachne into a spider—which is why biologists refer to spiders as Arachnids.

4. (c) The style of flame-like needlepoint stitching known as bargello was named for the Bargello Palace in Florence, Italy. The medieval building is now a museum, which houses chairs stitched in a zigzag "bargello" pattern.

5. (a) Billed as the world's largest community art project, the NAMES Project Memorial AIDS Quilt was displayed for the first time in Washington, D.C., in 1987. Created to honor victims of AIDS, it contained 1,920 3-by-6-foot panels at that time. Today there are 44,000 panels honoring more than 84,000 individuals—with more added every day.

6. (a) Granny squares were conceived in the 1890s as a way to use up random scraps of yarn left over from larger projects. They're crocheted individually, then pieced together to form an afghan.

7. (c) The weeping willow was a common motif in the somber samplers known as mourning embroidery. After George Washington died in 1799, it became fashionable to stitch elaborate depictions of grave monuments, urns draped in black, and weeping figures—first in his memory, and later in the memory of any departed friend or relative.

8. (c) Quilt block patterns have been named for all sorts of things, from Flying Geese to Courthouse Steps. Two were named for U.S. first ladies. Dolley Madison Star honors the wife of James Madison. Dolley was an outstanding Washington hostess who defined the first lady's social role. Some 75 years later, Frances Folsom married President Grover Cleveland (they were the only presidential couple to marry in the White House), and she became the toast of Washington. Mrs. Cleveland's Choice, an intricately pieced pattern, was named for her.

9. (a) Blackwork, a type of embroidery using pure black threads on white or cream-colored fabric, was popular in England during the Tudor period of the early 16th century. Though the stitches are simple, blackwork motifs were very intricate, with interweaving patterns that looked like fine calligraphy.

10. (b) Crochet is the French word for hook, which is the tool you use to make crocheted items.

8-10 correct: A stitch in time
4-7 correct: Loose threads
1-3 correct: Dropped stitches

Selected Bibliography

Books

Benét, William Rose. *The Reader's Encyclopedia*. New York: Thomas Y. Crowell Co., 1948.

Buttolph, Angela, et. al. *The Fashion Book*. London: Phaidon Press, 1998.

Carnegie Library of Pittsburgh. *The Handy Science Answer Book*. Detroit: Visible Ink Press, 1994.

Folkard, Claire, ed. *Guinness World Records, 2003*. London: Gullane Entertainment, 2003.

George-Warren, Holly. *The Rolling Stone Encyclopedia of Rock & Roll* (3rd edition). New York: Fireside, 2001.

Goring, Rosemary. *Larousse Dictionary of Beliefs and Religions*. New York: Larousse, 1994.

Halliwell, Leslie. *Halliwell's Film Guide* (7th edition). New York: Harper & Row, 1989.

Hendrickson, Robert. *Facts on File Encyclopedia of Word and Phrase Origins*. New York: Checkmark Books, 1997.

Herbst, Sharon Taylor. *Food Lover's Companion*. New York: Barron's, 1990.

Jones, Constance. *1001 Things Everyone Should Know About Women's History*. New York: Doubleday, 1998.

Kowalchik, Claire and William H. Hylton, eds. *Rodale's Illustrated Encyclopedia of Herbs*. Emmaus, PA: Rodale Press, 1987.

Leach, Maria, ed. *Funk & Wagnalls Standard Dictionary of Folklore, Mythology, and Legend*. San Francisco: HarperCollins, 1984.

Mariani, John F. *The Dictionary of American Food and Drink*. New York: Hearst Books, 1994.

McHenry, Robert, ed. *Merriam-Webster's Biographical Dictionary*. Springfield, MA: Merriam-Webster, 1995.

Netzer, Corinne T. *The Complete Book of Food Counts*. New York: Dell, 2001.

Panati, Charles. *Panati's Extraordinary Origins of Everyday Things*. New York: Harper & Row, 1987.

Simon, Henry W. *100 Great Operas and Their Stories*. New York: Anchor Books, 1989.

, M.D., M.P.H. *Taber's Cyclopedic Medical*
(17th edition). Philadelphia: F.A. Davis
/3.

, ed. *Butler's Lives of the Saints*. San Francisco:
*er*Collins, 1991.

rjorie P.K. and Jean S. Arbiter. *Womanlist*. New
ork: Atheneum, 1981.

Websites

cdc.gov

emilypost.com

factmonster.com

greatwomen.org

harry-winston.com

imdb.com

procheer.com

toonopedia.com

tvland.com

usda.gov

Other Sources

The Fragrance Foundation

Society of American Florists

About the Author

*L*eslie Gilbert Elman is a frustrated *Jeopardy!* contestant (she passed the contestant search test, but never got "the call"), who has soaked up a lifetime's worth of trivial information just in case someone asked her to write this book.

A journalistic generalist, she has written about everything from crochet to ice hockey to honeymoons in the Poconos. She lives in New York with her husband.

The ladies' room has always played a significant role in her life.

To Our Readers

Conari Press, an imprint of Red Wheel/Weiser, publishes books on topics ranging from spirituality, personal growth, and relationships to women's issues, parenting, and social issues. Our mission is to publish quality books that will make a difference in people's lives—how we feel about ourselves and how we relate to one another. We value integrity, compassion, and receptivity, both in the books we publish and in the way we do business.

Our readers are our most important resource, and we value your input, suggestions, and ideas about what you would like to see published. Please feel free to contact us, to request our latest book catalog, or to be added to our mailing list.

Conari Press
An imprint of Red Wheel/Weiser, LLC
P.O. Box 612
York Beach, ME 03910-0612
www.conari.com